THE LUCID DREAMER

The
Lucid Dreamer

A Waking Guide for the
Traveler Between Worlds

Malcolm Godwin

SIMON & SCHUSTER

New York London Toronto Sydney Tokyo Singapore

SIMON & SCHUSTER
Rockefeller Center
1230 Avenue of the Americas
New York, NY 10020

A LABYRINTH BOOK
Copyright © 1994 Labyrinth Publishing (UK) Ltd.
Text copyright © 1994 Malcolm Godwin
Original illustrations copyright © 1994 Malcolm Godwin

Design by Malcolm Godwin & Magda Valine
Printed by
10 9 8 7 6 5 4 3 2 1
Library of Congress Cataloging-in-Publication Data

Godwin, Malcolm
The lucid dreamer: a waking guide for the traveler between worlds/ Malcolm Godwin
p. cm.
Includes bibliographical references and index
ISBN 0-671-87248-6
1. Lucid dreams. I. Title
BF1099.L82G63 1994
154.6'32--dc20   94-1701
                                                    CIP

C O N T E N T S

P R E F A C E

Twenty years ago my habitual life underwent an undeserved and totally unexpected transformation. One moment I was going about my admittedly bewildered and aimless life in London, and the next it seemed that a spiritual gold brick had fallen, narrowly missing braining me altogether, yet imparting enough of a glimpse of the *real* world, that nothing would ever be the same again.

As if in a dream I suddenly gave up everything I possessed, abandoned those I really loved and cared for, and was roaming India, afire with a divine madness and thirst, desperately seeking a spiritual master who might be able to give the last touches to what was obviously my final, and rather uncomfortable, stage of enlightenment. If anything was to be learned in the following two decades it was that, however close you may imagine *nirvana* to be, transformation is seldom instant.

Looking back on the last twenty years, seven being spent in India, what strikes me is just how much I have forgotten since returning to the rest of the world. Some of us seem to have an amazing ability to mislay even the most transforming and enlightening events in our lives. And it was during that period in an Indian ashram that I experienced lucid dreaming for the first time. It was just one of many extraordinary episodes of that period that had managed to completely slip out of my consciousness, along with all the other psychic esoterica and spiritual bric-à-brac, which I felt embarrassed to still carry.

So in one sense this book has grown from the almost nostalgic concern to re-examine many of the states which arose then. At the time my own master had frequently, and publicly, poked fun at my obsessive fascination with esoteric garbage. So there is still a certain wariness in experimenting with lucid dreaming. However it seems so natural to me that it is simple to adapt those time-honored techniques which induce the state, and which are common to many shamanic and mystical traditions.

In consequence the approach you will find within this book is neither from the professional standpoint of a psychologist, nor a scientist. Apart from being a Sunday mystic – a sort of naïve, religious primitive – my only credential is that I am a sporadic lucid dreamer, who is still lost in wonder at what I have felt. Anyone who has experienced this vivid state will agree that a large question mark begins to hang, like the sword of Damocles, over the dreamer's waking world, which by comparison suddenly doesn't seem so stable and reassuringly substantial as it once did. The lucid world is so rich, incredibly detailed, and alive, that the normal, everyday appearance of the waking realm can seem almost a flat monotone by its side. For not only is the dreamworld as clear and spatially real as anything in our waking state, but it also can be experienced with all the five senses, including taste and smell.

In my own search for some explanation of this phenomenon I have relied upon a background of popular shamanic and mystical traditions which are to be found within almost every known culture in the world, most especially India and the Far East. Yet it is only recently that I have also collided with a number of Western models and paradigms which seem to suggest that both scientific and mystical traditions are now, at last, speaking of exactly the same phenomena.

However, I am not a scientist, and, like most of

The Dream, _by Henri Rousseau._

our metaphysically orientated generation, have to take on trust many of the fashionable and popular ideas on such subjects as the new physics, quantum mechanics, metamorphic fields or holgraphic neuro-physiology. I offer no apology for this; the very com-plexity and utter abundance of the information at our disposal in the contemporary world prevents any single-focus view. We have all become cut-and-paste experts, gathering diverse harvests, shuffling the var-ious gems from each discipline, and sticking them on the wall in an effort to find some pattern or signif-icance. And from what has been learned from study-ing the realm of the new physics, it appears that scientists are also suspecting that our seemingly stable and solid world turns out to be, what the mystics of the East have always claimed, about as substantial and

real as a dream. Which can be both a great comfort and, simultaneously, a terror to behold.

My own unscientific experience of lucid dreaming appears to mirror a number of these new theories about the nature of reality, which imply that we actually create the physical world in which we live, in just the way that we create the dreamworld we inhabit when in a conscious dream. And it is from a standpoint of sheer wonder that this might really be so – that we can also awaken from this daytime dream we have all created – that this book is writ-ten.

Malcolm Godwin,
West Dorset, England, 1994

Part I

THE LUCID REALM

Chapter 1

Awake and Dreaming

Chapter 2

Transforming Illusion into Illumination

Chapter 3

The Secret Dreamers

Chapter 4

The Forgotten Realm

Chapter 5

Ghost in the Dream Machine

Ittal, from a house in Kattumeru, Orissa, India (copy).
The Saora tribes of central India paint these ittals, or pictograms, on the walls of their houses. They are believed to be dream communications from the spirit worlds. Such images transform the wall upon which they are painted into a doorway between the spiritual kingdoms and the material world. This particular image was said to be dreamed by the husband of a woman suffering from a nervous disorder. The image is a representation of the marriage feast of Jaliyasum, the god who was said to be responsible for the woman's condition. Shamans are asked to mediate between the dreamer and the spirit by either praising or criticizing the work, suggesting modifications or additions.

CHAPTER 1

AWAKE AND DREAMING

All is like a dream or a magic show

Tibetan Buddhist Treatise, 11th century

THIS BOOK IS NOT, LIKE MOST DREAM WORK-SHOP MANUALS, concerned with the content, interpretation, analysis or symbolism of dreams, but rather with the very stuff that dreams are made of. And in begging the question as to what makes up a dream we are immediately confronted with our own cherished and habitual ideas of what makes up our waking state. The alive and vivid reality of a lucid dream forces anyone who experiences it to undergo a transforming re-appraisal of what they perceive to be the reality of their waking lives. We will be primarily concerned with two states — *waking while dreaming* and *dreaming while being awake*. The bridge which links these two states is built from alert awareness, both in our so-called waking state and within the lucid dream.

The phenomenon of the lucid dream doesn't fit any traditional ideas about dreaming and only in the past decade has there been any interest shown in this state by the scientific community, or awareness of it in popular culture. Ten years ago many psychologists and neurophysiologists refused to even acknowledge its existence. However, through the persistent efforts of such researchers as Stephen LaBerge at Stanford University or Keith Hearne in England, the lucid dream has been suddenly enthusiastically embraced as a scientific reality.

Lucid dreaming is a state in which the sleeper becomes alert and conscious that he or she is dreaming. The actual imagery experienced in this state is often claimed to be far more vivid and full of life than in normal, non-lucid states and it is extremely difficult for even the most veteran lucid dreamers to ascertain whether the experience is a waking reality or not. In this state the dreamer is able to take control over who appears and what is dreamed, and the experience is most often accompanied by a marvellous and euphoric sense of power, delight and heightened faculties. It remains a relatively rare state and does to some extent depend upon a natural inclination or knack. Although some people undeniably have a certain talent for this type of dreaming, with care, patience and persistence, almost anyone can experience becoming conscious while actually still asleep and technically dreaming. You can learn to control your dreams, directing and producing them in any way you desire, with the most miraculous results and insights.

Mystery and Melancholy in a Street, *by Giorgio de Chirico.*
Each object in the surrealist scene above has a sense of immanent
presence, enhanced by their shadows which seem almost alive. Lucid
dreamers report that dream-things appear to possess an inner life of
their own with a magical sense of reality which is far greater than that
encountered in the normal, everyday waking world.

Above: **View of a Street,** by Adelchi-Riccardo Mantovani. It is not known how the brain can create detail as precise as in this scene drawing only from past memories. Where such memory is stored and how the brain reassembles new vistas and combinations remains a mystery.
Opposite: **Alice Entering the Mirror,** from Lewis Carroll's Alice

Through the Looking Glass, illustrated by John Tenniel. Alice appeared to have fallen asleep as she entered a separate, mirror image of her own room where everything was reversed, and yet even though many of the laws were bizarre and impossible, the actual world seemed as real as her own. Lucid dreaming is often experienced in much the same way.

ONE of the central issues to be examined, is whether there is any essential difference between the experience of being awake and the experience of being lucid and conscious when asleep and dreaming. If these two states prove to be more similar than we suppose, then what the psychics, shamans and mystics have always claimed is true. Throughout all cultures, persuasions and periods these visionaries have asserted that our perceptions of the normal world are distorted and that the world we are used to is really nothing but a dream. Some of us cheerfully take note of what they say but then proceed with our lives as if we had not heard a word. Perhaps this is because so few of us are prepared to undergo the rigors of either the shamanic or the mystical life in order to verify first hand what they claim. But what if they are right, and the world we inhabit is really nothing more than a dream? Is there any way that we can directly know this without the demanding disciplines and often dangerous initiations of both sage and sorcerer?

There is a method, available to almost anyone, which does allow a glimpse of what the sages talk about, and this is the phenomenon of lucid or conscious dreaming which has been gaining considerable interest of late in both America and Europe. This little understood state of consciousness turns out to be the master key which can open doors of perception into the nature of both the dreaming and the waking worlds.

Although the existence of this rare form of dreaming has only recently been publicized enough to reach a popular audience in the West, it is in fact one of the most ancient and treasured of human talents. It appears to have formed the central core of virtually every shamanic and mystical practice from the dawn of consciousness. Lucid, or conscious, dreaming allows shamans or "travelers between worlds" to visit the realms of the spirits in order to gain healing power and insight for both themselves and their peoples.

In the East, this form of dreaming has long been recognized by mystics as a great signpost on the way to enlightenment and to spiritual freedom. However, to both mystic and sage the essential purpose of lucid dreamwork is not to gain the shaman's power, but ultimately to wake up. And this waking up is not just within a dream, but in what we all know of as our waking

life. It is this awakening that lucid dreaming mirrors so evocatively, from what the mystics call our world of illusions and dreams, which is the central theme of this book.

Many of the dream states discussed in the following pages carry with them certain dangers for the unstable, the unwary or even the most rational and stolid amongst us. To a shaman or sorcerer, dreaming, quite literally, can be a very dangerous business. If we are to be honest, there are many obscure and dark corners which can have perilous consequences when disturbed if you as a dreamer venture into them without due care and warning. If readers were to take too seriously any of the visionary works of the shaman which have appeared on the market, then they might well find themselves out of their depth in very alien territory.

I have purposely kept away from many of the darker aspects of moving the dream body into other realms. It is not the intention of this book to do anything more than explore the borders between the various dream and waking states in order to understand that we are just as asleep when we think we are awake, as we are in dreams. All the various exercises and practices you will find have one purpose — to give the reader a real taste of lucid dreaming and let him or her trust their own inherent nature to guide them beyond this point.

However the ultimate object is to wake up — not to get lost in an even greater labyrinth of dreams. With this firmly in mind we will often be introducing practices which are more meditative than is usual in dream work. For one thing, working on

dreams often releases a great deal of energy which has quite simply no outlet. Simple meditations reduce the internal restless confusion and have an effect of grounding the dreamer and of creating a silence in which the noise of the mind is absent. The selection of meditations ranges over the entire spectrum of the world traditions from Tibetan Tantra through Buddhist and Hindu practices and the self remembering techniques of the masters of the Sufi world of Islam. In attempting to represent and express what we believe to be our reality, we create models and ideas which are simpler and easier to grasp than reality itself. The problem is that we often confuse the two, imagining when we have a word for matter that we have grasped its nature. For the last three hundred years our Newtonian perspective has given us all an idea of the universe which, in this century, has been proved to be false. The new physics has begun to show that the universe is not the solid machine-like structure we once thought it to be. But both these views are only ideas about reality and not reality at all. They are words, labels, and we tend to give them substance and forget they are not the existential reality.

Opposite: ***Reflections***. Above: ***Man in a Bottle***. *Both paintings are by Richard Hess. The problem faced by every lucid dreamer is how to tell the difference between a waking reality and a waking dream. A lucid dream can be every bit as substantial and convincingly real as normal, waking life. But both realities increasingly appear to be extraordinary, artistic creations of the brain and its inherent and programmed workings.*

WORDS FOR THE UNWARY

THIS communication is limited to words; words with which you will either agree or disagree. But words are second-hand and only *about* experience. At the very best we have a situation that the Taoist master Chuang-tzu, talks of,

"Fishing baskets are employed to catch fish; but when the fish are got, the men forget the baskets; snares are employed to catch hares; but when the hares are got, men forget the snares. Words are employed to convey ideas; but when the ideas are grasped, men forget the words."

This is the reason for including the various methods, so that the reader can directly experience what is discussed. The trouble is that the territories steadily get more and more unknown and often disturbingly far from the safety of familiar surroundings. Many of the techniques border upon territories of the "siddhic" powers, those seemingly magical abilities which arise from certain yogic or mystical practices, like the raising of Kundalini, seeing colored auras, having intuitive glimpses of the future or entering ecstatic trances and having out-of-body experiences. All these can be very bizarre indeed. So it is important to stress that these are not methods for the unwary, the timid or the unstable. They require courage to put into practice.

However there is a safety net; the very persistence needed to do any of them will exclude those who are not ready for their effects. All the same, if at any time you begin to enter states which you find intolerable, then immediately stop the technique and follow the one meditation which transcends them all, which is to just sit and watch the thoughts go by and not to identify with them. This brings a clarity and sense of calm amidst what otherwise can be very disturbing. If you have been single minded enough to trigger such a strong response from following any method, then you are certainly well equipped to follow this one.

But above all don't take yourself, or your dreams, too seriously. After all they are only dreams.

DREAM PRACTICE

Before continuing to the next chapter, try a very simple experiment which will give you some idea of the quality of your daytime visual imagination. Many times we daydream, but we are seldom attentive as to how visually substantial the images we create might be. Choose one of the objects from the painting opposite and, with eyes closed, bring the image into focus in your mind. Try turning the object around, watching the light change over its surface.

It will be rare for any readers to have a photographic replica floating in the darkness in front of them. Most of us find it difficult to keep any consistent image at all. Perhaps this is because many of us use words to give form to our inner images of eggs, hats and things. Such imagery is about as stereotyped as a children's spelling book, yet our non-verbal imagery is often vague and shadow-like, like that reported in normal dreams. In a lucid dream, however, the brain appears to bypass all verbal needs and presents to everyone, irrespective of ability, clear and immensely detailed imagery which can be touched and closely inspected and found to be substantially real.

La Clef des Songes, 1930, by René Magritte. *The artist links everyday objects with ordinary words. But the words are independent and in no way describe the visual object. Magritte is pointing out, with some humor, just how attached we are to verbal descriptions. But not only are we dependent upon words to experience reality, but also upon the culture which lies behind them.*

CHAPTER 2

TRANSFORMING
ILLUSION INTO ILLUMINATION

When the state of dreaming has dawned,
Do not lie in ignorance like a corpse,
Enter the natural sphere of unwavering attentiveness.
Recognize your dreams and transform illusion into luminosity.
Do not sleep like an animal.
Do the practice which mixes sleep and reality.

Tibetan Buddhist prayer

THE QUOTATION, ABOVE, PERFECTLY ENCAP-SULATES the essence of the world we are about to explore. Two thousand five-hundred years ago Gautama the Buddha, when asked *what* he was: whether an Incarnation, a God, a Deva, or a Saint, simply replied " I am Awake." No one had ever described the ultimate state of enlightenment in such simple terms. And when he said that he was awake, he was talking of awakening from the state which the rest of us consider our waking lives.

The *"practice which mixes sleep and reality"* describes a threshold which lies at the border of what the sages call our whole enchanted and dream-like condition, and reality. And mystics do not make any distinction between whether that somnambulism occurs while we are asleep and dreaming or while we are awake and also dreaming.

The prayer itself could just as equally have originated from the Hindus, Taoists, Jainas, Sufis, Siberian shamans, Australian Aborigines, or the Native American medicine men. In the East mystics especially stress that we human beings, with very rare and notable exceptions, are somnambulists virtually our entire lives, and it is only a few sages who manage to step outside of this dark wheel of illusion into the clear light of what is real. Now whether any of us agree, in theory at least, with these enlightened beings is irrelevant. The simple fact is that we will never truly *know* until we are also in their luminous condition.

From polls and surveys taken in both America and Europe it would seem that at least thirty percent of us, at some time in our lives, have had some sort of a glimpse into states of consciousness which challenge and shake all our preconceived ideas of reality. These can

The Sleeping Gypsy, by Henri Rousseau, 1897. The mystery of this painting is partly due to the tension felt as to whether the ▮▮▮▮ is a dream or whether it is real. Is the sleeping figure dreaming of the lion or is the lion a real menace in the waking world. Perhaps the lion is the beast-like unconscious awaiting its moment to roar into life. The dreamlike landscape, illumined by a full moon, is rendered all the more silent by the quietened stringed instrument lying b▮ ▮▮▮ figure's side. The viewer does not really know whether the scene is a dream any more than lucid dreamers are able to tell if anything they experience is real or not.

Jiddhu Krishnamurti, *1895-1986 . Intensively prepared by the Theosophists to become the vehicle for the Maitreya or the World Teacher, he disbanded the very organization which was to have carried his messianic message. His true awakening came in 1948 and he devoted the rest of his life to giving lectures up until his death at the age of ninety-one. But even after years of tirelessly giving talks, often to the same people in the audience, he would publicly despair of ever communicating how we might wake up.*

Meher Baba, *1894-1969. An Indian mystic who was on a devotional Sufi path. Feeling the pointlessness of trying to communicate at all through words he remained silent for over forty years, only communicating through a sign language which was translated by one of his close disciples. His essential message was love and his constant credo —"Be happy." It was Meher Baba who recognized that many people who seemed crazy were actually close to a spiritual awakening, but were so confused as they began to awaken that they could not cope with normal dreaming life.*

Osho Rajneesh, *1931- 1991. Enlightened at twenty-one, this controversial master devoted the rest of his life to speaking on how to wake up out of our habitual dreams. He was famous throughout India and the West as a mesmeric speaker and, unlike Meher Baba, gave a ninety-minute discourse every day, in either English or Hindi, for over three decades. Yet he admitted to his later disciples that his words were useless in transmitting his teachings for these could only happen through communion and not communication. Of all the mystics of this century he managed to disturb most people deeply enough for them to at least recognize they were sleeping.*

U.G. Krishnamurti. *1918-( ). In 1967 U.G. entered the natural state, or what he was pleased to call "the calamity." When asked to sum up his teachings in one sentence, his reply was,"The phrase is — I cannot help you." He is uncompromising in his message that all ideas about enlightenment, meditation, self, or god-realization are nothing more than sweet dreams. Reality, he insists, is a very different affair and most of us, living in our dreams, wouldn't touch it with a bargepole. He simply states that no communication is possible between someone in their natural state and someone dreaming, and anyway, he insists, none is necessary.*

range from the fairly common out-of-body-experiences, near-death-experiences, through telepathy, precognition, seeing energy fields and auras, to earth-shaking mystical visions, direct experiences of altered consciousness, or simply waking up from our so-called waking dream.

Such insights can come about through prolonged meditations, practice of various spiritual methods, or quite simply because we were just standing on a particular spot at a particular time when a gold brick of enlightenment descended. Even then, from what the masters and gurus tell us, those heightened states of awareness of which we are so proud, are merely a little flash illuminating a few square inches in the otherwise vast territory of the unimaginable Void. Such glimpses only seem to have the effect of making the darkness seem even deeper than before.

Anyone fortunate enough to have been with, or to have listened to, an enlightened man or woman, will have realized that their awakened condition is so radically different from the rest of us that there appear to be no words which seem adequate to describe the state or how also to enter it.

The sage, J. Krishnamurti, for instance, was, more often than not, reduced to tears in front of his audiences trying to impart his understanding. But the more he persevered the more both he, and his listeners, seemed to end up exasperated and unsatisfied, as if one was talking in Swahili and the other in the alien dialect of Alpha Centauri. And it was not as if his audience were stupid, any more than the mystic teacher, Georges Gurdjieff's disciples were simpletons. These two men of the spirit attracted some of the most aware and intelligent followers of our century and yet from what we learn virtually none of their thousands of disciples and followers ever reached enlightenment. Words certainly don't seem to be the right medium for imparting the truth of reality.

But what has this to do with lucid and conscious dreaming? Simply that lucid dreaming can directly help in understanding what these mystics are trying to demonstrate without the need of words.

All of us sleep, and as far as is statistically known, all of us dream. We are also capable of experiencing these powerful conscious dream-states that can penetrate even our most cozy, habitual worlds of normality and make us aware that what we thought was wakeful consciousness was perhaps nothing more than a dream. This is not going to give anyone *samadhi* or guaranteed enlightenment within this lifetime, but it can alter your sense of reality enough to radically change your perceptions and the understanding of who or what you are.

The particular territory we are about to explore is the strange twilight zone or threshold between dream and reality which can give any of us, with a little persistence and dedication, a real taste of what the psychics and mystics are describing. And that experience is readily available to all of us now. If we care to examine this unique inner world then at least we might realize just how deeply asleep we are; and that might trigger a real desire to eventually wake up.

Mystics from every religious persuasion seem to share at least two things in common. Firstly, they insist that we are dreaming all the time, whether we are awake or asleep. But telling us that while we still snore doesn't seem to help at all. For these beings are truly awake yet can't seem to enter our dreams in order to show us how to wake up. However hard they seem to try, their reality appears to be so radically different from our own that they are often seen to despair of ever communicating their discovery.

Four of the great mystics of this century, appearing opposite, have persistently, in different ways, tried to transmit their understanding, but the equally persistent failure on the part of their disciples and followers to grasp what is being shown, remains the second constant that mystics have in common. Lucid dreaming is a natural way to bypass words and to experience what they indicate, directly.

W H E N   D R E A M I N G   D A W N S

THOSE who have experienced this type of lucid event more often than not acknowledge it has been one of the high points of their lives. For those who have not been in such a state, what is it actually like?

"When the state of dreaming has dawned"

Typical to most accounts is the fact that the sleeper is at first in a normal non-lucid state. There is such a complete and non-critical involvement in the dream event that it is unquestioningly believed to be completely real. Then something odd happens, or is seen, that suddenly doesn't make sense to a part of the critical faculty of the mind and the dreamer snaps into alert attentiveness. We will later discover that one of the most effective methods of inducing lucidity is to remember to awaken if you witness anything outlandish or abnormal.

"Enter the natural sphere of unwavering attentiveness. Recognize your dreams and transform illusion into luminosity."

Immediately the dreamer consciously recognizes that it is a dream, it takes on a radically new quality, becoming less vague and ill-defined and infinitely more real. Its reality is truly uncanny although paradoxically, *the dreamer maintains a clear and lucid awareness that it is still only a dream*. This is a crucial distinction from the state of our normal awareness.

This stage of being sharply alert and attentive, without falling into an uncritical identification with the actors, the scenery, or the dream-self, must be maintained if the dreamer is not to slide back into normal unconscious dreaming.

The next stage which arises, after recognizing that you are awake in your own dream, is that you know that you can, quite literally, *do* whatever you want to and *be* whoever you want to. You have complete control of the dream. For instance, almost every dreamer wants to fly. It appears to be a wonderful, fundamental and natural human urge to immediately test your wings in a dream, and very few first-time "luciders" can resist the opportunity. These exhilarating flights are often followed by a careful and curious scrutiny of the world in which the dreamers find themselves.

Knowing that every desire can be fulfilled the subsequent pattern is entirely up to the dreamer and his, or her, taste.

A very common phenomenon is the false awakening which follows a lucid dream. The dreamers believe they have woken up. This can be so real that the dreamer is quite convinced that he or she is awake, getting up to have a shower, prepare breakfast and leave for the office. The majority of long-term lucid dreamers experience many such "awakenings," almost

as if they are in a series of nesting, dream-dolls, much like the painting by Magritte on the opposite page. Each awakening is at first believed to be the true one, until some small detail is found to be in some way "out of place" and then the whole, of what had been up until then the real world, collapses, and the dreamer is once again aware that it is yet another dream.

For the beginner there really seems to be no way to verify that, standing in what appeared to be the normal waking world of his room, it was not yet another dream. This can hardly be stressed enough to those who have not experienced this phenomenon. Lucid veterans learn to test reality in two ways; pain and gravity. If you can fly it is ninety-nine percent certain that you are dreaming. If you hurt yourself you are likely to be awake. So pinching oneself still

seems one of the best tests of all.

But even when finally awakening into the normal world there can be a bizarre phenomenon awaiting the sleeper which is often associated with lucidity. On arousal from sleep, the dreamer sometimes sees fully formed and what appear to be completely substantial images set within the framework of the actual waking space. These are not as uncommon as

Opposite: *The Importance of Miracles*, 1927, by René Magritte. Above: *The Subway*, by George Tooker. Many of our dreams are influenced by the stresses and fears of our waking lives. Nightmarish situations are often encountered in seemingly normal and everyday places. In non-lucid dreams we are victims, helpless to change the scenario. But being lucid means that such a potentially threatening scene as the subway above can be completely altered as the dreamer has total control over the action and its eventual outcome.

Above: **The Dream of Vishnu-Narayana,** eighteenth century, South India. Hindus maintain that the creation of the physical world is the dream of the god Vishnu. Brahma, who is credited with the actual creation itself, is seen here issuing from Vishnu's navel, seated on a lotus blossom. The true nature of the experienced universe, awake or asleep, is then seen as a dream, maya or an illusory play. Right: **Satchakra,** detail of a nineteenth-century painting from Rajasthan. This represents the energy within the body of the rising female creative principle, or Sakti, which in Tantra is believed to be responsible for the creation of the universe.

we might suppose. Such waking visions are generally known as *hypno-pompic hallucinations* and seem to occur when the brain cannot manage, for some reason, to switch instantaneously from the dream to the waking state.

But the seamless reality of such visions, set as they are within the framework of the normal waking world, once again challenges what is understood as the indisputable stability of our normal cherished environment.

So this is the typical territory we will be exploring. Such conscious dreaming can be induced by persistent effort. Yet this is only the beginning of what promises to be a transforming journey for anyone, for once the "traveler between realms" gains confidence and a resolve to examine just what makes a dream and what reality, then a vast new realm is opened up which transcends all our previous perceptions.

The question that arises after the first lucid experience is, simply, how does one really tell the difference between this form of dreaming and the normal waking reality, when both seem as real, or as dreamlike, as the other? Modern science has, up until the last decade, been deafeningly silent about the nature of dreaming and reality. This cannot be said for the mystics, who have been broadcasting for millennia that our waking world is an illusion and a dream. But any direct link between spirituality and lucid dreaming is virtually unknown in the Western traditions.

In the East, on the other hand, lucid dreaming has long been acknowledged as an important milestone on the route to enlightenment. This seeming oversight in

the West is probably due to a predominantly Christian distrust of the paranormal, that is except when it appears in history as authorized by the Church. The Catholic Inquisition hardly offered encouragement for experimentation in this field and while there is a rich tradition of dreams in the Old and New Testaments, lucid dreaming became a secret science more associated with alchemy, freemasonry and magic than with the mainstream of religion.

Dream practices have long been at the very heart of most Eastern traditions. The Tibetan Bonpo school, which uses lucid dreaming extensively as a form of meditation, predates Buddhism by over 12,500 years, according to the records of their founder, Tenpa Shenrab, while the Hindu *Upanishads,* which allude to a conscious dreaming world, reach back well over five thousand years .

Buddhism is based upon the proposition that we are dreaming all the time anyway, and the Hindu concept of *maya* clearly tells us that everything we appear to experience is actually an illusion, or a playful dream created by God. The original deity was supposedly either bored or lonely, so split itself into fragments which have forgotten who they are, and who play a sort of hide-and-seek with God in a universe of dreams.

Too many mystics and enlightened beings have independently arrived at an understanding that our world is a dream for us to ignore what they say. So, in exploring the threshold between dreams and awakening, that twilight area where illusion, imagination and

Girl at the Window, *by Micheline Boyadjian, Belgium. The two windows look out like the two eyes in the head. The same girl seems to be gazing out of both, like the left and right hemispheres of the brain. Increasingly we learn from both mystics and scientists that our cherished reality "out there" beyond the windows is actually a creation within the brain itself. Lucid dreaming gives a direct experience of this fact, for the dream world is every bit as real as the waking one even when there is no external stimulus available.*

reality meet, we will discover that there are dream and visionary states which allow us glimpses of *the real world*. Such states are our natural birthright and are in no way the exclusive territory of the mystic, the shaman or the enlightened ones.

For we all dream. We all spend years of our lives, when asleep, living in alternative universes with radically different structural rules and natural laws. Yet, for the most part, we casually forget them all in our so called waking life, until perhaps some little act triggers a memory which can bring back a dream of epic proportions, capable of giving the deepest insight into our natures and actions.

"Do not sleep like an animal,
Do the practice which mixes sleep and reality."

This book is essentially a dream manual, designed to help the dreamer remember and explore territories which have been visited and forgotten. It has two essentially different types of readers in mind. Those who like to know *about* things, and those who have a compulsion to actually *experience* them. These two categories each have twin subsets of their own, being those whose nature is to thunder down the beach, hurling themselves at the glistening waves, and those who prefer to dabble a long time at the ocean's edge, testing the coldness of the water and slowly acclimatizing themselves to the idea of actually submerging themselves in the stuff.

The main text is *about* the no-man's land between dreams and reality. But alongside these theories and hypotheses there are a selection of dream methods for those who want *a direct experience* of lucid dreaming.

As a word of caution, however, there is much within

F.W.H. Myers was a founding member of the British "Society for Psychical Research." Although he had a poor opinion of his own psychic abilities, he championed work on conscious and lucid dreaming.

these pages which could challenge the way you view the world. The need for such caution very much depends upon how you, the reader, approach this subject.

For those who heed the warning and wouldn't touch the methods with a barge-pole anyway, you also have your particular dangers. If you only wish to know *about* the subject, it simply means that you must take someone else's experience for the truth (which just burdens you with the dead noun of *knowledge* and not the active verb of *knowing*). If you do decide to *know* directly, then it is imperative to remember that seldom is something worth much that can be purchased cheaply. To explore some of the shamanistic dreamworlds presented in the later chapters requires a long, arduous and often exceedingly painful apprenticeship which is alien to most Westerners who are used to instant results.

Wisdom, it is said, is a lonely business and few are prepared to persist with a method for long enough for it to bear fruit. And time is what is especially needed when it comes either to exploring the dreaming world, or to what a mystic might call an awakening.

So, on the one hand, you can read *about* the nature of dreams and the creator or creatrix of those dreams whom we refer to as the Dream Maker. On the other hand, if you follow some of the methods, meditations and techniques scattered throughout the book, with diligence, you will directly *experience* those dreams and the Dream Maker. *But it takes time.* Anyone who wants lucid dreams after one evening's practice would do better to put this book down now.

Georges Gurdjieff, who was one of the greatest charismatic "teachers"or masters of our century, would give his disciples at least six months of intensive practice before they would have even the smallest glimpse of conscious dreaming. For Stephen LaBerge who, more than anyone, has brought the lucid dream to the attention of both scientist and public alike, it took over two-and-a-half years before he could satisfactorily invoke conscious dreaming on a regular basis.

One man who must hold the world record for sheer perseverance was Frederic W.H. Myers, one of the founding members of the British Society for Psychical Research. This Cambridge classics scholar by "painstaking effort" only managed three lucid dreams in three

Georgei Ivanovitch Gurdjieff was a charismatic teacher, writer and mystic who maintained that everyone was actually asleep, and only when awakened we would understand that we were only dreaming we were awake.

thousand attempts. Although he considered he was too poorly endowed as a psychic to be able to achieve more, he still managed to enthuse, "I have long thought we are too indolent in regard to our dreams; that we neglect precious occasions of experiment for want of a little resolute direction of the will." That was in 1887. Perhaps they were more persistent in those times.

Although, today, there are an increasing number of experimental lucid dream workshops which can justly claim the most astounding and speedy results, the question which arises is whether those who participate are prepared for, or can cope with, the radical changes in consciousness which conscious dreaming invokes.

To explore one's own dream life is a perilous undertaking. Not everyone is suited to it and some of the techniques in this edition can land you in very sticky territory.

It is not just that the ego can become inflated with a sense of power, which it does anyway, but that the more one travels in a borderland between what we think of as real and what we believe to be dreams, the more we tax our own sanity.

And it is precisely the same no-man's land that appears to be shared by the psychotic and the schizophrenic, that will be explored in these pages.

So in one breath you are encouraged to use the various tried and tested dream methods found within these pages, some of them thousands of years old, while in the next you are being warned to take it easy.

Maybe the simplest and best advice is to not take it all too seriously, or yourself for that matter.

Avoid being too identified with what you experience, for the master-key to exploring both a lucid dream and a waking world is to maintain an alert attention but to avoid becoming too identified with what is going on.

And, when backed up against a dream wall with your most monstrous and murderous nightmare relentlessly bearing down upon you, the greatest weapon you have is laughter, as laughter dispels the fearsome.

The more serious you get the more substantial both your fears and your dream realms will become.

In this regard lucidity, lightness, love, laughter and life, really do appear to be the five guardian allies of any traveler in the extraordinary worlds we are about

DREAM PRACTICE

ONE of the first practices which will help to establish some conscious rapport with your dreaming self is to recall the most important and powerful dreams you have ever experienced, either as a child or an adult. It takes considerable conscious effort to remember either the important or the recurring dreams you might have had, but with perseverance brief memories will begin to surface. Write them down briefly, as they are only notes to trigger further memories.

Without trying to analyze them, search for some overall pattern to the situations or images which are unique to *you*.

It might be that you have dreams of being chased or of finding yourself in embarrassing situations. Your dreams might be comic or overly serious, but whatever the case consciously recall the type of dreamworlds you usually inhabit.

If there is a recurring scenario, or one to which you feel strongly attracted, examine it more carefully. This will be the familiar base from which you can always operate and where you can direct your attention. Then simply intend to go there in your dreams, and when you do so determine that you will remember all that happened in them. This is a deceptively simple yet powerful means of focusing one's attention on a dream spot.

It might be a strange landscape or a particular room in an old house which has doors which you have never opened; it could be a city street where many of your dreams are enacted. Whatever the situation or place, try to fix it in your mind, telling yourself that this will be the place where you will become conscious when next you dream of it.

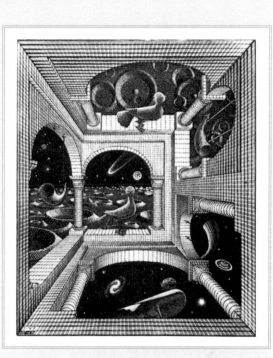

This simple method of imprinting the idea that whenever you find yourself in that spot you will remember it is a dream, is one of the most effective triggers for lucid dreaming.

Opposite: **Drawing** by William Blake. This nineteenth-century English artist said of his visions, "A spirit and a vision are not, as modern philosophy supposes, a cloudy vapor, or a nothing; they are organized and minutely articulated beyond all that mortal and perishing nature can produce. He who does not imagine in stronger and better lineaments, and in stronger and better light than his perishing and mortal eye can see, does not imagine at all." It is now believed that many of Blake's mystical visions were actually lucid dreams. This in no way reduces his mystical imagery but makes us realize the essentially sacred and visionary nature of the phenomenon.
Above: **Engraving**, by Escher.

CHAPTER 3

THE SECRET DREAMERS

We are in a time so strange
that living equals dreaming,
and this teaches me that man
dreams his life, awake.

Life is a Dream
by Calderon

THE VERY FABRIC OF THE PSYCHOANALYTI-CAL PROCESS over the last hundred years has been squarely based upon dreaming. Freud saw dreaming as the "royal road to the unconscious" and this view has been dominant throughout the century in virtually all schools of psychology.

With so much emphasis on the interpretation of dreams it is truly remarkable that so few reports of lucid dreaming have surfaced from the volumes of case histories during these years. So why, after this long period of neglect and total silence from the professional dream analysts, has lucid dreaming suddenly appeared like a comet in popular consciousness? Is it a talent which has only just evolved in the last decade, or has humankind always possessed this extraordinary gift of becoming awake within a dream?

We learn from ancient texts that lucid dreaming has been around for as long as there have been written records, which might come as a surprise as so little is known about the state to either mainstream Western religion or science.

In Freudian terms, dreams are invariably seen as mirrors of repression and psychological ill health. In order for an effective cure to take place, the patient's dreams have to be analyzed, dissected and interpreted so that the patient can clearly see the nature of his or her imbalances. Lucid dreaming appears to be at the opposite end of the spectrum, being more connected with a psychology of the healthy. Contrary to a pathology, lucid dreaming apparently elicits from the dreamer such descriptive superlatives as *real, true, ecstatic, blissful, revealing, wondrous, full of gratitude, magical* and *divine.*

Chumash cave painting, *California (copy by Campbell Grant).*
The Chumash shamans of California were known to induce lucid
dreaming in order to travel into the spiritual realms. They created
the mandalas above as representations of their soul journeys, much
in the same way that the ittals, or pictograms, are painted by the
Saora tribes of central India (see page 9) or the dreamwalkers of
Australia.

Above left: **Sigmund Freud**, 1856-1959. In the light of modern neurobiology, many of Freud's assumptions are found to be unscientific and inaccurate. Many workers in the field now believe the dominance of his unproven ideas about the repression of instinctual drives has led to the study of the unhealthy mind rather than that of the healthy.

Above right: **Havelock Ellis**, 1859-1939, was a pioneeer of his time in advocating a more natural expression of sexuality, both for homosexuals and heterosexuals. But he appeared to have a blind spot for lucid dreaming, discounting the possibility of its existence.

Below: **Carl Gustav Jung,** 1875-1961.

Curiously, Freud himself did not mention lucid dreaming at all in the first edition of his mammoth *The Interpretation of Dreams*. He did, however, add a very small footnote to the second edition in which he briefly acknowledged that:

"...there are some people who are quite clearly aware during the night that they are asleep and dreaming and who thus seem to possess the faculty of consciously directing their dreams. If, for instance, a dreamer of this kind is dissatisfied with the turn taken by a dream, he can break it off without waking up and start again in another direction — just as a popular dramatist may under pressure give his play a happier ending."

This is virtually the sum total on lucid dreaming given by the founding father of the psychoanalytical method, on the road to the unconscious.

But, in this at least, he is hardly to blame and merely compounds the almost complete lack of interest shared by his own profession and the entire scientific community. At the time Freud was penning the revisions to his second edition, the eminent English psychologist, Havelock Ellis, was dismissing lucid dreaming altogether. "I do not believe that such a thing is really possible, though it has been borne witness to by many philosophers and others from Aristotle... onwards."

What he was probably referring to was a reference made by Aristotle in his treatise *On Dreams*, in which the philosopher writes, "For often when one is asleep, there is something in consciousness which tells us that what presents itself is but a dream." At the time he wrote this, in the fourth century BC, his compatriot Greeks were visited by dreams rather than having them. Night had given birth to Hypnos, sleep, and to "the people of dreams." And that dream world had existed long before the son of Hypnos, Morpheus, was elevated to become its god.

Some time before the ninth century BC, Homer had divided dreams into the true dreams that arrived through the "Gates of Ivory" and the false that came through the "Gates of Horn." But both were still, supposedly, messages from the gods. Only the followers of Pythagoras and the eccentric Heraclitus, four centuries later, broke with this tradition, holding that the soul was freed from the body in sleep and was able to converse with higher beings, and not the other way around.

In the West the Greek belief that dreams were messages from the divine, persisted. The Christian Church inherited much of the mythology of the Israelites, who also asserted that dreams were God's messages which needed to be interpreted by the patriarchs, prophets or dream tellers.

Both the Old and New Testaments are chock full of dreams. We constantly hear in one form or another that, "If there is a prophet among you, I the Lord will make myself known to him in a vision; I will speak with him in a dream." Jacob dreams of a ladder, Joseph dreams of the sheaves of corn and of himself rising above all others. And

Above: **Hypnos**, *Greek, fourth century BC. The Greek God was believed to touch a person with his wand bringing sleep. But it was his son, Morpheus who brought the dreams. One of Jung's great contributions to the psychoanalytical movement was the idea that psychological health was a balance between the unconscious and the conscious. He believed that there is a collective unconscious which we tap in our myths, just as we are in touch with our personal unconscious when we dream.*

it was, after all, Joseph who interpreted Pharaoh's dream. But the only dreams that were of interest to the Jews and the early Christians were those songs of the night which were from God Himself.

Christ's birth was announced to Joseph in a dream, and Pilate's wife told her husband to have nothing to do "with that righteous man, for I have suffered many things because of him today in a dream."

All the biblical dreams are presented as super-natural revelations. The Vision of John on the island of Patmos is the superlative example. But while such dreams, divine or lucid, were commonplace in biblical accounts, such divine outpourings were likely to catch the eye of the Inquisitors only twelve hundred years later, only to be reinterpreted this time as demonic. Having powerful dreams became a dangerous practice, as many so-called witches and heretics found to their cost.

In religions other than Christianity, the lucid dream is reserved for the most valued members of the society – the saint, the soothsayer, the shaman or the mystic. As part of the secret doctrines and rites of initiation, such dreams of power brought spiritual gifts to both the individual and the tribe, or peoples, and conferred great prestige upon the dreamers.

It has been especially so in the lives of such peoples as the Native Americans or Australian Aborigines. The Vision Quest, a method to induce spiritually potent dreams, is not just unique to the North American tribes. It appears in various forms and colors throughout the world. At its core, its essence is always the sacred.

To many, Mohammed's *Laylat al-Miraj,* or night journey, is just such a vision quest – a lucid dream if ever there was one, in which the Angel Gabriel led the prophet through Jerusalem, past the seven celestial spheres finally to ascend to God.

So, any reader contemplating entering the realm of lucid dreaming would do well to meditate upon the quality of sacredness inherent in the lucid dream, irrespective of creed or religious persuasion. You will be entering your own inner psychic space in full consciousness. The realms of the spirit, even in the dark recesses of the unconscious mind, are still spiritual, being both wondrous and awesome.

Historically speaking, records of lucid dreaming go back far further than Aristotle. If we are to believe the Tibetan Bonpo School of dream masters, their founder, Tenpa Shenrab, lived over fifteen millennia ago. If this does not readily fit your cherished historical time-frame then you will probably find it as difficult to accept that the Australian Aborigines, who have the oldest spiritual traditions on earth, are said to have been around forty thousand years ago. The oral traditions of the Hindu Vedantic and Upanishadic texts of India are believed to have existed as far back as 5,000 years ago, while the Jaina traditions claim even greater antiquity.

While many traditions have varied instructions on how to induce or invoke lucid dreaming, all appear to regard being conscious while dreaming as a prerequisite for any spiritual path.

The clearest writings on the subject seem to be found in an ancient tantric text, the *Vigyan Bhairav Tantra,* which is one of the greatest treasures of the

---

Jacob's Ladder, by Adalbert Trillhaase. *Many of the biblical visions, like that of John on Patmos who witnessed the heavenly revelations, are suspiciously similar to lucid dreams. Few of those early visionaries could distinguish between waking or dreaming reality, and would have been surprised to have been asked if there was a difference.*

Hindu world. These are *the hundred and twelve* meditation techniques given to his consort, Devi, by Lord Shiva. *Vigyan* can roughly be translated as consciousness, *Bhairav* is one who has gone beyond, and *Tantra* is the method. (Some of these methods are to be found in Part II.)

Two-thousand-five-hundred years ago one of the Buddha's greatest disciples was Sariputta. We are told in texts of the time that as his meditations deepened many strange visions and lucid dreams started to occur. They were so real, so perfectly actualized, that he insisted they were not phantoms but were as real as the Buddha himself.

What must have been the golden age of lucidity came during the period from the eighth to the twelfth centuries in Tibet. At that time there was a gathering of some of the greatest Buddhist mystics ever known, who devised the most sophisticated techniques of Dream Yoga, which have never been surpassed. It was in this extraordinary atmosphere that *The Tibetan Book of the Dead* was conceived and written.

The dream yogis created a highly developed, experientially based science of lucid dreaming, which our own scientific age is only beginning to recognize as being far in advance of anything we know of today.

The earliest Western account of lucidity appears in a letter written, about seven hundred years after Aristotle, by Saint Augustine, who was quoting an earlier dream of a physician from Carthage, one Gennadius. This man had a dream in which a youth of "remarkable appearance and commanding presence" interrogated him. In a subsequent sequence of nightly dreams, the youth quizzed him on the nature and state of his dreaming. Gennadius was asked whether these events had taken place in sleep or wakefulness. When the dreamer replied that he knew he was in fact still sleeping, the youth reminded him that

even so he was still seeing in his sleep. This startled the dreamer into waking up within his dream. The youth continued his inquisition. "Where is your body now?" To which Gennadius replied that it was in his bed. "Do you know that the eyes in this body of yours are bound and closed, and that with these eyes you are seeing nothing?" questioned the youth. "As while you are asleep and lying on your bed these eyes of your body are now employed and doing nothing, and yet you have eyes with which you behold me, and enjoy this vision, so, after your death, while your bodily eyes shall be wholly inactive, there shall be in you a life by which you shall live, and a faculty of perception by which you shall still perceive." Which is as heartening to hear for us today as it was no doubt for Saint Augustine.

While Persian Sufis were practicing spectacular telepathic and shared lucid dreams, the twelfth-century Spanish Sufi, Ibn El-Arabi, asserted that one should learn to control thoughts in a dream and that through this alert lucidity the disciple "will produce great benefits for the individual. Everyone," he maintained "should apply himself to the attainment of this ability of such great value."

The Christian theologian, Thomas Aquinas, even gives a rare and valuable clue as to when a conscious dream would be most likely to occur, and in doing so he predates the findings of our present sleep researchers by over five-hundred years. He says that lucidity is most likely to occur "Towards the end of sleep, in sober men and those gifted with strong imaginations."

Although there were a number of isolated cases of lucid dreamers, few seem to have survived the lean years from the fourteenth to the eighteenth centuries. It was probably a combination of the zeal of the Spanish Inquisition on the one hand and the new Age of Reason on the other.

So it was not until the middle of the nineteenth

Dancing Dervishes, detail of painting from Rajput, India, 1740. The Sufis of both Persia and India used lucid dreaming extensively in their meditations. One of the most effective methods to maintain lucidity within a dream if it begins to fade is to start whirling. Why this is so effective remains a mystery.

century that a real dream pioneer managed to describe his experiences in a fascinating volume called *Dreams and How to Guide Them*. This was the first methodical examination of lucidity in dreams, written by the Marquis d'Hervey de Saint Denis. He described how he had learned to recall, awaken in and control his dreams, in a journal which documented twenty years of careful dream research. But his work was received with scepticism and little enthusiasm by the scientific community of the time.

Even when a famous philosopher like Friedrich Nietzsche made an obvious reference to his own lucid dreams in saying, "And perhaps many a one will, like myself, recollect having sometimes called out cheeringly and not without success amid the dangers and terrors of dream life: 'It is a dream! I will dream on!'"– even then few rallied behind this nineteenth-century flag to explore such phenomena.

The twentieth century did not fare much better, although it began promisingly enough. The author, poet and psychiatrist, Willem Frederik van Eeden, who was well known and respected in Holland, and who was the first to coin the phrase "lucid" dreaming, was also the first to seriously and systematically research the state of being asleep, especially that dreaming state which included a full recollection of daily life, the awareness of the sleeping self and the ability to act voluntarily within the dream scenario.

In a paper presented to the British Society for Psychical Research, just before the outbreak of World War I, he outlined more than three hundred and fifty of his own lucid dreams, gathered over a period of fourteen years. He insisted that the sleeper "reaches a state of perfect awareness and is able to direct his attention, and to attempt different acts of free volition. Yet the sleep," he was quick to point out was, "undisturbed, deep and refreshing."

In his address he gave one, by now famous, example of how he attempted to experiment within the dream. He began to try to break a glass goblet within the dream. He used two stones, but the glass stubbornly refused to break. He then took a "fine claret-glass from the table and struck it with my fist, with all my might, at the same time reflecting how dangerous it would be to do this in waking life; yet the glass remained whole." Disappointed at first, van Eeden then discovered it had shattered "but a little late, like an actor who misses his cue." He concluded that the dream world, however ingenious an imitation it might be, still had many slips and failures. He then threw the broken remains of the glass out of the window in order to hear the tinkling. "I heard the noise alright and I even saw two dogs run away from it quite naturally. I thought what a good imitation this comedy world

Above: **Drawings** from the Marquis d'Hervey de Saint Denis'
copious notebooks showing the imagery which appears at the onset of
sleep. Opposite: **The Marquis d'Hervey de Saint Denis**
spent five years in continual observation of his own dreams,
managing to fill twenty-two notebooks with colored images during
that time. He was one of the first to experiment with lucid dreams
and showed that it was possible to gain access to one's own dreams
simply by paying attention to them.

was. I saw a decanter with claret and tasted it,
and noted with perfect clearness of mind: 'Well,
we can also have voluntary impressions of taste in
this dream world; this has quite the taste of
wine.'"

This particular dream experiment echoes one
made by Hervey de Saint Denis over half a century
before. He had also wondered what a familiar
porcelain tray would look like if he broke it in his
dream. I can well understand his fascination as to
how good the creator of the dream might be at
representing a broken tray. For this had never

happened in actual waking life, so there were no
previous experiences to draw upon.

When Saint Denis examined the fragments closely
he was amazed to discover the precise detail of the
"sharp edges of the lines of breakage, and the jagged
cracks which split the figures in several places. I had
seldom had such a vivid dream."

Van Eeden appeared to have experienced his
tactile and auditory senses as well as his sense of
taste in full, regardless of being in what would
otherwise be considered a hallucinatory world. He
discovered that "the sensation of having a body —

having eyes, hands, a mouth that speaks, and so on — is perfectly distinct; yet I know at the same time that the physical body is sleeping and has quite a different position." He was convinced that, however bizarre it might appear to others who had not experienced this state, he really had a second dream body which he thought might correspond to the astral body, which was a popular concept at the time, having Annie Besant as the chief esoteric spokeswoman on its behalf.

The Englishman Hugh Calloway, who is better known as the occult writer Oliver Fox, was another self-taught lucid dreamer who had little previous knowledge of other cases. His first experience came at the age of sixteen. The instant he recognized he was awake and yet dreaming, the quality of the dream changed in a manner very difficult to convey to one who has not had this experience.

"Instantly, the vividness of life increased a hundred-fold. Never had sea and sky and trees shone with such glamorous beauty; even the commonplace houses seemed alive and mystically beautiful. Never had I felt so absolutely well, so clear-brained, so inexpressibly free! The sensation was exquisite beyond words; but it lasted only a few minutes and I awoke."

This description is one of the most evocative and at the same time most typical of the phenomenon. Fox called these conscious and alert states "Dreams of Knowledge" in which he said he could move around "like a little God."

The Dream of Knowing might be an even better term to express lucidity. Knowledge is far too static and second-hand to be a true description of the state. The essence of the dream is one of truly knowing beyond doubt that it is simultaneously both a reality and yet a dream.

In the period between the two world wars little was heard of lucid dreaming other than such odd cases as in the work of Georges Gurdjieff, the charismatic mystic who often used Sufi-inspired devices in order to awaken his followers and disciples to their true situation. He specifically tried to induce conscious dreaming in them, often saying that most men are asleep when they think they are awake.

One of his techniques to inspire lucidity within the dream was for a person to watch his or her hands during the day and then to be able to visualize them with the eyes closed. The moment they actually dreamed of their hands they would then remember it was a dream and awaken within it.

One of Georges Gurdjieff's most brilliant disciples, P.D.Ouspensky, had already experimented with dreams even before meeting him. Ouspensky had wondered if it was possible to preserve an alert consciousness in dreams. He eventually mastered what he was to term a half-dream, in which he became conscious and could exert a certain amount of control over his dream material.

Except for an odd and isolated magazine article or two, the whole subject of lucid dreaming vanished

from popular and scientific consciousness for decades. The Western silence and ignorance on the subject prompted an Australian Aboriginal to comment, "White mans got no dreams. He go 'nother way." The phenomenon of being alert within the dreaming state even managed shyly to sidle past the psychedelic years of the 1960s and early '70s when research into dreams and drug-related "higher" states was at its peak. However, by the late 1970s there was a sudden flurry of interest which blossomed into an entirely new attitude on the whole subject.

Back in 1948 it was an American psychiatrist, Nathan Rapport, one of those few and isolated individuals who had something to say about lucid dreaming, who in article called "Pleasant Dreams!" eloquently summed up the elusive yet pragmatic nature of our subject.

"Those magic fantasies, the weird but lovely gardens, these luminous grandeurs; they are enjoyed only by the dreamer who observes them with active interest, peeping with an appreciative, wakeful mind, grateful for glories surpassing those the most accomplished talents can devise in reality.

The fascinating beauty found in dreams amply rewards their study. But there is a higher call. The study and cure of the mind out of touch with reality can be aided by attention to dreams."

He really seems to have put his hand on the pulse of our whole generation. For that is what lucid dreaming really does offer — a cure of the mind out of touch with reality. At first you will feel that lucid dreaming makes you question the whole fabric of reality, for we have to ask, if the dream is so real, what is the reality? And in posing the question it will be discovered you have already found the answer.

Celia Green, an English parapsychologist, published the most extensive review of conscious dreaming in a book simply called *Lucid Dreams*. But even in 1976, ten years after its publication, she seemed to be talking to a brick wall as far as the scientific community was concerned.

Her words were certainly rational enough, but fell into a scientific desert.

"It might be thought that it would be interesting to discover what the neurophysiological state of a person was when their mind was in a state of rational activity although they were physically asleep. If this state should turn out to be exactly the same as that of a person who was asleep and dreaming in the ordinary manner, this would be strange and interesting. If it should turn out to be different, the nature of the differences might shed light on the true nature of sleep and the true nature of mental functioning."

Green was followed by three other major writers in the field, being Charles Tart, Patricia Garfield and Ann Faraday, all of whom were fascinated by the phenomenon of lucid dreaming. Faraday went as far as saying that, "This remarkable state of consciousness is in my view one of the most exciting frontiers of human experience."

Opposite left: **Celia Green** was one of the first parapsychologists to investigate both out-of-body experiences and lucid dreaming. Her work was met with considerable scientific skepticism although her evidence was substantial. It took the stringent laboratory experiments of Stephen LaBerge to finally convince the scientific community that lucid dreaming not only existed but that it opened up entirely new avenues in neurophysiology. Above: **Stephen LaBerge** has created a number of simple technological devices, such as those which deliver mild electric shocks or having colored lights which alert the sleeper that they are entering REM sleep. Many of his subjects induce a lucid episode after only a few sessions in the laboratory.

بودچون بدرغاریسیدندشبان ازبیش درفت انکه ایشان برارومی اندرشد ندچون شبانگاه بو

IT was not until Stephen LaBerge joined the Stanford University dream laboratory for his doctoral thesis in psychophysiology under the direction of the sleep and dream-research pioneer, William Dement, that any experiments under scientifically acceptable laboratory standards were undertaken.

LaBerge's first major achievement was to induce intentionally lucid dreams in laboratory conditions. But what caught the attention of the scientific community was that he and his research subjects were able to send messages to the waking world from the dreaming realm. Using both eye and hand movements, both he and other investigators were able to send signals while still asleep yet consciously dreaming to the technicians monitoring the experiment.

Since those pioneering cases in the early 1980s there has been a boom in experimental dream workshops specifically designed to induce lucid dreaming, for it has been found that there are so many therapeutic ways in which lucidity can help dreamers in facing recurrent nightmares, or to understand the symbolism of their inner worlds. Many who would not dare to do something in the waking world feel suddenly free to do it in a conscious dream. This has proven to give people confidence in their waking state as well.

Learning something in a lucid dream is far easier than in the waking state. This is why mystics encourage their disciples in learning how to dream consciously. Many meditation techniques, which are easily embraced in a dream, might, in the waking state, take years to practice before any results are forthcoming.

LaBerge has also developed a number of excellent techniques and even some technological devices to aid lucid dreaming. Still, it is acknowledged that lucid dreaming only comes naturally to about five to ten percent of the population, and even then usually needs some triggering device. But even those who do not spontaneously have such dreams can develop the ability if they are strongly motivated and develop a good dream recall.

The major obstacles to the successful invocation of lucidity in dreams can be simply identified as amnesia and habit. The next chapter is devoted to the first — amnesia. We examine why we forget and what we can effectively do about it. The problems of habit are far more entrenched and take up the rest of the volume.

Left: *The Seven Sleepers, illuminated manuscript, Iran, 1550.*
In twelfth-century Persia there were a number of Sufi masters who used conscious and shared dreaming as a meditative practice. The extraordinary ability to be part of a collective dream, in which each dreamer experiences the same world with identical details, challenges all our comfortable ideas about the nature of reality. The painting represents the seven levels of human development, being the degrees of "waking" consciousness we experience before the real awakening.

CHAPTER 4

THE FORGOTTEN REALM

To write something and leave it behind us,

It is but a dream,

When we awake we know

There is not even anyone to read it.

From the doka of Zen master Ikkyu

DURING THE LAST FEW DECADES much has been learned of the process of sleep and dreams, and the major breakthrough which triggered all this activity is acknowledged to be the discovery at the University of Chicago of the sleep phenomenon known as REM, short for rapid-eye-movements. Many readers might well be familiar with the discoveries of Eugene Aserinsky, Nathaniel Kleitman and William Dement and the flood of research which followed them. As it is crucial to any understanding of what might occur physiologically when we dream, be it lucid or non-lucid, a brief survey of what they uncovered will be helpful.

The physiologists first found that within our sleep cycle there were periods when the eyes beneath the lids became very active. These alternated with periods when the eyes moved very slowly or not at all. It was also found that subjects who were awoken during the REM sleep could usually remember their dreams with great clarity, whereas those roused from non-REM sleep could seldom remember even a fragment of a dream. The

breathing and heart rate was irregular and generally faster during the REM period, but both slowed and became more rhythmical as soon as the period passed. We now know, from extensive research which has been conducted worldwide since that initial discovery, that the nightly sleep cycle is made up of a number of clearly defined stages.

At the very threshold of sleep, as the muscles begin to relax, there is a transitional state, often referred to as the *hypnagogic*. This is distinguished by a sense of drifting or floating off, which, for some, is accompanied by vivid, almost psychedelic images. Many sleepers even experience a *hypnagogic startle* as they literally *fall* asleep. This can often be so disturbing as to awaken the subject.

In laboratory conditions as the sleeper drifts into the first stage, the electro-encephalograph, or EEG, which records the changes in brain-wave patterns, detects spiky, rapid *alpha* waves of the relaxed but awake brain. These gradually give way to the slower and more rhythmic *theta* waves of light slumber. This

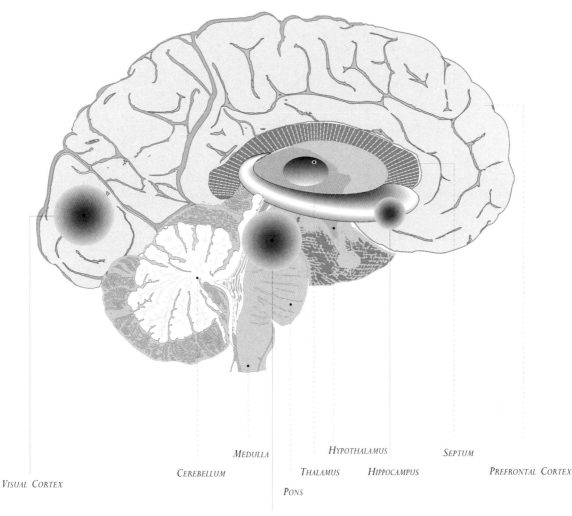

VISUAL CORTEX

CEREBELLUM

MEDULLA

PONS

THALAMUS

HYPOTHALAMUS

HIPPOCAMPUS

SEPTUM

PREFRONTAL CORTEX

NEURAL FIRING WITHIN THE BRAIN STEM

The Dream Machine. *A diagrammatic section through the brain showing the main regions involved in dreaming.*
Together with the neocortex, the hippocampus is believed to provide the neural basis for memory storage. The hippocampus has been thought to play an important role in deciding if information received through the senses is worth committing to memory. It is now known that it is also the source of theta rythms. These appear to be generated in all mammals during periods which are crucial to their learning. It reflects a neural process whereby particular

information essential to the survival of any species is imprinted. What is significant is that while theta rythm is only present during periods of specific behavior pivotal to the survival of each species (rats while exploring, cats while hunting and rabbits while sensing danger), all placental and marsupial mammals share theta rythm during REM sleep.
This suggests that dreaming is intimately connected to learning and is triggered at certain times during the night by neurons firing in the brain stem and by the synchronous presence of theta rythms.

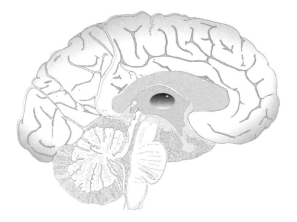

stage can be as short as a few seconds or as long as ten minutes. The theta waves are then joined by rapid bursts of brain activity, shown on the EEG as groups of sharp jumps known as *spindles*. These are synchronous with other waves known as *K-complexes* which show as steep inclines and deep rifts. This is thought to signify the phase of true sleep, although many subjects when roused from this state report that they have been thinking and some even insist they were not asleep at all but still perfectly aware and conscious.

About twenty minutes after the beginning of the sleep cycle the large and relatively slow *delta* waves begin to replace the spindles and K-complexes. This marks a stage which the physiologists consider to be the really deep plunge into the void of sleep. Subjects awoken from this stage often feel fuzzy and disorientated and want to return to sleep again and report that their mental activity is more akin to thinking than to dreaming.

Now we come to what some scientists call the "third state of existence," so distinct is its nature from either deep sleep or wakefulness. It has been referred to as "paradoxical sleep," for while the blood pressure rises, the pulse quickens and the brain waves become remarkably similar to those when we are awake, the rest of the body, except for the rapid movement of the eyes (REM) and tiny spasms and twitching of the fingers and toes, *becomes virtually paralyzed*. It is thought that this is nature's way of protecting sleepers by preventing them from taking violent action which might be

Awake and Relaxed while drifting off to sleep.

STAGE ONE: Light sleep begins

STAGE TWO: Light sleep continues

STAGE THREE: The onset of deeper sleep

STAGE FOUR: Very deep sleep

Above: ***The Four Stages of Non-REM Sleep.*** *The distinctive brain patterns picked up on the electro-encephalograph, or EEG, show the four major NREM stages found in the usual 90 minute sleep cycle. Groups of brain cells generate tiny electrical impulses and as these discharge the EEG shows their activity. Each non-REM cycle is followed by as little as five to as much as thirty-five minutes of REM, or dreaming sleep, which has brain-wave patterns remarkably similar to those found during waking hours.*

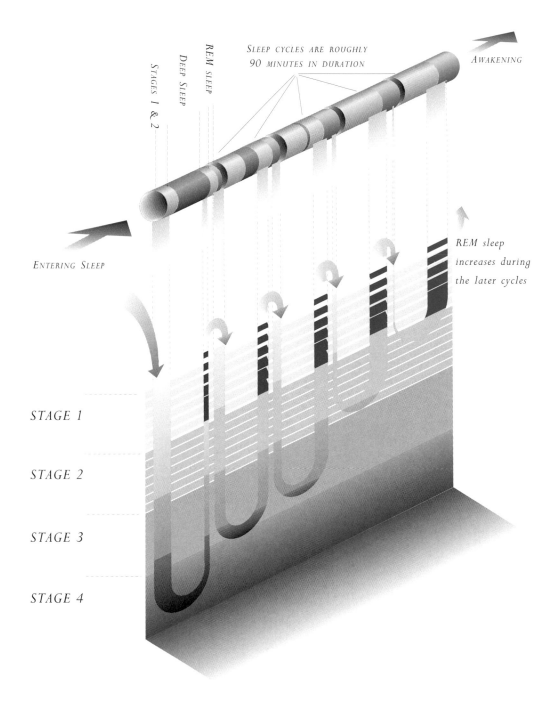

STAGES 1 & 2

DEEP SLEEP

REM SLEEP

SLEEP CYCLES ARE ROUGHLY
90 MINUTES IN DURATION

AWAKENING

ENTERING SLEEP

REM sleep
increases during
the later cycles

STAGE 1

STAGE 2

STAGE 3

STAGE 4

THE FIVE SLEEP CYCLES SHOWING REM AND DEEP SLEEP

appropriate to whatever was being dreamed. This paralysis may have evolved to limit sudden movements by a sleeping animal which might alert a nightly predator.

A person abruptly awoken from REM sometimes has difficulty moving for a few seconds. This phase of *paralytic immobilization* seems to be controlled by nerve centers in the primitive brain stem. This state might account for many of the nightmare situations in which the dreamer is being chased or trying to move within a dream and finding his or her limbs are being dragged through treacle.

The first REM period of the night usually lasts about ten minutes, after which the sleeper almost awakens before slipping back into stage two. The cycle then becomes highly variable with each individual. The deep *delta* sleep may not occur again at all, with the sleeper just alternating between stage two and REM. But usually the complete REM/non-REM cycle lasts about ninety minutes, which means we experience some four to five full cycles of sleep each night.

As each cycle of ninety minutes passes, the proportion of REM to non-REM increases, so that by the early hours of the morning the REM has increased from ten minutes, at the onset of sleep, to as much as one hour during the last two hours of sleep.

This means that "dreaming sleep" accounts for as much as twenty percent of an individual's sleeping life; so that, on average, we can expect to spend almost five years in dreamworlds, and experience over 150,000 dream adventures within a single lifetime.

But just as we have seen the two antithetical conditions of the REM state as being a wakeful and energized brain within a paralyzed body, so we must also consider what at first appears as a natural "brainwashing" process which happens on the border between dreaming and awakening.

We forget.

This almost chronic amnesia is shared by both territories. In dreams we forget about our waking lives as much as we forget our dream existence upon awakening. It is curious that while dreaming we are calling up memory after memory with which to people our plots and scripts. This intensification of and increased access to memory within the dream contrasts markedly with our almost complete inability to grasp the full memories after the dream has terminated. Researchers estimate that more than ninety-five percent of all dream mentation is lost upon waking.

No really satisfactory explanation as to why this might happen has been proposed. However, as virtually all the dream experiments have been conducted on Western subjects, who have no social or spiritual context which particularly values dreams, the reason might simply be cultural rather than biological. As far as is known, many pre-industrial cultures, or those for which the dream has some particular significance, have no problem in recalling dreams.

For any traveler between the realms of sleep the major obstacle to overcome is amnesia. As we move from the everyday world of wakefulness into sleep or from the realms of dreaming into that of awakening, we tend to forget all that we had experienced at the checkpoint on the borders. In order to dream lucidly the traveler must be able to remember both realms simultaneously.

WAKEFULNESS

EYE MOVEMENT

EEG

MUSCLE TONE

HIPPOCAMPUS

The three states of wakefulness, slow-wave and REM sleep. A cat, in its 25 minute cycle, shows that during wakefulness its eye movements and the generation of theta waves in the hippocampus are active while the muscle tone shows a marked decrease during REM. Other than this the two scans seem almost identical.

SLOW-WAVE SLEEP

EYE MOVEMENT

EEG

MUSCLE TONE

HIPPOCAMPUS

REM SLEEP

EYE MOVEMENT

EEG

MUSCLE TONE

HIPPOCAMPUS

BOTH SIDES OF THE BORDER

WHAT is pertinent to our particular quest is that such forgetfulness *on both sides* of the border – in dreaming and in waking – can be overcome, but that in our normal and often stressful Western lives it takes, for most people at least, persistence and self-discipline to do so.

So from the outset of our journey into lucid dreaming there appear two simple rules of thumb. Firstly, as the cycle of sleep nears its end, the amount of time spent dreaming is at its maximum. And, as far as lucid dreaming is concerned, the most likely times that we can become conscious of dreaming is near dawn, at the very end of the cycle, which gives a marvellous excuse for those experimenting in the genre to stay in bed late.

The second rule for the dream journeyman or

Dreaming of Immortality in a Thatched Cottage, by Chou Ch'en, sixteenth-century handscroll, China. As we view the two figures, one flying through the air, and the other asleep, we must ask just who it is that is dreaming. Is it the phantasmal one in the air who experiences the dream, or the apparently solid sleeper whose body is firmly rooted to the ground?

52

woman involves breaking the memory barrier. Any would-be dream seeker *must keep a dream journal.* Of all the many pitfalls and hurdles which will be met if anyone chooses to use the various techniques given this book, the most difficult to overcome is the memory barrier — the built in inertia which blocks the recall of our dreams. Once you begin to remember your dreams with some clarity and detail, then the rest of the process becomes steadily easier and easier as you gain confidence that the important sequences are not forgotten. This cannot be stressed too much.

My own experience as a sporadic lucid dreamer is typical. For when I really decided to invoke conscious dreaming methodically it took me almost three months to gain a measure of success in remembering two or three prominent dreams beyond fragmentary images. And this ability is crucial to any other success. You will find a number of simple methods which, perhaps, just because of their modest aims do not initially appeal to most people. Somehow we all want the pyrotechnics, the dramatic visions and dreams of power immediately — to dance before we have learned to walk.

Above and right: ***Two pages from Jung's Dream
Journal.*** *Carl Jung kept a diary of his dreams which was
known as the "Red Book." In it he painted a record of what must
have been one of the richest dream lives in history. It is strange,
therefore, that he never seemed to have had a fully lucid dream.
If he had, what a contribution he might have made to our
understanding of the collective unconscious when he could have
explored it at first hand.*

KEEPING A DREAM JOURNAL

From this day forth I shall be called a wanderer,
Leaving on a journey.
Thus among the early showers,
you will sleep night after night
Nestled among the Camelias

THE RECORDS OF A TRAVEL-WORN-SATCHEL
Bashō, 1680

KEEP a pen, paper, or a tape recorder by the bed, and if you have a partner be merciful and use a small flashlight to prevent waking them. The journal should be small enough to keep under your pillow or carry around during the day, in case something triggers a memory of an earlier dream. Both pen and pad should only be used for recording dreams. Rituals even as small as these create a sense of something unique, personal and special. It also means that even the sight of these objects, having their special purpose, can be a focus which prompts memory. These are, after all, your passports into another world.

Make a point of consciously deciding that the journal is the place where you will be recollecting your experiences in the dreamworld.

However odd the details might appear, they are only a device to help jog your memory. Most of us have spent our whole lives ignoring our dreams and now you will be carefully recording every detail of them, so do not be impatient. Also remember that dreams, like memories, always

have a context. No memory is an element by and of itself. Very young babies apparently can only recognize objects they have seen before when the whole context in which they originally saw them is precisely the same. Put the self same object on a blanket with a different arrangement of patterns or flower motifs, and the object will appear to be something entirely new. Likewise, our adult memories are always put into an overall context. Sometimes when the context is recreated then the memory of the object also appears, even though the actual object is not there, and so seems surreal or bizarre.

I always tend to remember the same spot in a landscape when listening to a particular piece of music. The whole orchestra playing Beethoven's Ninth Symphony always summons up a country lane in an English village where I was evacuated as a child in the war.

Why this happens within my waking memory is probably because the old church which appears within the scene was where I must have heard choral evensong, and now I superimpose the Choral symphony – first heard ten years later – on the evensong within the context of the village lane.

PRE-SLEEP ACTIVITIES

DIRECTLY before going to bed, there are a number of useful tips. The first is simply to go to bed with a clear head, unbefuddled with alcholol, sleeping pills, or just being too tired. Sit and relax, and allow the mind to clear itself of all the junk accumulated during the day. Of all exercises, relaxation is probably the most difficult for a Westerner under the usual stress of daily life. The most important element in calming the body, to allow an easy entry into sleep, is through regular and rhythmic breathing exercises. Simply breathing slowly or breathing in to the count of five and out on the second five, does seem to be beneficial to many would-be dreamers who find it difficult to drop off. One method is to tense each muscle throughout the body, starting at the feet, as you inhale and let it relax as you exhale. Continue this until you reach the head.

CALM ATMOSPHERE

If you are to make any progress on the royal dream road then it is essential to create an atmosphere of calm. It is almost useless to try any of the methods if you cannot set aside a peaceful time for them.

The room itself where you sleep should be filled with light and calming colors, or for those with more exotic taste, candles and incense. If you have a sympathetic, as well as compassionate, partner, then a gentle foot massage usually works charms on even the most hardened insomniac.

Herbs such as rosemary, thyme and lavender beneath the pillow are noted for inducing a quiet and natural sleep, as will a hot bath immediately before retiring. Some psychics recommend a handful of powdered ginger thrown into the water, which according to them cleanses the aura.

Whatever the case may be, it certainly relaxes any tension in the muscles. If you find these instructions a little daunting, you might remember that a mystic would have probably taken years to enter a deep and meditative state where he or she could access their dreams, while a shaman would have gone through elaborate rituals or a long and often dangerous initiation to be worthy enough to meet the spiritworld. It is common, however, that armchair-shamans tend to expect instant gratification. If we pay for a book on dreams, then surely it should deliver the goods on demand. But the realm or particular aspect of ourselves that we are about to enter does not allow for quick solutions or forced entry. So you might as well relax and prepare for what might be a long wait. Now, in a quiet, calm but clear state tell yourself that you will recollect your dreams during the night.

And to really implant the suggestion firmly into an otherwise often reluctant brain, write it down.

The Dream, by Marc Chagall. The content of most of our dreams
is largely determined by what has happened during the previous
waking hours. Most scenarios are creative variations on particular
strategies acted out in the day and carried into sleep. Lucid
dreaming allows the sleeper an almost limitless spectrum of creative
possibilities, quite beyond our wildest imaginings.

OATH TO ESSENCE

Afirm resolution focuses your attention upon the subject. Nothing will happen without a real commitment, and persistent and regular practice. But once you have made a commitment, or as Gurdjieff might have said, taken an "Oath to your Essence," then your resolve takes on a kind of substance, something that gives a grip to what otherwise is completely ephemeral. If you merely sit in bed saying to yourself that you are going to remember your dreams that night, it is common just to listen to the words without them sinking in to any depth where they might actually work. It is very much like self-hypnosis, and if you are familiar with any hypnosis techniques then these would be of immense help. However, at this stage we are more concerned with the initiate than the adept, so if you can allow the message that you "want to remember your dreams" to really sink as deeply into your being as you can manage, that will suffice. *Intention* or *intending*, as we shall shortly discover, is the single most powerful tool that any dreamer can possess.

DIFFERENT SLEEPERS

No two people fall asleep in the same way. And the very method of falling asleep can affect the particular techniques we will be using. So it is good to touch upon the subject here at the outset. One person might fall asleep on closing his or her eyes, whilst another might take restless hours finally to drop off. Some of us sleep fitfully, constantly surfacing from semi-sleep, while others are dead to the world the entire night.

If before sleep one is given a simple visualizing technique, those who usually fall asleep immediately only need to be distracted from their practice for a second and they are snoring. Give the same technique to someone who finds it difficult to fall asleep, or is apprehensive or nervous, and they might be awake all night thinking about it.

And then there is indigestion. If the surveys are correct, we must assume that sixty percent of you readers suffer as you lie in bed at night. The Tibetans, who really must be the most compassionate meditators on the planet, even have Agar 35 pills for meditators who suffer from chronic stomach cramps and who find difficulty in relaxing. For those who do suffer with this, early nights and really warm conditions help.

A possible addition to your normal vitamin list might be niacin and B6. It has been hazarded by some researchers that a lack of vitamin B6 for some reason makes recall of dreams more difficult. I have no scientific way of verifying this except to say that in my experience it really does seem to help.

REMEMBRANCE

This is a very powerful technique, especially known in Indian Tantra. Before going to bed sit with closed eyes and slowly unravel the day which has passed. Start from the evening and travel back through the whole day until you remember the very way you woke up and what thoughts you encountered in doing so. It is important to be completely accepting and non-judgmental of anyone's behavior, including your own. Be as dispassionate as possible — an observer on the hillside who does not identify with the dramas and passions of what he or she watches. This is an excellent way of ridding the mind of unwanted and irrelevant clutter. The quality of your dreams increases and the number of simple rubbish images which are collected during the course of the day seems to diminish. At the end of the procedure some practitioners visualize compressing the whole day's experience into a hot air balloon and letting it rise skyward or popping it in a bottle and throwing it out into an imaginary ocean. This discipline also helps you to attain a far greater dream recall than normal.

It is known from the Dead Sea Scrolls that the religious Essene communities of biblical times believed that sleep was a small death, and treated it with as much respect. As members of the community went to sleep there was an acceptance that they might not awaken, so when the next morning dawned it was greeted as if it were a new life, a new birth. It appears that these people made it a point to leave nothing undone or unsettled at the end of the day. All arguments had to be resolved, wrongs forgiven and quarrels settled so that each person might be released from the life-day to enter the dream-death-night. Such a way of

Above: **Painting** by Max Ernst. In dreams the brain goes over the day, rearranging scenes and creating new situations in complex new and often bizarre combinations, as in the surrealist painting above. By having a conscious review of what you have experienced throughout the day, before going to sleep, you allow your dreams to become more intensely motivated and to carry far less dross and garbage than normal. In this state of clarity, any choice of a venue you wish to dream, becomes accessible.

entering sleep would mean that one is unburdened by unresolved garbage, so that dreams would be free to pick up deeper and richer threads.

59

ORACLE OF THE FOX

THERE is a lovely dream device, which if my recollection is right, was used by the Dogon in northwest Africa, called the "Oracle of the Fox." It can be creatively adapted in whatever way the reader might like to employ.

When a man seeks the help of the wise man or oracle-teller, he is instructed to order his life in the sand outside his dwelling. He does this by means of various stones and wooden sticks, which represent each part of his life. They might stand for his wives, his cattle, his relatives, enemies and friends. They can represent a spiritual problem which haunts him, or a particularly difficult decision he has to make. Once the man has ordered his life in a big circle on the ground completely to his satisfaction, the wise man places small offering bowls of meat and other foods within the "life arrangement," and the man retires to bed.

Now a number of things occur during the night. Firstly, the subject has decided something must be done about his particular problem. He has acted upon that need and has committed his energies to discovering a solution. Secondly, he has laid out his life in all its various elements before himself. Everything is clear and defined in his mind.

He then *goes to sleep on it*. This phrase and its psychological implications seem to have had a healing counterpart in almost every culture.

Having slept on it and then arising the next morning he and the wise man inspect the arrangement. In the night the foxes have come to take the food in the bowls, knocking over some of the stones or sticks representing the man's life and household and leaving tracks and marks. These physical traces along with the man's dreams are then interpreted by the wise man. The psychological advantages of this system are self-evident. The subject has ordered his life, apportioning each element a size and place within his scheme of things. He has then gone to sleep on it and his dreams, along with the physical oracle outside his house, are then interpreted.

This whole and healthy process demonstrates another aspect of keeping a dream journal, which is to keep waking thoughts alongside those of dream recall. Sometimes dream symbols suddenly make sense during the day, and you understand the significance of an image you encountered in sleep.

The purpose of all the methods in this book is not to enter into the usual dreamwork of interpreting, analyzing or even working actively with dreams. The ultimate goal is the triggering of a lucid dream experience. If you are already a regular lucid dreamer then many techniques can be set aside, except for the dream journal.

U P O N   A W A K I N G

THE CULMINATING part of all the previous preparations comes at dawn. Do not open your eyes immediately upon waking, or if you forget, have some object by the bed to cue or jog your memory. Prepare this before going to sleep the night before by telling yourself that when you see it in the morning you will remember your dreams.

Otherwise, with eyes still closed, try to remember even a fragment of the dream which will act as a magnet for the rest. We all know just how ephemeral dreams can become when you really want to remember them. They seem to evaporate, leaving a general feeling of something having happened in an otherwise empty space. To recapture those memories, they must be allowed to emerge gradually and spontaneously into your consciousness. To attempt to hunt them down ruthlessly is futile. So simply relax with eyes closed and wait for a stray clue to arise. Avoid following any thoughts which bring up all the habits of the morning – like what the mail will bring or whether you forgot to pay the electricity bill last week. Just lie quietly, gently fishing for a hint, and the dream will suddenly rush back. If there is no image forthcoming, write in your journal the sort of images which appear in your waking moments instead. There is no hurry.

Give each dream a title in your journal and record the date. List all the details of who was in it, what they wore, and particular objects or obvious symbols present in it along with your general emotional state. Don't be surprised if what you dream seems a bit dull at first. Only when you have written it all down will you suddenly realize that in some peculiar way it was unique and revealing. They invariably are.

These methods are only a preparation for the subsequent techniques, and are designed to break through the amnesic barrier. Inducing lucid dreaming is certainly not easy but without preparation the reader will discover it is impossible.

The simple practice of keeping a dream journal also gives you a fascinating record of your inner workings. If you also keep a diary at the same time, you will begin to see immediate correspondences between the daytime and nightime realms. As we will later discover, the very act of giving something your full attention gives it substance.

Opposite: **Amma;** *copy of drawing by Griaule and Dieterlin, from the Dogon tribe of Mali, Northwestern Africa. The shamans of the Dogon people have a huge repertoire of signs and symbols which have a complex significance. Amma is the creator who gives rise to 266 signs alone. So the shaman, when called to interpret the signs made by the fox in a dream oracle is considered a highly skilled and respectable practitioner of an ancient tradition.*
Right: *A fossil embedded in a beach pebble is the type of object which can hold a personal reminder for the dreamer. Any small and otherwise unimportant object can be of help, before going to sleep, to enter a dream consciously and to remember that dream when seeing the object upon awaking. In short, the preparations for waking should be as careful and detailed as those for going to sleep.*

CHAPTER 5

GHOST IN THE DREAM MACHINE

If the human brain were so simple that we

could understand it,

we would be so simple that we wouldn't.

Emerson Pugh

LUCID DREAMING HAS MADE A SUDDEN, and what many see as an unnerving, impact on Western assumptions of what has until now been understood to be dreaming. How does this novel phenomenon fit into any of the current theories of how, where and why we dream?

To begin with, how are dreams described or defined in the Western world? Apparently, according to the consensus of workers in the field, dreams are defined as vivid, hallucinatory events occurring in sleep which can involve the entire spectrum of the senses.

While vision appears to be the dominant dream faculty, tactile and auditory sensations do appear in most of our dreams. Taste and smell seem to be poorly represented, and pain is oddly absent, even when many dreamers have excruciating nightmares of physical ruin and threat.

Normal, non-lucid dreaming is seen by many neuro-physiologists and psychologists as hallucinatory and delusional simply because non-lucid dreamers *have no insight into the true nature of the state which they are experiencing*. During a normal dream one adopts an uncritical acceptance of the events as being completely real; that is, until one either wakes up within

the dream and becomes lucid, or wakes up out of sleep, at which point, in both cases, the imagery is seen as a fantasy.

In dreaming we apparently lose that waking faculty which might best be called a critical perspective. Instead, we establish a state of extreme credulity in which all self-reflective awareness appears to be suspended or dormant. The dreamer experiences a single-focused reality, and is utterly absorbed by the magic of the dream event.

A similar lack of insight is found in the delusional states of psychotic patients suffering from what we understand as mental illness. It is also true to say that some of the most basic characteristics of the dreaming consciousness are actually delusional, and in the case of the bizarre quality of the imagery, closer to *delirium, dementia,* and *psychosis* than to any normal

Parable, by Samuel Bak, 1975. Non-lucid dreamers do not recognize the true nature of either their dream environment or themselves. Alert, conscious, and lucid dreaming opens up the possibility of not only gaining insights into one's psychological attitudes or resolving personal dilemmas of the waking world, but also of the actual exploration of the brain itself. One might then discover the location of the one who is creating the whole affair.

The Waiting Room, by George Tooker, 1959. Freud's "pressure cooker" model of the mind is reflected in this Kafka-esque painting of people waiting in cubicles for some unspecified bureaucratic reason. Freud believed that the unconscious mind was a turmoil of socially unacceptable desires and impulses, and was always on the point of exploding, but that we somehow suppressed these drives. It is only in the privacy of our own dreams that we supposedly can let off our anger, lust, frustration and fears. Freud based his assumptions on a limited understanding of how the excitory nerve cells worked in the brain. He was not to know at the time of the existence of the inhibitory neural cells, which are now understood to play a greater role in the higher brain functions.

and sane consciousness. Many researchers would maintain that, if it were not for the fact that we were asleep, we would probably be pronounced crazy. Our sensory illusions, while dreaming, appear to be identical to those of the schizophrenic; the disorientations of time and space, or the non-critical acceptance of dream effects, are as weird as any of the most outlandish assertions of the manic depressive. And even our curious amnesia over what happened in the dream could be likened to the loss of short-term memory found in premature senility.

So, at the outset of our investigation, our seemingly innocent and private dreaming process could be likened to madness. There are even some classical psychologists and traditional neurophysiologists who seriously maintain, and make their living out of that assumption, that the study of dreams is the study of a model of mental illness.

The trouble is that no scientist is really certain why we dream at all. While there are any number of plausible explanations, they are all still only a matter of conjecture, and no single hypothesis seems to match all the facts.

There have been two distinct and opposing schools of thought regarding the question of the dreaming mind, although recent research has begun to blur the edges somewhat. Team A has claimed that dreaming is essentially a *physiological* affair, in which the psychological content and significance of the bizarre events found within a dream is irrelevant and devoid of meaning. Dreams are seen merely as the meaningless debris thrown out by the purely biological upkeep of the brain's neural highways and byways. This physiological, and especially the behavioral, view

has been hotly contested by Team B, which sees dreaming as a *psychological* event in which meaningful images surface in the mind to give valuable insights and hints as to the inner health and behavioral well-being of the individual. Both groups can be forgiven the single-minded fanaticism with which they defend their theoretical standpoints. After all, they both earn their livelihoods by what they each defend so passionately. The truth, however, as it so often does, appears to lie somewhere in the middle.

The classic Freudian view, which came under fire as soon as scientists began using more sophisticated physiological tools, is founded upon the belief that the unconscious mind is somewhat like a cauldron or a pressure cooker, seething with socially unacceptable desires and impulses. Freud believed that it is always on the point of boiling over, or exploding, but that somehow we manage to suppress our personal hotpots sufficiently in order to prevent this happening. Even so, sometimes the pressure cooker must use an outlet or something will simply blow up. One safety valve is the dream, or what we have already heard Freud call the road to the unconscious. Dreams, according to him and to most of his followers, allowed a relatively safe peek at the goings on within the inner recesses of the patient's mind. But the part of the mind responsible for the dream is very tricky and often subtly disguises the truth it contains so as not to be too shattering for the poor, over-sensitive, waking ego. And it is this disguise that needs a trained psychoanalyst to unmask, revealing the hidden face of truth.

HYPOTHESES

IT is now known that Freud had only a partial understanding of the working of the neurons within the brain. At the time he was working only the *excitory* neurons were known to science, so he had reasoned that on occasion they might build up a tremendous electro-chemical charge, which in some way had to find release. Much of his psychological theory rests upon the "pressure cooker" model, with the repressed emotional charge seeking some outlet or safety valve. Freud had no way of knowing at the time that the brain has two types of nerve cells, one *excitory* and one *inhibitory*. And generally speaking it has been found that it is the inhibitors which play a greater role in the higher functions of consciousness within the brain.

This is just one of the many discoveries which challenge the Freudian view of a psychological basis for dream imagery. Throughout the last three decades, there has been a gradual drift away from the somewhat discredited psychoanalytical and interpretive approach to dreaming. In reaction there has been a decided movement towards a materialistic and mechanical explanation of dreams as existing in the brain on the basis of the very nature of its electrical wiring, its chemistry and the miracle of its neuronic interconnectedness.

In using physiology alone to understand dreaming many researchers have fallen into a subtle trap. For it all sounds so plausible, knowing that there are actual physical sources for what we experience which can be measured and fixed by an awesome array of new technologies. But whether dreaming is simply created by the inherent mechanisms of the brain, or dream-machine, or whether the sophisticated technology determines what we discover, is a matter of personal opinion.

One particular physiologically based scenario which has proven to be more resilient, and at the same time more controversial, than most, was that put forward by J. Allan Hobson and Robert McCarley in 1977, which they have called *activation/synthesis*. Since it was introduced it has gone through many awkward revisions and it is by no means the only valid brain-based theory, but it does address some very fascinating issues. Among other things it highlights what was already known, that our brain-minds are actively creative. What the theory suggests is that the brain is so hell-bent on finding significance in the images thrown up by the random firing of its nerve cells, that it will find it even when there is none. What is also remarkable about this hypothesis is that it sees the brain as a dynamic, self-sustaining organ which *generates its own information*. The brain-mind appears to deal with the external world by having *ideas* about that external world. It then automatically

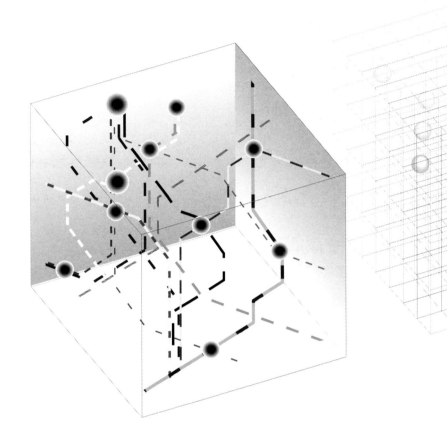

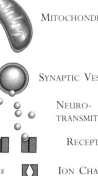

Opposite: **Diagram of a synapse**. This appears at the end of the axon, or the main trunk of a neuron. Any neuron that has been excited conveys information to other neurons by generating spikes of electrical activity known as action potentials. These impulses propagate like waves down the length of the axon to their terminators which are the contact points

MITOCHONDRION

SYNAPTIC VESICLE

NEURO-
TRANSMITTERS

RECEPTORS

ION CHANNEL

between neurons — the synapses — and are converted into electrical and chemical effects that inhibit or excite activity in the connecting neurons. The impulse releases neurotransmitters which diffuse across the synaptic cleft and bind to receptors, which in turn give rise to the generation of new action potentials. When a neuron is excited sufficiently to override the inhibiting input, it sends an electrical charge down its axon. Learning appears to occur by altering the relations of inhibitor and exciter sufficiently so that the influence of one neuron on another changes. Up until now we have tended to see the brain as a huge network of boxes, each with a discrete memory as in the diagram on the right, above. In actuality it is more like a railway network in which some stations, or junctions, are used more than others, as on the left.

ACTIVATION/SYNTHESIS HYPOTHESIS

Synthesizer *both integrates and assigns meaning to otherwise meaningless firings.*

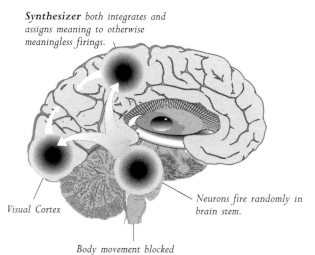

Visual Cortex

Neurons fire randomly in brain stem.

Body movement blocked

PSYCHOANALYTICAL DREAM THEORY

Scrambler *symbolizes and disguises the true meaning of the images and dream events*

Waking experience

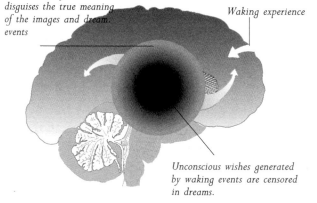

Unconscious wishes generated by waking events are censored in dreams.

Above: *The old psychoanalytic model attributes the strangeness of dreams to the inner censor disguising unacceptable unconscious wishes. The activation/synthesis model is physically brain-based, the strangeness of dreams being attributed to the distinctive physiological nature of REM-sleep generation itself.*

sets about imposing those ideas, which it sees as its own truths, upon that external world. So it could be said that the internally manufactured dream world is then presented to the consciousness as the external universe.

Early researchers expected to find the brain in some sort of resting state during sleep and were surprised to discover that, on the contrary, in sleep our brains appear to be more active than when we are awake. Not only are there heightened bursts of intensity, but also a seemingly wider spectrum of "sights" can be seen during dreams. The sheer ingenuity of the outlandish events and bizarre imagery found in dreams often surpasses our normal experience of the everyday waking world. It has been a frequently observed phenomenon that many creative solutions to apparently insoluble waking problems present themselves far more easily in sleep.

Hobson and McCarley suggested that dreaming-sleep is determined by a "dream state generator" located within the brain stem which periodically triggers the dreaming state in sleep. They showed that the periods in which the generator was switched on coincided with REM periods. At the same time *sensory input* and *motor output* are inhibited, which has the effect of leaving the body partially paralyzed in REM sleep. The forebrain, or cerebral cortex, is then showered in each REM period with internally generated impulses from the brain stem. Under this bombardment the forebrain is believed to attempt to assign meaning and significance to these semi-random firings, making familiar or bizarre images fit as best they can. In other words it interprets these random bombardments as dreams.

Hobson expands the idea. " I believe that dreaming is the sign of a genetically determined, functionally dynamic blueprint of the brain designed to construct and to test the brain circuits that underline our behavior – including cognition and meaning attribution. I also believe that this test program is essential to normal brain-mind functioning, but that you don't have to remember its products to reap its benefits." In other words the content of the dream imagery has no psychological meaning at all.

Unfortunately the phenomenon of lucid dreaming tends to cut swathes into this theory. For if the activation/synthesis assumption – that the forebrain passively creates dream imagery from a semi-random bombardment of impulses from the brain stem – were true, then how could a lucid dreamer control the outcome of his or her dream? And why are there so many reports of an exhilarating response to discovering that one is lucid, which suggests an encounter with high order perceptions rather than with random stimuli?

Hobson recently revised the earlier theory, acknowledging the deep psychological significance of dreams and suggesting that the brain stem activity may act as a switch from one dream episode to another.

A more curious theory is one advanced by the Nobel laureate, Francis Crick of the Salk Institute in La Jolla, California and his partner Graeme Mitchison of Cambridge. They claim that the function of dreams is to remove "certain undesirable modes of interaction in network cells in the cerebral cortex. We postulate that this is done in REM sleep by a reverse learning mechanism, so that the trace in the brain of the unconscious dream is weakened, rather than strengthened by the dream."

This idea of a kind of reverse learning suggests that in REM sleep the complex associative network of neurons might become overloaded by such vast amounts of incoming information. The neo-cortex could then develop what the scientists call "parastic" thoughts that could act like a virus within an otherwise orderly memory store. The researchers concluded that we actually "dream in order to forget."

But once again, while this might fit our ideas of normal dreaming, any lucid event does not fit this scenario at all. The dreamer can go in whatever direction he or she cares to choose, either following the dreaming imagery which is about to be forgotten or summoning up entirely fresh narratives which have been previously chosen while awake. For experimental work in dream laboratories has shown that the dreamer can determine to a surprising extent what is to be dreamed.

The two researchers, like Hobson and McCarley before them, have had to revise their intial ideas by saying that only the bizarre dream content was the result of erasing parasitic thoughts and the "dreaming in order to forget" should now read "dreaming to reduce fantasy."

So we are back to the original question: what is sleep and dreaming *for*? What is its function? Although sleep includes rest and we feel restored and refreshed after it, there seems to be no physiological reason which would find sleep any more effective than just lying down and resting. Sleep and dreaming must have some other real function which has yet to be discovered. And we know that nature is not likely to be so unhandy as to create a biological state which is enjoyed by most mammals, without something more purposive than just giving the brain a chance to let off fireworks at random.

Jonathan Winson, on the evidence of his research at Rockerfeller University on memory processing during sleep, has come up with what appears to be the most reasonable reason for dreaming in mammals. He proposes that dreaming,

> "reflects a pivotal aspect of the processing of memory. In particular studies of theta rythm in subprimate animals have provided an evolutionary clue to the meaning of dreams. They appear to be the nightly record of a basic mammalian memory process: the means by which animals form strategies for survival and evaluate current experience in the light of those strategies."

It would appear that REM, or dreaming sleep, is initiated in the brain stem which also is responsible for generating theta waves in the hippocampus, or the "seahorse," which, along with the neo-cortex, is believed to provide the neural basis for memory storage. There is substantial evidence that theta rythm encodes memories during REM sleep *(see page 47)*.

This would also neatly fit the prevailing theories that, while non-REM sleep evolved about 200 million years ago when warm-blooded mammals began to appear alongside their cold-blooded reptilian cousins, REM sleep, and probably dreaming, evolved about 50 million years later when those early "transitional" mammals had stopped laying eggs and began to give birth to live offspring.

As shown in the diagram opposite, nature appears to have opted at that time for the software of REM sleep rather than increasing the size of the hardware needed in order to evaluate experience and store new information. The echidna or spiny anteater, an egg-laying mammal (a monotreme), provides some insight into the way this might have happened. Monotremes were the first mammals to develop from reptiles and the echidna reflects the dilemma facing nature's engineering design. In order to be able to build up memories to aid in future survival, the echidna needs a large, convoluted prefrontal cortex. In relation to the rest of its brain the size of this is truly spectacular and greater in proportion than any of the primates, including humans. But the echidna does not have REM sleep, so it does not appear to dream. Theta rythms occur while it is foraging and it builds up maps of territory and memories for survival but there are no theta rythms as it sleeps, so it cannot process information during that time. But if, using this prefrontal hardware to fix such memories, the anteater were to develop higher faculties, its cortex would have to be vastly too big for any skull to house it.

With the evolution of REM and the generation of theta waves during that sleep period, the new mammals could process information crucial for their survival like the location of food or the ways of hunting or escape, all activities which have theta rythms present. During dreams this information is once again accessed, to be integrated with past experience to provide a constantly upgraded strategy for behavior.

While scientists don't really seem to know why nature designed sleep at all, given this evolutionary scenario, it is possible to hazard a

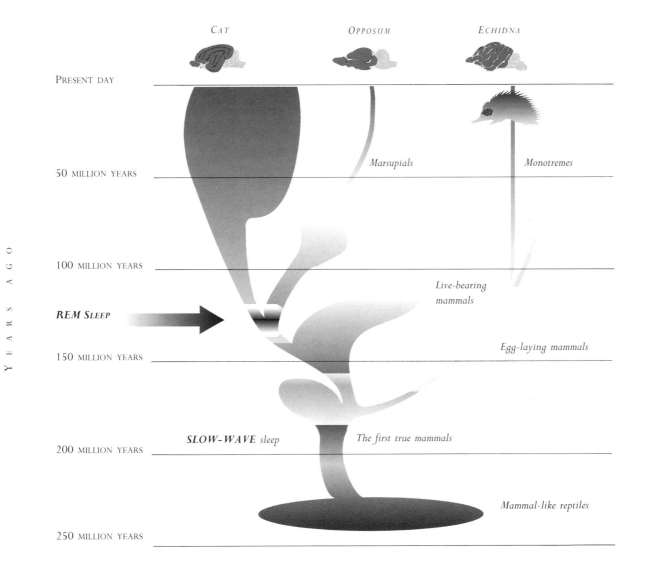

The mammalian evolutionary tree, showing the divergence of placentals and marsupials from the egg-laying monotremes. The first mammals to appear over 200 million years ago are thought to have possessed dreamless, slow-wave sleep and it was not until 50 million years later that true REM sleep developed. The echidna, which is a living example of the divergence of the monotremes, does not possess REM sleep at all. Nature seems to have engineered an alternative solution to the theta waves believed to be responsible in REM sleep for memory retention, by choosing "hardware" as opposed to "software." So this animal has an enormous pre-frontal cortex relative to the rest of the brain, which is relatively larger than any other mammal including humans, but does not have the more effective learning program of dreaming. (Diagram from original by Jonathan Winson)

guess as to why we dream. Dreaming may reflect a memory-processing mechanism inherited from lower species which ensured that information essential for its survival was reprocessed and imprinted during REM sleep. This accumulated information might just be the great unconscious that Freud had proposed. In this memory store the information would be primarily sensory, which is consistent with what we find in our own dreams which are essentially non-verbal, and visual.

One likely advantage of the new evolutionary gift of sleep and dreaming for humans was that human infants have to be born with craniums small enough to emerge through the birth canal — not large enough to operate successfully in the world. But once the organism leaves the womb there is a phenomenal compensation, for the brain enlarges prodigiously within the first year of life. It is during the first few weeks after birth that the brain grows at its most spectacular rate. And it is in those early weeks that the infant has as much as nine or ten hours of REM sleep a day. Some neurophysiologists propose that this internal source of stimulation is both preparing the child for what it will shortly face in its waking environment, and stimulating that astounding neurological growth in the brain itself. Dreams would certainly be the perfect way to test and practice instinctual behavior without the need for the corresponding motor responses.

In adults this ability could have been retained for learning and memory functions. But nature is breathtakingly economical. For not only does she create a learning tool which can be utilized in the peace and calm of the nest or home, but

The cortical neurons in a newborn child have virtually no connections though either the branch-like dendrites or the terminating synapses.

SIZE OF NEWBORN BRAIN

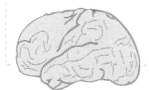

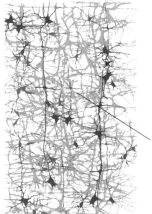

SIZE OF TWO-YEAR OLD BRAIN

Cortical neurons at two years. Through a tremendous surge of hemisphere growth, cortical dendrites (the fine branches from the main neural trunk) grow and glia cells multiply. This is the great age of synaptic development.

Growth of cells in striate cortex. *It would appear that the phenomenal growth of connecting cells during the first two years is accelerated by a child's high proportion of REM sleep.*

apparently she also provides rest for a very particular part of the brain. But which part needs rest?

It is known that most neurons in the brain do not appear to need rest at all. The most likely fatigue-sensitive area of the brain found by Hobson and McCarley turned out to be those metabolic events that synthesize and supply neuro-transmitters to the neural endings. It would appear that the *aminergic* neurons of the brain stem are the most likely candidates for transmitter depletion, for these groups of cells dramatically decrease their activity during sleep, falling to their lowest levels during REM sleep. It also appears that rather than being a period of renewal, or of recovery from the previous day's activity, these neuro-transmitters, by their inactivity, are being *conserved for the next day.*

The functional significance of these aminergic neurons is specifically related to the *critical attentional* and *learning* tasks. So the absence, rest or inhibition of these neurons would perfectly fit the pattern one finds in dreams of a completely non-critical consciousness which blandly accepts the most bizarre events floating before it without ever questioning how such things could possibly happen.

When the aminergic neurons appear to be turned off in REM sleep, all our muscles are also inhibited. This phenomenon occurs in the sleep cycles of all mammals. It appears to be another of nature's dazzlingly economical methods of not only resting the muscles and conserving the transmitters, but also inhibiting physical action when dreaming.

But if these small aminergic neurons, which are

so sensitive to fatigue, are conserving their synaptic efficiency for the coming day, then why is there such a wild festival being celebrated so noisily each night by the other neurons and the rest of the brain? The activation/synthesis hypothesis proposes that the bigger and seemingly indefatigable neurons are firing off in order to ensure the brain circuitry remains open and operative. So here we see the intense activity of the brain during REM sleep as being nothing more than an active maintenance program, keeping the brain channels clear.

But, once again, nature ensures that not only does such maintenance clear the main routes; it also changes the functional capability of the brain through increased activity, consolidation of memory traces, comparative testing of information, repetitive learning patterns and creating solutions to waking problems.

The physiological explanation as to what might be happening within the brain when we have either a lucid or non-lucid dream is still probably best described by using the hypothesis of activation/synthesis. This might best be summarized in this way:

Images arise in the brain when dreaming, even though there is no external sensory input. Such hallucinations are the result of the specific activation of senso-motor brain circuits which appear to link the brain stem to other sub-cortical centers and to the upper motor neurons of the cerebral cortex, or forebrain. If the higher-level neurons of the visual system are excited in the same way that makes them "see" during the daily waking state, they will process that signal *as if it came from the outside world.* In other words, our cortical neurons are simply tricked into believing the signals come from outside. The brain can only recognize what true state it is in from its context, and since most perceptions originate from our waking state, the REM-sleep activated brain assumes the context is the normal one of being awake.

Because the smaller aminergic neurons are inhibited in some way during REM sleep, or are simply resting up, waiting for the next waking and working day, the brain loses all its contextual and referencing faculties, and so accepts the most outlandish behavior of its inner happenings while still imagining its context as being "out there." The brain ascribes *meaning* to internally generated signals simply because there is no external input, only memory, with which to build. Because the brain has lost its normal ability to be alert to both context and self-reference, it has no integral stability which tells it that you are hallucinating in a dream. Only when, for some mysterious or accidental reason, the self-referencing faculty suddenly awakens within the hallucination, do we find ourselves in a lucid dream. Somehow the aminergic neurons have managed to throw off their inhibitions and are suddenly actively awake.

Normally REM sleep is switched on when the firing of the aminergic neurons is subdued. These appear to modulate, or control, the instruction to the forebrain and one of these instructions could be an order to record or remember a particular experience. During REM sleep these neurons fail to sense any message simply because they are inactive. This suggests that a sleeper on immediately awakening should be able to remember his or her dream and so be able to write it down. But that if there is a gap of only a few seconds between waking and trying to recall the dream, it will probably be lost altogether.

This summary still doesn't really answer the questions of why we dream or who is pulling the strings. But we do know that dreaming is a natural activity of the brain, rather than a message from the gods. So we might now ask what function brain activity itself might serve.

The brain is certainly a miraculous and extremely efficient biological tool. It is instrumental in furthering our survival as an organism and it does so, at its highest levels of cognition, by being able to adapt to environmental changes which are totally unexpected and to which our more instinctual, reflexive and habitual reactions are inappropriate. This is known as our *reflective* consciousness. This creative attentiveness is the self-same cognitive function that we find in dreams when we speak of lucidity. And as Stephen LaBerge points out with considerable insight, "Lucid dreamers are thus able to act *reflectively*, instead of merely *reflexively*. The important thing for lucid dreamers is their freedom from the compulsion of habit." In saying this he could be quoting a mystic about the habitual compulsion of seeing our waking world in such a fixed and unchanging way. In lucid dreams we are able to respond reflectively to our dream content. LaBerge continues, "Seen in this light,

Diane, by Ludwig Schwarzer, 1972. The question remains as to who or what actually dreams. Is there a "dream maker" located within a particular region of the brain, or are dreams just the hallucinatory result of our interpretations of random firings in the brain stem?

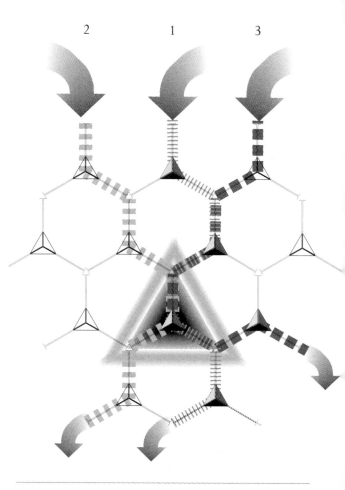

lucid dreaming does not at all appear as a mere abnormality or meaningless curiosity; rather, it represents a highly adaptive function, the most advanced product of millions of years of biological evolution." Bravo!

Perhaps the most recent proposition as to how the brain-mind works is both the most radical and exciting of all, for it is the first to be based upon biology. The Nobel prize winning scientist, Gerald Edelman, and his team believe that the brain is not a biological computer but an evolving ecosystem of competing cells. Edelman feels he is finishing off what Charles Darwin started in picturing the brain as the most complex organism which adapts to its environment by a process of natural selection. Just as species have to learn to adapt to ever changing situations or perish so, in this neural Darwinism, Edelman proposes that "neural selection" helps the brain to adapt to its ever altering environment.

In this spectacular imaginative leap, Edelman and his co-workers are finding how neurons might build up links between each other, so that certain random actions that are rewarded by pleasure or pain have those neural pathways operating at that moment strengthened, while those which are not, shrink. This theory of the survival of the most useful neural networks and their continuing ability to "reproduce" or expand could be carried into the nightly activities of the sleeping brain. During REM sleep the neural pathways which have already been strengthened would play back the events of the day and such a feedback would widen highways into superhighways *(see diagrams)*, while at the same time creating associative

Above: *The brain can be seen as a process of "neural selection" whereby certain cells are favored over others, simply by the number of their ability to create interconnecting pathways with other active cells. These cells are the ones which tend to expand and explore, making new contacts, while others, off the beaten track, cease to grow at all. Dreaming appears to be a method to try new pathways and strategies (2) based upon original waking experiences (1), which, if confirmed by subsequent waking events (3), widen the neural pathways creating super highways and massive interconnecting cells.*

connections which could be tested the next day, once again either surviving or going to the wall. The beauty of this elegant theory is that it fits what we know of nature and what is suspected about dreams.

Apart from lucidity, we see that non-lucid dreaming has biological meaning and significance

2   1   3

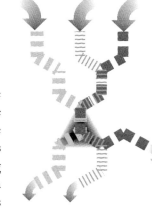

simply because it allows us to practice for our waking environment. The details and the content are unimportant, but the overall process is paramount. If one talks of the meaning and significance of dreams from a psychological standpoint, then this entirely depends upon the particular dream, for not all dream types are the same. While Freud might have believed that dreaming is an urgent communication from the overloaded unconscious, and the modern therapist might claim it to be an inner process for psychological growth, change and transformation, LaBerge suggests it is more like an uninterpreted poem. That we are all nightly poets really does seem to make sense – with some dreams little more than inconsequential doggerel, some like witty limericks, while others are sublime epics. In lucid dreaming poets can consciously choose the form, the meter and the outcome and can relish the effect upon their dream audience – in truth themselves.

If the brain is the physical basis of mind and if consciousness is synonymous with that brain-mind, as Hobson and McClarey so clearly imply, then the question which next arises is which came first – the witnessing consciousness or the brain-mind.

Many mystical traditions maintain that early in childhood the witnessing consciousness gets caught in the trap of identifying with memories stored in the brain. And just as we get lost in our thoughts or dream without being conscious and alert that we are dreaming, the "witness" somehow got lost in the labyrinth of the brain-mind. It is this loss of lucidity and alertness which results in becoming identified with and being attached to thoughts, ideas and ways of perceiving. It is the basis for the false and egoic sense of self, as well as the dream actor who struts his nightly stage. It could be that lucidity, or alert attentiveness, is closest to the original state of witnessing consciousness.

Do any of our current physiological theories give any indication as to the location of the ghostly creator/creatrix within our dream machines? There seems to be a general consensus among researchers that the whole process of dreaming starts in the brain stem which appears to send triggering messages to both the hippocampus and the neo-cortex. This initiates the generation of theta waves in the hippocampus which appear to be a neccessary ingredient in the processing of memory. As far as the physiologist is concerned, the dream maker itself is an inherent mechanism of memory. To some the dream maker is the ghostly spirit of REM, a poet-bard who sends songs into the cortex-self, while others still believe there is no dream maker at all, just the random outbursts of a noisy, robotic, maintenance gang sallying forth from the fortress of the brain stem. But it still looks as though, if we wish to find the elusive creatrix of our dream realms, we must look beyond the essentially physiological theories of our day. All the same, they do offer possible foundations for what apparently is going on, and can be used as a stepping stone when we explore the nature of the lucid dream itself.

DREAM FOCUS

IF after having examined the physiological basis for dreams we have arrived at a somewhat mechanical explanation for our sleeping process, this method makes a welcome psychological balance. It shows that you can influence the subject matter and outcome of your dreams.

Choose a subject that is in some way absorbing your interest during your waking hours. It could be some unresolved problem which bothers you, some uneasiness in a relationship, some worry over your health, or simply how to solve a business dilemma. Whatever shape it takes, spend some time in the day to contemplate the various facets of the situation. Once you have laid out the problem in your mind, in much the same way as the man in the "Oracle of the Fox" in the last chapter, inform yourself that you will find a solution in your dreams that night and that you will remember what it was upon awakening.

Write down whatever is remembered the next morning. You may discover that you have immediately had a clear and obvious dream of the particular subject you had selected. However, it might be the dream images are more subtle and roundabout. A concern, for instance, with a problem of your health might give you images of a city or a complex machine rather than an actual fleshy body. There again you might wake up with the solution to your problem without even remembering dreaming

about it. Do not expect immediate, instant results, but you should be able to have a positive response within the space of a week.

If you follow this simple procedure you will quickly find that regular practice will enhance your dream recall and help to solve many everyday problems, clarifying many dilemmas or confusing situations of daily life.

This is one of the most creative ways of communicating with your nightly dreamer, and if you can establish a rapport with that inner entity and determine what programs you want to dream, then lucid dreaming is already well within reach.

Above: **Screen** (detail) by Tohaku, Japan, 1590. Opposite: **The Emperor's Dream**, watercolor, China. Legend tells of the Emperor Kao T'soy who lived during the Shang dynasty, who dreamed of a man who would help him rule the vast Chinese empire. He then had a likeness painted and sent search parties throughout the land. Eventually a peasant was found who matched the portrait. He was immediately recognized by the Emperor who promptly installed him as Prime Minister.

Part II

TRAVELERS BETWEEN WORLDS

Ittal, *from the Gangan District, Orissa, India. This shows the lucid
dream voyage of the shaman, Gamru, in honor of his wife. The
house is that of their favored deity and the lovers are shown in an
embrace which depicts them as one. Their union has been blessed by
two dream children seen riding an elephant.*

CHAPTER 6

THE FOUR GATES

Why does the eye see a thing more clearly in dreams

than the mind while awake?

Leonardo da Vinci

ALTHOUGH THERE ARE AS MANY TYPES of lucid dreams as there are dreamers, it is useful to examine them within fairly obvious general patterns, each class having its own specific *milieu* largely determined by the attitude of the dreamer.

Anyone stumbling into a dream with eyes open, suddenly finds his or her life transformed beyond recognition. The very act of being able to pull the strings above the dream theater, with its puppet actors engaged in strange dramas, with bizarre scripts in an ever unfolding play, alters, for all time, one's perception of both the dreaming and the waking self. How this metamorphosis expresses itself is largely determined by the dreamer's background.

To be a lucid dreamer in an aboriginal society marks you firmly as a *karadji,* a "clever man," shaman, or a wise woman. You are one who follows the "aerial rope." If you had been brought up in a Tibetan Buddhist environment, you might have sought the guidance of a Lama or dream yogin who could direct your explorations towards a spiritual goal. There again if you live in a North

American or European community which values healers and therapists, then this will influence your aims and determine how you perceive the dream realm.

When we dream it is never a single state. Rather, it is more a number of qualitatively different and altered states of consciousness that we experience, of which our normally vague and unspectacular "garbage" dreams are only the first step on a remarkable visionary stairway. The very original English psychologist, Mary Arnold-Foster, who taught herself to wake up in dreams, wrote as far back as 1921 that, "There are dreams and dreams, and we must get rid of the assumption that they all resemble each other."

In lucid dreaming this is especially good advice, yet it is still difficult to assess whether it is the nature of the dreams that change or whether it is the nature of the dreamer's attitude which alters. In the case we are about to examine it will be seen that, by changing the emphasis, a single input

The Enchanted Realm, by René Magritte, 1953. Detail from a mural in the gaming room at Knocke-Heist/Le Zoute, Casino.

could be interpreted in at least four different modes. When newly awakened dreamers begin to explore the vivid and clear world of the lucid dream, they sometimes encounter a dazzlingly bright light. The fifteenth-century Sufi mystic, Shamsoddin Lahiji, experienced this cosmic light in a lucid dream, and felt that "the whole universe, in the structure it presents, consists of light." He tells of rays of light which joined within him and rapidly pulled the whole of his being upward. After reaching what he called the Sphere of Spheres, he finds himself covered in light without quality or dimension and he is simply annihilated to himself and appears to cease to exist at all. "But," he continues, "once I had found my super existence in God, I saw that this absolute light was I. Whatever fills the universe is I; other than myself there is nothing. The eternal being, the demiurge of the universe, is I."

When confronted by this luminosity the Sufi mystic, who already has certain spiritual expectations and aspirations founded upon his own mystic traditions within the Islamic faith, might see it that way. A North American, on the other hand, involved in the holistic therapy movement, might see the self-same energy phenomenon in terms of a Jungian mytho-poetic event reaching far down into the collective unconscious. The light might then appear as a fountain issuing from the the Earth Goddess and raining its healing vibrations upon the dreamer. A shaman, or sorcerer, more likely would see this whole energy phenomenon in terms of the spirit world.

Someone who is dying, or has a near-death-experience, would see the luminosity in yet a different fashion. There is, for instance, a remarkable consistency in the reports of near-death-experiences which could be summarized in the following account.

The deceased first appears floating above his or her body, only to be drawn into a tunnel towards a dazzling luminosity. In this light-filled world there is an overwhelming feeling of peace and ecstasy and the deceased meets beings of light who emanate a sense of great compassion and warmth. Frequently the whole episode is accompanied by beautiful music and images of the most exquisite landscapes, mountains and rolling meadowlands – a veritable paradise.

In *The Tibetan Book of the Dead* the instructions whispered in the ear of the deceased are briefly summarized as:

Now the pure luminosity is shining before you; recognize it. At this moment your state of mind is by nature pure emptiness, possessing no nature, no quality of color, or substance whatsoever. This pure emptiness is the female Buddha-nature. But this mind is not only emptiness for it is also sparkling, pure and vibrant which is the male Buddha-nature. These two are inseparable, both vibrant luminosity and emptiness in the form of a great mass of light. On recognizing this pure nature as being your mind liberation is assured.

It cannot really be said that these four classes of experience are clear cut modes of lucid dreaming, but rather classic attitudes, or better still, gateways through which the dreamers enter into what appear to be closely parallel experiences.

Each gate leads to a major highway or, to adapt Freud's famous phrase, gives access to the "Royal Road to Awakening."

In many cases, especially in those in which the subject has had no previous instruction, or doesn't belong to any spiritual tradition which has clearly defined maps or simple strategies of action, the dreamer is a solitary traveler. The dreamer has only trust in his or her own ingenuity to fall back on when dealing with some of the bizarre happenings and entities they might meet on the way. Certain Tibetan Tantric schools even use the device of terrifying and awesome divinities and demons to shock the novices into lucidity. When they encounter such monsters within their dreams they consciously recognize they must be dreaming.

Having achieved their objective the dream masters leave the poor lucid novices to deal with the consequences — twenty-foot dream demons, hellbent on unspeakable retribution for having been summoned.

In India the process at least seems less fraught. Here the Yogi uses techniques of breath control and *prana* to ensure a continuity of consciousness in the dreaming state. But for most of us, any venture into the lucid state is without a guide. So it is useful to examine the four gates to the realms of dreaming. Each has its own specific territory and very particular scenery which you might recognize from your own travels. And even if you have not yet experienced lucidity you will probably have a sympathetic feel for the landscapes you would feel most at home in. The four realms we will explore are, Dreams of Power, Dreams of Wholeness, Dreams of Death and Dreams of Awakening.

Opposite: *Target. Even in this abstract target we can begin to see associated imagery after staring at it for only a few moments. It is easy to observe how we all "fill in" information, creating whatever image suits our culture and background.* Above: ***Shaman dancing**, detail from an illuminated manuscript, fifteenth century, Turkey.*

DREAMS OF POWER

THIS "gateway to power" is the one most used by the Shaman, the Sorcerer, the Medicine Man , the Clever Man or the Witch. None of these terms adequately describes the peculiar nature of the calling. And a "calling" is what appears to define it best. A shaman is one who is somehow called or chosen – often being dragged screaming and kicking against his, or her, magical destiny – by simply having certain psychic or spiritual gifts or talents. Strangely many of these receive the calling after a long and protracted illness, which parallels in quite a remarkable way the experiences of psychotics and schizophrenics. The delusional symptoms of psychosis of the mentally ill are those encountered by the shaman who yet somehow learns to integrate the dream world within his or her own reality. As the respected historian of religion, Mircea Eliade, writes in *Shamanism*,

> "The shaman is not only a sick man; he is, above all, a sick man who has been cured, who has succeeded in curing himself. Often when the shaman's vocation is revealed through an illness or epileptoid attack, the initiation of the candidate is equivalent to a cure."

These often reluctant mediums, through trance, vision, or lucid dream, are able to penetrate diverse universes and realms of being. To the

Owl totem,
from the prow of a
Tlingit canoe, Northern
Canada. It is not
surprising that
elusive night birds like owls
have been associated with death,
the spirit realm and dreams
throughout the world.

shaman the cosmos is alive with gods and spirits, energies and vibrations which are all subtly interconnected. In ecstatic trances or lucid dreamings he or she can travel at will in often uncharted territories and perceive the myriad patterns which lie beneath our usual day-to-day existence. In essence the shaman is an interspecies interpreter, a "traveler between worlds," who interposes himself on behalf of his tribe, clan or people, and the content and mode of his lucid dreaming is very much dictated by the traditions and needs of the people he or she serves.

The inward "Dream Journey" that an Australian Aborigine *karadji* makes, for instance, is a pilgrimage typical of shamans anywhere in the world. This dream route is scattered with psychic terrors and sly perils which are to be avoided or overcome. Many of these threatening denizens of the spirit kingdom seem to possess quite gruesome powers, bent on destroying the dreamer if he or she does not have the inner integrity and certitude with which to resist them, or to remain alert and watchful. So real are the dangers that the dreamer must seek the guidance of an elder magician. Only such teachers know the safe routes deep into the dreamings, which can be truly perilous and sometimes even result in actual death or madness.

One of the shamans of the Tamang people from Nepal related to the anthropologist, Larry Peters, how he journeyed to the highest heaven to meet the local shamanic deity, Ghesar Gyalpo. The training which this *bombo* had received is part of what must be the oldest lucid dreaming tradition in the world, stretching back thousands of years. It is the same shamanic tradition which was embraced along with mystical Buddhism in Tibet. The informant told Peters:

"I walked into a beautiful garden with flowers of many different colors. There was also a pond and golden glimmery trees. Next to the pond was a very tall building which reached up into the sky. It had a golden staircase of nine steps leading to the top. I climbed the nine steps and saw Ghesar Gyalpo

at the top, sitting on his white throne which was covered with soul flowers. He was dressed in white and his face was all white. He had long hair and a white crown. He gave me milk to drink and told me that I would gain much *shakti* to be used for the good of my people."

Left: **Little Owl,** *by M.Catesby, eighteenth century.* Above: **Portrait mask,** *from the Haida peoples of Queen Charlotte Islands, Canada.*

DREAMS OF WHOLENESS

THE second gateway to dreams leads more down Freud's royal road to the unconscious than to awakening. The fact that dream workshops and therapies proliferate at an almost alarming rate in the West, is testimony both to the fascination with our inner dreaming world, and to what appears to be a desperate need to integrate all aspects of a personality into a healthy and unfragmented whole. The participants in many of these workshops devoted to self-improvement bypass the traditional role of the professional analyst entirely. As one do-it-yourself dream worker somewhat smugly, yet still with some truth, remarked, "Once dreams belonged exclusively to oracles or psychiatrists. Now dreams belong to the dreamer."

In lucid dreamings this is especially true, for the possibility of being able *consciously* to walk down that royal road and clearly choose which of the various side-roads to explore, in the full knowledge that all the imagery holds vital clues as to the health of your inner being, presents an incredible opportunity for self-growth.

All the personal dream symbolism is available to the dreamer and every psychological waking technique can be used, as it were, directly at the scene of the incident. A technique like Fritz Perl's Gestalt therapy, in which you would normally revisit your dreams in waking life and re-enact them from every angle and from every role, can be used by a lucid dreamer on the spot. The dreamer can alter viewpoints, change the symbols, enquire of each player what they really are within the dream and what they represent. The possibilities are seemingly endless.

If psychologists are correct in assuming dreams to be entirely the reflections of our own inner minds, then each element within the dream must be an indivisible aspect of one's self . If this is so, then each of the elements is playing a part in a rehearsal of strategies to be employed in dealing with the following day, or attempting to resolve particularly unsuccessful past dilemmas. Then to be consciously aware of the patterns flickering into existence must surely be what Fritz Perls claimed was the "Royal Road to Integration."

Gustav Jung had many powerful dreams which he methodically recorded in what was known as the "Red Book," which is justifiably the most famous journal in the history of dreaming. While he did not record many lucid dreams, this particular example has all the hallmarks of one which hovers on the edge of consciously entering the state.

"I was walking along a little road through a hilly landscape; the sun was shining and I had a wide view in all directions. Then I came to a small wayside chapel. To my surprise there was no image of the Virgin on the altar, and no crucifix either, but only a wonderful flower arrangement. But then I saw that on the floor in front of the altar, facing me, sat a yogi in lotus posture,

in deep meditation. When I looked at him more closely, I realized that he had my face. I started in profound fright, and awoke with the thought: 'Aha, so he is the one who is meditating me. He has a dream, and I am it.' I knew that when he awakened, I would no longer be."

Opposite: *Macrocosmic man, from an illustration of the vision of the German abbess, Hildegard of Bingen. Known as the "Sybil of the Rhine," many of her visions appeared as she was sleeping and are thought to have been exceptionally powerful lucid dreams.*
Above: *Mandala-yantras, Tibet. Jung stressed the importance of the mandala as a foundational symbol of integration and wholeness which could be found in individual dreams and collective myths.*

89

DREAMS OF DEATH

THIS is paradoxically the gateway to the "Royal Road to Rebirth." No other culture has ever given so much attention to the journey supposedly taken by the deceased than Tibet. *The Tibetan Book of the Dead*, unlike its counterpart in Egypt, is strangely not really based upon death at all. It would probably best be described as *The Tibetan Book of Dreams*. Originally it arose from a strange marriage between the exotic, demon infested, shamanic traditions of the ancient Bön civilization which survived in Tibet, and the meditative ideas of the Indian Buddhists.

From this unlikely union a whole Yoga of Dreams began to emerge which culminated in the period between the eighth and twelfth centuries when most of the death practices were developed. These were concerned with the psychic force left behind by the deceased and the *bardo*, or gap which happens at the point of death. In it the deceased encounters the entire illusory fabric which he or she has to project and maintain in life. At the point of death it is supposed that we can come to realize that the entire fabric of our universe is self-created. At death we are presented with this fact in what appear as six stages.

But the "bardo" experience itself is that of a luminosity which appears to be the very ground of being. There are two traditional attitudes to this. In one, the Tibetan tantric path, the yogi attempts, through lucid dreaming, to pre-empt death by a sort of dress rehearsal. This is accomplished by penetrating the true nature of the phenomenal world through understanding that it is yet another dream. By becoming conscious in the nightly dreams, gradually the practitioner recognizes that the normal waking world is, in essence, created of precisely the same stuff as

dreams. At the moment of death this is shown to the deceased who – if they are not overcome by the intensity of what, after all, are only their own projections of heaven and hell, and can cease to be identified with the images and events which happen – will realize their own true light and not be born again into the waking dream.

Other traditions like the Dzogchen, whose origins stretch far back to the Old Bön, the most ancient and indigenous shamanistic religion of Tibet, see lucid dreaming as only a secondary effect, arising out of their practices of the natural light. They go directly to the *luminosity* of the "bardo," ignoring the lucid diversions almost entirely. They believe that they don't have to search for enlightenment, for they are already enlightened, having only forgotten this by identifying with the phenomenal world of memories and events. All they need is to be reminded in their practices, and the essentially natural state of illumination is there, as it has always been. No one has to be transformed, only illuminated.

Even though they give little energy to conscious dreaming, they do find that their meditations are far more powerful and effective when they dream rather than when they are awake and have too many trivial diversions. The techniques they use are in essence identical to those of Awakening.

Ascent of the Blessed, by Hieronymus Bosch. This detail from Bosch's famous painting depicts the most commonly observed phenomenon in near-death experiences; that of a tunnel with a bright light at its end. To a Christian there would be the expectancy of angels of light. To those on a more Eastern path, the light might be seen as emanating from the Buddha, Krishna or Mahavira. Our brains are eager to fill in data with past memories of our own expectations.

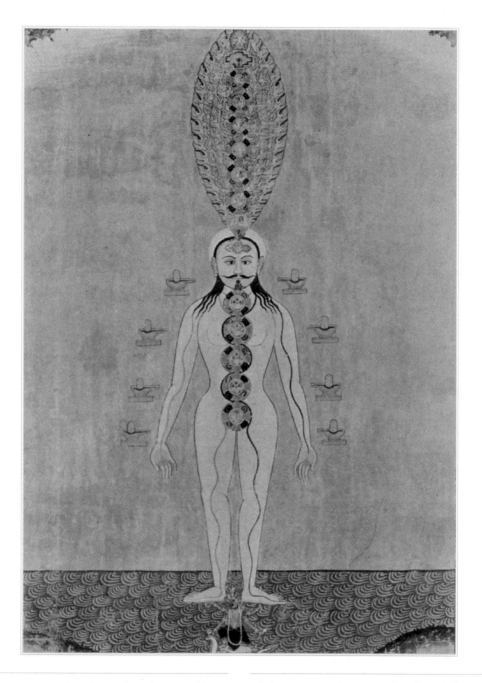

Yogi and energy centers, *Rajasthan, eighteenth century. The Eastern approach to the mysteries of consciousness have been as rigorous as the pursuit of any Western science. However, each spiritual discipline has confusingly different maps of the inner world. Depicted above are the psychic centers which appear within the etheric body of the yogi according to Indian Tantra. The text which accompanies this painting lists thirty chakras; only the major seven are shown. Other disciplines, such as certain forms of Buddhism, only list five chakras which are intimately linked with the five sheaths or bodies. Reading from the base chakra to the crown of the head we find the Muladhara, Svadhisthara, Manipura, Anahata, Visuddha, Ajna, and the Sahasrara.*

DREAMS OF AWAKENING

A TRUE dream of awakening is traveling through the fourth gateway to the Royal Road to Reality. It is the road where you are most likely to meet the mystic and the sage.

According to the perennial philosophy of the Hindu Vedanta, we possess three major states of consciousness. These are waking, dreaming and imageless sleep. There is a fourth state, Turiya, which transcends and integrates them all and is the final destination of all dreams of awakening. Each of these states can be entered into in full lucidity and supposedly make up the full human potential.

THE FIVE SHEATHS

In the classical Vedanta texts it is said that the Self is ensheathed by five bodies which are identified as the *food* or *gross* sheath, the *vital*, the *mind*, the *intellect*, and the *bliss* sheaths. The food sheath is the physical body, the abode of the waking state. The vital sheath is that which determines the internal forces of vitality and the actions of external sensation. The mind and intellect sheaths are the sources of discrimination and identification which make up the separate subject of "me" and "mine." The vital sheath and those of the mind and intellect make up the subtle body, the abode of the dream state. The bliss sheath is said to project the other sheaths in the waking and dreaming states. All the sheaths merge into this causal sheath in deep sleep.

This is but one way of describing the dream bodies. Instead of five sheaths we discover there are seven lucid dream bodies known by Tantric traditions and by the Sufis of the Near East. These bodies pretty much correspond to the five already discussed, but are known in a hierarchic

order of spiritual awareness as the *physical*, the *etheric*, the *astral*, the *mental*, the *spiritual*, the *cosmic* and the *nirvanic*. Each dream body apparently dreams according to its own set of rules or laws, and within realms and territories specific to it. As the lucid dreamer gradually explores each level and approaches the nirvanic level, so the dream worlds take on greater and greater "reality."

The foundational dreaming body is the *physical*. It has its own simple projected fantasies, its own body-related dreams of seeking wish-fulfilment. These are partly the "garbage" dreams we have met in previous chapters. In lucid dreaming they will be found in the sexual fantasies or other desires which the dreamer has denied in the waking world. From evidence of the journals of lucid travelers, satiation of sexual, material or other bodily desires rather surprisingly gives way quickly to curiosity, especially about the dreaming state itself, and thus activates the other dream bodies in turn.

The *etheric* body is the one which is most likely met in out-of-body experiences. When the dreamer is in a non-lucid state the etheric traveling is only remembered as a dream, but when one becomes alert and aware the dreamer can direct his body anywhere desired.

The *astral* body can move into the past and can be equated with visiting Jung's collective unconscious, although it is more often than not confused with the etheric.

The *mental* body is said to travel both into the dreamer's past and into his or her future and in the case of a shaman, the past and future of his or her peoples. This is also the body of power used by sorcerers and shamans. It is, without doubt, the most dangerous dream body of all, because it is said to be able to create whatsoever the dreamer desires. Which means that the dreamer has to be constantly on guard and alert, so as not to create actualized dream entities which can range from demons to Buddhas.

When a Zen master tells his disciple, "If you meet a Buddha on the road – kill him!" it is the false dream road of the mental body he is talking about, a road, it is claimed, which can easily be routed into the waking world. This visualization-actualization tradition is one of the major pathways of the Tibetan sect which has Milarepa as its founding master. He was able to dream consciously, and create whatever forms he wished for. However, in order to reach this state he had been meditating for over eight years in the solitude of a walled-up cave. Such unswerving discipline and perseverance, along with the guidance of one of the greatest masters of the age, Marpa, is very different from the casual attitude of a modern dreamer dabbling with an unexplored region purely out of curiosity.

The *spiritual* body is said to be able to enter eternity where, as Christ once said in describing the Kingdom of Heaven, "There shall be time no longer." Supposedly this is the realm of the archetypal myths which form the basis of the collective dreams of peoples. In this region there is no distinction between dream and reality, the moon or its reflection in the water.

The *cosmic* body dreams of the infinite, beyond space and time. This is the realm of the so-called "Big Dream" where matter and mind have become one. This is the body that the Sufi mystic,

Shamsoddin Lahiji, might have been using when he saw the realm of light.

The final, *nirvanic,* dream body is one which can only be described by the enlightened being, a Buddha, a Mevlana Rumi, or a Lao-tzu. Even then each manages to say something completely different about it. This body is said to "dream" simultaneously of Nothingness and Suchness; the sound and soundlessness. There is no duality, only the present moment unfolding and enfolding.

The separation of a fluid, ephemeral counterpart to our physical body is often given the name "astral projection." Strictly speaking there are many layers of such bodies, as we have just encountered. The etheric is the first and probably the one which most people experience either in out-of-body experiences or in flying dreams.

The dream-body which, in mystical or psychic terms, most lucid dreamers seem to inhabit, as the experiences go deeper, is that of the astral. Those dreamers who are unfamiliar with the Eastern or Western jargon of esoterica often call it the "Dream Body" or even the "Second Body," and this seems a far simpler and more pragmatic coinage, which also avoids the trap of adopting a tradition with unfamiliar terms and concepts which don't quite fit the experience anyway.

As Western lucid dreamers in laboratory conditions have confirmed, this second body is apparently able to explore other dimensions of existence in just the way Eastern mystics have claimed.

While most Westerners' out-of-body experiences have been the result of accidental or fortuitous happenings, and most have a suspiciously similar quality to lucid dreaming, there are many

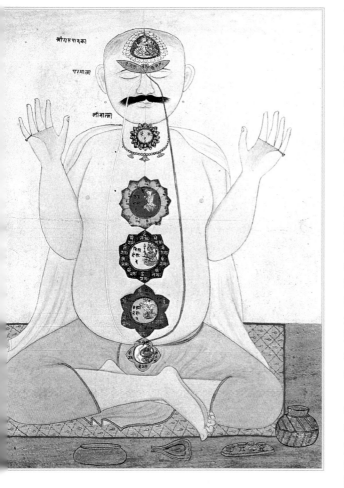

Chakras in the subtle body, *diagram from Himachal Pradesh, India, c. 1820. While the East has the greatest tradition of understanding the nature of consciousness and the subtle energy centers, Western science and neurobiology is beginning to contribute to its wealth of knowledge. Many states, like out-of-body experiences, which were once thought to be the sole domain of those who devoted their lives to ecstatic religious practices, are actually readily available to everyone. And many of the more exotic and visionary states are suspiciously like lucid dreaming.*

techniques which allow a person to transfer consciousness from the physical bodies we accept as real, into a more ephemeral perceptive organism. This dream body allows a person to float up through the ceiling, visit a friend in the normal framework of the natural environment, or radically to alter perspective and encounter bizarre entities from other planes which even appear to have mythic and legendary status.

It is reported from surveys on paranormal experiences in the United States, that as many as forty percent of those interviewed had an out-of-body-experience, or OBE, at some time in their lives, or believed that they had suddenly acquired a second, non-physical body. Many of those interviewed consider the astral counterpart to be the real self, and the physical body to be nothing more than a shell for the perceiving consciousness. Depending upon the religious backgrounds of those experiencers, the second body is seen as a spiritual, higher self or a soul.

Astral or etheric projection of the second body, commonly found in out-of-body and near-death experiences, does resemble dreaming; and, particularly in its clarity and apparent realism, it is almost indistinguishable from, and often interchangeable with, lucid dreaming.

After Oliver Fox had arranged to rendezvous with a friend on the astral plane he was in bed when, his friend, "appeared instantaneously in an egg-shaped cloud of intense bluish-white light and stood by the bed regarding me. He was dressed in a white robe." He continued, "I saw that inside the bluish white ovoid surrounding him were bands of color."

Frequently the dream body of another is seen as

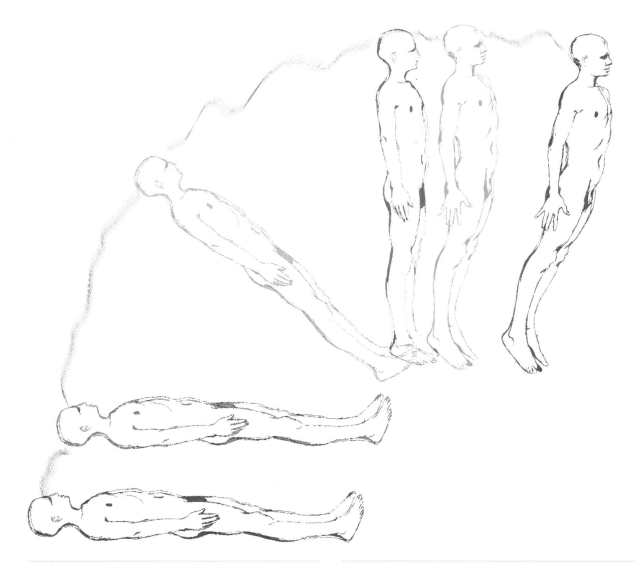

Left: **Sylvan Muldoon.** *In 1929 a book entitled "The Projection of the Astral Body" was published. The authors, Hereward Carrington and Sylvan Muldoon, claimed that astral travel was within everyone's reach if the intention was strong enough.*
Above: **The projection of the astral body,** *as envisioned by the authors who claimed that "The astral body, then coincides with the physical body during the hours of full, waking consciousness, but in sleep the astral body withdraws to a greater or lesser degree, usually hovering above it, neither conscious nor controlled." Muldoon developed methods for astral projection which are very similar to the "pineal door" technique (see 98-99), but he insisted that the astral body is joined by a silver cord which, if severed, results in instant death. The illustration shows the astral body lifting clear of the physical one on the bed. According to Muldoon, when it is about six feet above the bed this incorporeal body rather abruptly rights itself and from then on can move unhindered. However, in retrospect, his accounts are remarkably like those of any lucid dreamer.*

an egg-like mass of auric colors. The Irish seer,
George Russell:

"There was at first a dazzle of light, and then
I saw that this came from the heart of a tall
figure with a body apparently shaped out of half-
transparent or opalescent air, and throughout the
body ran a radiant, electrical fire, to which the
heart seemed the center. Around the head of this
being and through its waving luminous hair,
which was blown all about the body like living
strands of gold, there appeared flaming wing-like
auras. From the being itself light seemed to
stream outwards in every direction; and the
effect left on me after the vision was one of
extraordinary lightness, joyousness, or ecstasy."

Now while many out-of-body experiences are
induced by the dreaming state, the simple
principle is that, in order for a second body
projection to occur, all that is necessary is for the
body to become inert while the mind remains
alert. A deep relaxation of the physical body
followed by a willed excursion of the second body
can induce the self-same lucid state as in
dreaming.

One beautiful method was devised by Oliver
Fox, who gradually had to teach himself as there
was no precedent in his immediate culture to
guide him. He devised a technique in the 1930s
which is as valid and effective as it is pragmatic.
Simply because it was created for a Western
audience, it has many advantages over the more
obscure Eastern methods. This one parallels the
method given in Shiva's one hundred and twelve
tantra techniques.

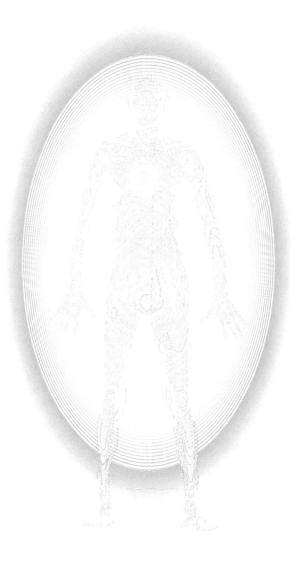

There are simply too many independent reports by psychics, mystics
and visionaries, of seeing humans as ovoid or egg-shaped beings of
light, to ignore their claims. In many shamanic accounts, like those
of Carlos Castaneda, which he claims to be the authentic teachings
of a Yaqui Indian sorcerer, Don Juan, these luminous spheres are
supposedly the true nature of our bodies. Each of our luminous eggs
are said to be connected with a web of light fibers, which in the
East are known as the "hairs of Shiva." By shifting the position of
the center of these clusters the sorcerer is said to be able to visit
other realities and realms, especially in lucid dreaming.

THE PINEAL DOOR

THE practitioner should relax the body and begin to visualize an imaginary trap-door within his or her brain. Breathing should be deep and regular and the eyes rolled backwards, directed at a point between the eyebrows. After a while a certain calm numbness will settle over the body, probably starting at the feet. For some this may be experienced as a muscular rigidity which can become quite painful in the beginning, especially centered in the jaws. A pressure is felt in the head, but if the subject perseveres a pale radiance will illuminate the room, accompanied by brief flashes of light and an increasing noise. The noise can often reach almost deafening pitch.

The subject now may be experiencing the sensation of having two bodies, a static outer body and a more fluid inner body which may appear to be trapped within it. The trick is to visualize, with all one's intent, the subtle body escaping through the trap-door of the brain. The incorporeal self gathers at the pineal gland, as if preparing to leap out through the door. This gland is located in the centre of the brain and has long been associated with the third eye. It was once even believed to be the seat of the soul.

The illumination around the subject now appears to become intensely bright and the noise increases until there is a strange sensation of passing through the trapdoor and with a kind of "pop" you have passed through the "Pineal Door." The noise ceases and the light calms and the student, as Fox then relates, "can get out of bed in leisurely fashion and walk away, leaving his entranced body behind him on the bed."

The plane that the second body inhabits appears to operate under the law of "what you imagine is what get." It is precisely the same realm of the will that is to be found in the controlled lucid dream.

Another explorer of the inner dimensions who had to find his own "sink or swim" technique was Robert Monroe, who later worked in co-operation with Dr. Charles Tart of the Department of Psychology at the University of California. Monroe was tested during his out-of-body experiences. It was found that the wave patterns of the brain corresponded to those found during dreaming. They were accompanied by REMs, although, unlike dreaming, his out-of-body experiences were almost immediate and did not follow the normal sequence of a sleep cycle.

His early experiences were fascinating visitations to friends who were unaware of his presence, and exploring his familiar and known environment, which he was later to call "Locale I." Gradually a new plane of events began to claim his attention, which he described as:

"an immensity whose bounds are unknown, which has depth and dimension incomprehensible to the finite, conscious mind. In this vastness lie all the aspects we attribute to Heaven and Hell."

He was to call this realm "Locale II." This is a place where time is non-lineal, and in one sense completely non-existent. There is only a "now," in which just to imagine or to think something, immediately made it happen. He believed that it was a dimension whose imagery was created by minds who had access to it in dreams, in thought or in death.

The Secret of the Golden Flower, China. This is a Taoist treatise on how to circulate the light within oneself, to release the primal spirit through the square inch between the eyes (the pineal door), and to liberate the heart from the material world. 1.Gathering the Light. 2.Origin of a New Being in the Place of Power. 3.Separation of the Spirit Body for Independent Existence. 4.The Center in the Midst of the Conditions.

Monroe insists that this Locale II is the *natural* environment of the second body.

The techniques employed by both Fox and Monroe echo those of the nineteenth-century Hermetic Order of the Golden Dawn, in which one would relax the body and visualize a radiant white light moving down the spine to the feet. It would then be channelled up through the body as a vortex spinning upwards to the head, leaving the body inactive and dormant as it did so. Finally only the head would be awake as the adept would enter a twilight zone between sleep and lucid dreaming. The magical visualization would then be accomplished by concentrating on various symbols and colors for each of the four elements or for the spirit. These give some focus for where the practitioner wishes to journey.

Having established the existence of these four gateways to lucid awareness and the possibility that the dreamer actually uses a second body to travel within them, we can explore each of the portals in turn and the royal roads that lead from them.

CHAPTER 7

DREAMS OF POWER

I am accustomed to sleep
and in my dreams
to imagine the same thing
that lunatics imagine when awake.

Meditations on First Philosophy
René Descartes

IT HAS OFTEN BEEN COMMENTED UPON by workers in fields as divergent as comparative religion, anthropology and psychiatry, that there is a remarkable resemblance between the inner dimensions of a traditional shaman and those of many patients with psychological disorders. Often the shamanic call – that point at which the subject first manifests talents and abilities to travel in other dimensions of the spirit – comes at times of great misfortune or debilitating physical or mental illness. The difference between how the traditional shamans, or wise women, are treated in their communities and how what is loosely called the schizophrenic is treated in our own Western society, might be summed up as the difference between a "breakthrough" and a "breakdown." Both the shamanic and the psychotic appear to have experiences of an awesome state, often cosmic in dimension, in which the subject is surrounded, and even penetrated, by threatening forces of both good and evil. These must be placated, fought or communicated with, in order to survive.

To both the sorcerer and the psychotic the whole of Nature, and its parallel spiritual dimension, is teeming with spirits, gods and powers, with each and every object having its own unique life and place within the cosmic scheme of things. But while both medicine man and patient seem able to travel between the different realms and states, only the shaman has learned to integrate the various realms and their natural laws into his or her consciousness. The great sickness, the near death rituals, or the mental anguish which has propelled the shaman or shamaness into these other realms, and from which he or she finally emerges, proves able to heal as well as to initiate.

It is small wonder that, in earlier communities, such strange states as epilepsy and schizophrenia came to be regarded as a manifestation of the spirit world, and the subject to be marked as the spirits' chosen representative. But not all those who showed such tendencies survived to become shamans. Only those who managed to master the phantoms of those inner worlds were deemed truly "called." This spon-

Shaman, *Siberia, 1900.* Opposite: *Shaman's rattle from the Haida peoples of Queen Charlotte Islands. Shamans are often chosen for their ability to dream lucidly, which gives a sense of voyaging in two worlds at once. As the dreaming world assumes greater reality so the waking one appears increasingly like a dream.*

101

taneous calling, usually through dreams and vision-trances, is to embody supernatural power and to act as a channel and intermediary between the different planes of existence.

What is pertinent to our investigation is that animistic shamanism (Latin *anima* or "soul") is not only apparently the most ancient of spiritual vocations, predating any religious or mystical equivalents by many tens-of-thousands of years, but it probably originally arose from the experience of dreams. Dreaming of any sort showed that the consciousness of human beings could exist independently of a physical body. This meant that primitive people began to conceive of themselves as essentially two, co-existing beings – one that lived during the day as a waking entity and one that emerged at night as the dreaming soul; the latter being able to take spirit journeys beyond the body and into unknown realms of power. What becomes fascinating in our present context is that most of these shamanic experiences appear to have their origins firmly anchored in the natural process of lucid dreaming.

Right: ***A Spirit Being***, *painting on bark, 1914, Western Arnhem Land, Northern Australia.* Opposite: ***The Flyer****, by John White. A painting of a shaman of the sixteenth century, Virginia. Lucid dreams empower the dreamer to fly. The sense of weightlessness and spiritual freedom is then naturally carried into waking life. From his nightly voyages this shaman, in his own vision, has transcended his material identity to become a bird.*

TRAVELER BETWEEN REALMS

IT is refreshing for a while to leave the current brain theories, with their flat, physiological concepts of the dreaming-self and, instead, reflect upon the magical dream experiences of the shaman.

The Menangkabau tribes of Indonesia believe that the real life force, the *sumanghat*, actually leaves the body in both dreams and serious illness. The shaman, or *Dukun*, must project his consciousness into the dream realm in order to placate or harry the malicious and malignant spirits who are hostile to the subject.

The nomadic Chukchee of Northeast Siberia believe that sickness is caused by the loss of one's soul. Spirits can, however, be enlisted in dreams to assist the shaman to find and restore them to the owner.

There are shamans of Siberia whose methods predate the Tibetan Masters who compiled *The Tibetan Book of the Dead*. Goldi shamans consciously dream-guide the dying or dead subject through the realms of the Otherworld, contacting long dead relatives to act as welcoming parties for the newly deceased. Much the same is recorded among the Karo Batak peoples of Malaysia. When a person dies, the shamaness guides the soul into the land of the dead in a lucid dream.

Native Americans all rely upon conscious dreaming for their vision quests, in which they encounter their unique totem animals who can reveal personal and tribal secrets of healing, omens and psychic hostiles or allies.

The Flyer.

In an account of a Jesuit priest living among the Hurons, we learn that,

"The dream often presides at their councils; traffic, fishing and hunting are usually undertaken under its sanction, and almost as if only to satisfy it. They hold nothing so precious that they would not readily deprive themselves of it for the sake of a dream. It prescribes their feasts, their dances, their songs, their games – in a word, the dream does everything and is in truth the principal God of the Hurons."

This is by no means an extreme case, for in varying degrees all Native American tribes held the dream to be central to life itself, and the very source and foundation of all matters of the spirit. They saw the dream as the inner being's travels in an alternative world which was so real and substantial that any event within it would have similar repercussions in the waking state. A warrior bitten by a snake in a dream would seek out a healer to administer to it in his waking state. And just as an Aboriginal of Australia might have learned a song or a dance in a dream, which he or she would then share with the rest of the tribe, so an Iroqois, Cherokee, Cheyenne, Blackfoot, Crow or Navaho might receive personal dream instructions about taking a totem or choosing a healing herb. Some dreams referred to the life of the entire tribe and gave the group songs, dances, cures and the designs of the complex sand paintings.

Lucid dreams of power were especially revered for they bespoke great spiritual gifts for the tribe and prestige for the dreamer, and many of the rituals and dances of the tribes were created in order to increase the yield of such blessed dreams. One such ritual to ensure a dream of power, was the vision quest. This usually was a particularly hazardous and difficult rite, often marking the passage from childhood, or adolescence, into adulthood. It usually included fasting, isolation, perilous circumstances involving lack of sleep or drug induced states. Many tribes insisted that a successful vision quest was essential for the full maturity of any member of the group. Another method used was dream incubation, which entailed isolation, meditation and sleeping alone in sacred places of power.

For a people like the Iroquois, the dream was an essential core of life, inseparable from all everyday activities. The dream instructed both tribe and individual on how to act and the meanings behind the acts. In cultures such as this, where dreams are so revered, the power of the myth interpenetrates the waking realm and the spiritual reality is lived out within the actions of the society.

By contrast our own Western approach to life seems impoverished and fragmented, the secular and the sacred forever split. Most of us have a terrible insensitivity both to the nature of personal dreams and to our collective dreams, which we know of as myth. Most of us are blind to the incredibly rich visions and inspirations of the dreamworld, whether that world is seen through lucid eyes or not, and so are cut off from the very collective source through which our society has been created.

Although many of the North American tribes used herbs to assist in invoking the vision – such as mugwort, the dream herb – the tribes of Central and South America have access to a far wider range of

hallucinogenic plants to invoke a trance-lucid-dreaming state in which they can remain completely conscious and alert. Peyote, sacred mushrooms, cannabis and mugwort are all used, much as the drink called Bhang is in India. Shamanism in such subtropical regions tends to have an even more exotic and psychedelic flavor than its Northern cousins, but the essential principle is the same – remaining lucid and alert both in dream and in trance.

Possum Spirit Dreaming, *by Tim Japaljarri assisted by Clifford Possum Japaljarri, Papunja, Central Australia. This spectacular dream account shows the whole terrain and the events which occurred to the lucid dream traveler who painted it. Few dream visions are so accessible and precise.*

A: Dream travel line
B: Resting place in the spirit journey
C: Wind breaks for the Corroboree men
D: Old Man's dreaming
E: Yam Dreaming   F: Running water   G: Campsites
H: Death spirit figure   I: Sun and Moon dreaming

DREAM DEATH AND TRANSFIGURATION

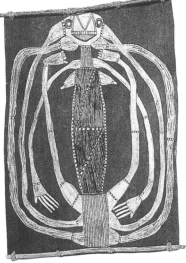

OF all peoples, it is, perhaps, the Australian Aborigines who possess the greatest shamanic awareness of the dreamworld. Their culture is said to extend back over 40,000 years, which makes it the oldest spiritual way known to this world. The shaman, *karadji*, or the "clever man," believes that illness or misfortunes are caused by magical or animistic events often connected to the mysterious spirits of the foundational "Dreamtime." Dreams continue to connect the Aboriginal peoples with what they call Dreamtime, a primal state which embraces the creation of the world at the very dawn of time. Dreamtime is the realm of the mythical beings who first breathed life into the universe.

Like most shamans, it is his task to act as intermediary between the primordial world and that of his tribe. The initiation of a karadji appears to be an archetypical and almost universal process. In dream or in trance, the candidate is killed or dies. Among the Arunta of Northern Australia, he is chosen by the spirits of the Dreamtime who throw an invisible lance which transfixes him through neck and tongue, and another which pierces his head from ear to ear. His dream-corpse is then given new internal organs and crystals are embedded in his wrists and at the third eye, which later will become the source of his magical power. He is literally reborn. This type of death and rebirth appears to be an essential part of the process of becoming a shaman in virtually all cultures.

The Rainbow Serpent is an essential image for the Aborigines. It was said once to have been a rainbow which descended to earth as a vast serpent whose huge body created paths and streams, mountains and rivers as it slithered across the land. It offered two boys shelter from the rain in its maw, but accidentally swallowed them, whereupon they changed into rainbow-coloured Lorikeets and flew into the sky. This is the Aborigine symbol for transformation. And transformation is what being a shaman or medicine man is most concerned with.

The karadji is taught by the *rai* or spirits, through conscious dreaming, to see with an inner eye, and the formalization of many of the "X-ray" paintings of the Northern Tribes hint at this ability. For the clever man can *see*. A Yaralde tribesman tells:

"When you see an old man sitting by himself over there in the camp, do not disturb him, for if you do he will 'growl' at you. Do not play near him, because he is sitting down by himself with his thoughts in order to *see*. He is gathering those thoughts so that he can feel and hear. Perhaps he then lies down, getting into a special posture, so that he can *see* while sleeping."

In Indonesia the Iban shaman in a dream-state has his head cut open; his brain is removed and carefully washed to give him clear vision, gold dust is inserted in his eyes to allow him to see the soul, barbed hooks are attached to his fingers to catch a wandering soul and hold it fast and an arrow is thrust into the heart to make him compassionate

towards the sick and the suffering. Which makes our fashionable "sofa shamans" of the West look a trifle diluted.

Just as the Aborigines are the oldest of the lucid dreamtimers, it is the Tibetan shamans who carry the process into the more exalted realm of mysticism. Here the shaman-monk is often concerned with the passage of death, and assists the deceased to enter into the Other realm. The Tibetan tradition of sorcerers long predates the religions of Hinduism and Buddhism and many of their practices have been absorbed into Buddhist and even Taoist ideas. Their greatest Buddhist saint, Milarepa, was originally a great sorcerer who, if the accounts of his life have any validity, could even bring about hailstorms and other spectacular effects. We will be looking especially at this culture in the next chapter because, at the time of Milarepa, in twelfth-century Tibet, there arose famous schools of Dream Masters who appeared to use lucid dreaming as a powerful method of meditation, which was reported to speed up the whole process of enlightenment.

In the Tibetan world of the shaman, as opposed to the mystic, the initiate is almost always "chosen" through a dream and invariably the dream has been lucid and conscious. The effect of such a dream was usually so powerful and overwhelming that the initiate had to die to his old ways of being, in order to be transformed into a radically new being. Many Western subjects entering lucid dreaming for the first time report experiencing nothing comparable in the whole of their waking lives, feeling as if they had been radically changed by the event and mysteriously transformed.

In the many accounts of magical shamanic experiences, the vast majority can be explained in terms of the radical, yet natural, function we call lucid dreaming. And in suggesting this, it in no way reduces the stature of the shamanic experience.

Opposite: ***Lightning Woman,*** *by Bilinyarra Nabegeyo, 1974, Western Arnhem Land.* Above: ***Rock paintings***, *depicting the Aboriginal myth of Dreamtime, Cape Peninsula, Australia.*

GODS, SPIRITS AND FREUD

WHILE the lucid dream event can radically transform the motivation of the initiate, the full transformation of the perceptual process seems to follow at a more leisurely pace. Entering a dream and waking up within it does not necessarily ensure a clear vision of the phenomenon being experienced. One carries the programming of one's culture and community right into the dreaming world and then projects it upon that world.

For instance when I, as a Westerner, enter a lucid dream I carry no ideas about gods and spirits, so it is extremely unlikely that I see any. However, I do carry some ideas *about* dreams and how they are structured and about the psychological interpretations of Jung or Fritz Perls or of such jolly mystics as Chuang-tzu with his butterfly paradox. So my perception and manipulation of the dream will be very different from that of a tribal shaman in Siberia. For one thing, his responsibility is to the tribe, while my very selfish Western concern is with what is happening to me.

Consider the beautiful account from the Tamang shaman of Nepal whom we have just examined. Once the dreamer mounted the steps, the ancient Ghesar Gyalpo "gave me milk to drink and told me that I would attain much shakti to be used for the good of my people."

Take this passage and imagine for a moment that you were having this dream, in which the essential ingredients were retained, but were now charged with the perceptions of your own cultural background. Without the shamans' sense of responsibil-ity the dream loses significance and meaning. If you were consciously aware of what was happening you would probably act very differently from the shaman and the instructions would be of a different nature. Yet the very fact of being offered a great gift, and told that you would have great spiritual power which would enable you to help others, could still have the effect of completely transforming your daily life.

Many of the reports of fantastic visitations by aliens and UFOs smack suspiciously of lucid or at least semi-lucid dreamings. If the very authenticity and reality of a conscious dream can even make a veteran of the genre seriously question whether he, or she, is awake or dreaming, then it is far more likely that someone, who is unprepared for such an experience and knows nothing of the phenomenon, will honestly but mistakenly believe that they have been visited by little green men.

If you already have had some experience of the remarkable reality of conscious dreaming, and also have a little psychological background, you might reflect that the message of Ghesar Gyalpo, rather than coming from some heavenly visitation, could equally have come from some aspect of yourself of which you were unaware and that for some mysterious reason suddenly surfaced into your consciousness. By having that insight, the sense of metamorphosis is in no way diminished, and might even be strengthened.

Above: **Shaman's drum**, *Denmark.* Opposite: **Diving bird mask**, *Canadian Indians. The bird is symbolically connected to the dream realms visited by the shamans and medicine men.*

THE SORCERER'S SIGHT

MANY reports suggest that to the eyes of a shaman or sorcerer, the essential reality appears as *energy and consciousness* and not matter, and the mind that perceives this energy is understood as a pattern and not as a substance. What shamans have in common with the sages is the desire to go beyond the perceptions of the everyday habitual environment in which somehow we have all been trapped. For, perceptually speaking, we appear to have encapsulated ourselves in one single, yet collective, vision of a stable physical universe in which effect follows cause with dogged persistence

To a psychic or one who can *see,* we all appear hopelessly imprisoned within a habitual energy field which is supported and maintained by our whole society and its beliefs. The fact that we all perceive the world in the same way is simply because we have all been programmed with the same "software" to believe it is that way. *Our expectancies are rewarded by substances.* And the very habitual mold into which we fit our view of the universe appears to prevent us from seeing it any other way.

Of course one might observe that the psychic is as much trapped as we are in a different habitual field. And of course that is true. But what both the mystic and the magician attempt to do is to break out of any perceptual jail and use remarkably similar tools to do so. Where the sage and the sorcerer appear to differ, is that while the shaman seeks other, spirit worlds from which to draw power and energy for both himself and his community, the mystic's only concern is with the mystery of *beingness* and the subsequent obliteration of the sense of being separate from the rest of existence. So one perceptual escapee tends to seek new worlds and their differences, while the other tends to lose the distinctions. But to both, the universe is still founded upon energy alone.

The mystic artist, William Blake, once said that "Energy is Delight," and that it is only our conditioning that makes us ascribe the significance of things and objects to that energy.

This tendency to give meaning and form to clusters of energy appears to be a simple function of survival, but it is to be hoped that, on occasion, we are more than just a mechanism for survival. Yet our long history of social programming, culminating in Darwin's concept of an existence in which only the fittest survive, seems to have created a perception of nature which has in its turn actually created the nature of our perceptions. We perceive only what we have learned to perceive.

If this is so, then the most ancient texts which assert that the phenomenal world is nothing but an illusion, and a dream, may well be right. The ancient seers believed that the energy of existence is real enough, but it is our interpretation or description of it that is entirely our own creation.

This reliance upon a description of "things" must have been necessary for the survival of our species, enabling our ancestors to see the world in the dualistic terms of "food" and "not-food," danger and safety, but after thousands of generations of per-

Opposite: *A Sioux medicine man* offers up a ritual tribute to the mystery of the land.
Above: *A Native American shaman.*
Both photographs are from The North American Indian, 1907-1930, *by E. Curtis.*

ceiving the world in this way we have, as a social species, built up such habitual expectancies of how the world should be, that we cannot see it any other way. We have all been programmed to believe collectively that the world is made up of objects and not an infinite web of interacting energy patterns.

Whenever we make a breakthrough and catch even a brief glimpse of the world in any other terms, we slam right up against our usual conviction of solid and physical certainty. We are unable, without extensive de-programming, to see the world as anything other than an indisputably hard and solid universe. And even when a few pioneering shamans manage to break out of the program into another plane, they more often than not persist in carrying the old habits of interpretation with them. So an Aboriginal karadji sees a Sun Woman, a Lightning Figure or Mimi Spirits, while an experimenter in a lucid dream laboratory might encounter the Earth Goddess, an angel or a wise old man.

It appears that in dreaming we can sometimes slip out of this straightjacket of blinkered perceptions and take the opportunity to visit other realms or to see the greater perspective of our predicament.

Even then we still manage to cloak the vision with our own predispositions as Christians, Muslims, Buddhists or even

Freudians. So, just as it is unheard of for Muslim saints and mystics to see Buddhist Devas when they dream of Allah or heavenly visitations, it is equally unlikely for Hindu brahmins to see Christain angels either.

If it is true that most of us are simply trapped within our own cultural programs, then it is only a short step to say that we perceive and actually create the world around us to fit that program. In psychological terms this is simply saying that we project the world around us, which at least seems a reasonable possibility. But the mystic and the sorcerer actually seem to be saying something far more radical. They claim that we are actually *able to create worlds of substance and matter around us*. Our dreams and desires can become actualized. If this is the case, then all of us are responsible for the world in which we find ourselves. Which could explain the inexplicable, magical and miraculous events which a shaman, a healer or a saint is able to manifest – from sacred ash or swiss watches from the hands of the Indian saint, Satya Sai Baba, to the extraordinary open surgery performed by Indonesian healers.

As we have already seen, psychic accounts of the energy world often describe it in terms of webs or filaments of light. Some accounts go even further, in which the strands are said to be not only energy, but consciousness itself. Each individual, when seen as an energy field, appears to be made up of globular or egg-shaped forms of light having filaments or threads which issue from the central core. Many descriptions also locate an intense cluster of energy which appears to be a focal point for the filaments

from the web-like spaces around. The location of these emanations, curiously, depends upon the particular tradition to which the observer belongs.

Many Eastern traditions, for instance, locate the point where filaments meet to the right of the physical heart; some insist it is at the third eye, while shamans from Central America say it lies a foot or so behind the body at shoulder height. Notwithstanding these differences, all seem to agree that the energy body of a human being is composed of light and that somewhere at the periphery of the aura of the central globe *a point of awareness*, or attention, appears as a smaller but far more intense glow.

Here we encounter, for the first time, parallel concepts to the new scientific theories of a holograph-like universe, which will be explored in Part III. For the present moment it will suffice to note that most mystical and shamanic traditions hold that the position of this *point of attentive awareness* is in some way directly responsible for whatever plane, realm or world the individual is experiencing. The realms experienced appear to be dependent upon which of the millions of filaments in the space around are focused by the cluster. If the point of attention moves from its accustomed position, the person will

Opposite: *Mandalas. Jung encouraged his patients to paint as part of their therapy. He believed that mandalas such as these provided a focus of attention for the patient, triggering deeper archetypal imagery which acted as a liberating and integrating force in the psyche.* Above: *Jung's own painting from his journal showing the archetypal winged and wise old man who used to visit him in his dreams.*

113

experience a totally different realm. It would appear that while the physicists are now theorizing about the possibility of parallel universes, the mystic and the shaman have long been exploring them and carefully mapping their territories. This would explain the insistence of virtually all such traditions, that in any initiation procedure the old person has to die in order for the new to be born. In other words, in order for a new vision of reality to be possible at all, the individual's point of attention has to move to another location on the vast existential matrix of light and energy. In order to shift its habitual spot, created by society's collective view of the nature of the world, and firmly imprinted by its programming devices, the would-be-visionary must clear his, or her, sight by unlearning all that has been programmed. So, as conditioned members of society, the shamans must die so that the programs are symbolically, or actually, erased from their minds to allow for a new *gestalt*.

It usually takes a psychological hammer-blow of considerable force to break through the perceptual barriers, and this would explain why there are so many tales of masters' apparently harsh behavior, and why there is such an insistence on trust on the part of the disciple.

After what is most often unremittingly arduous effort, the initiate might manage to drop some of the learned perceptual programs. Immediately the point of attention becomes more fluid and shifts from its chronic attachment to one cherished point. Having done so, it makes a quantum leap to arrive at a new location. Doing so, it will interconnect with millions of new filaments in a new configuration and a new world or universe will open up. That universe can be then perceived in a number of different ways, depending upon natural disposition, training and social background. This is the realm of the energy body. Those who are trained in certain techniques, or have meditated in particular mystery schools, may begin to see these realms for what they really are – light, energy currents, consciousness and vibrations. This is the resonating universe the Tibetans of the Dzogchen tradition speak of when they do their "practice of the natural light." It is that realm of the bardo which is described in *The Tibetan Book of the Dead* with such exactitude.

But most individuals still manage to interpret the energy currents and clusters as identifiable and familiar objects. A brilliant light may become car headlights or the intense spotlights of an auditorium, and these interpretations are then locked into an entire projected world-set.

It is claimed that many of the more intense and transforming dreams we have are due to a shift in the attention point while we sleep. For in dreaming we no longer seem to maintain such a strict habitual mode of perception, and our point of attention quite naturally shifts like those of children, whose own points are said to be very fluid – that is, before

Above: **The Morning Star.** *A bead ornament made by Crow Indians of the central plains of America.* Right: **Dance dress,** *of the Arapaho Indians, showing a crescent moon and a turtle. These symbolize the material, waking world being overcome by the crows, the magpies and stars of the dream-spirit realm which made up the deeper universe of the Native American Indian.*

shaman, mystic and visionary alike.

All mystery schools, whether they are created by a sage or a sorcerer, have learned methods which, by using lucid dreaming, can systematically shift that point of attention. The awareness of the dreamer is then connected with coherent, relatively stable, yet radically different energy configurations or worlds. These worlds are claimed to be as real as our own, and there are countless descriptions which bear out the dreamers' firm convictions that they have experienced something more real than a dream.

In the world of the mystic there appear to be two quite distinct paths or routes towards freedom and enlightenment. They are the way of the *will* and the way of *surrender*. In the first, discipline and control are essential. The sheer repetition of certain wilful practices slowly but surely wears down the conscious mind which maintains the illusion of our own everyday existence. The mind cannot seem to abide sheer persistence. Eventually it gives way, even if it reduces the participant to the point of exhaustion.

On the path of surrender one does not fight or try to swim upstream, but rather goes with the flow or bends with the wind. Both paths supposedly eventually arrive at the same awakening. The essential difference between the sorcerer and the mystic lies in the polarity of these paths. Using the power of will and imagination the shaman seeks freedom by passing through the myriad worlds of energy, while the mystic simply learns to bypass them, acknowledging them as fascinating but unnecessary diversions.

This brings us to a problem, which arises with virtually all the techniques we are exploring, and which should be addressed at this point.

I now find myself in a quandry, for paradoxically, as far as I am personally concerned, these methods which use *will* as their foundation differ completely from the form of mysticism that I follow. My own explorations under the guidance of a master have

social programming begins to fix the child's point of attention in one habitual spot.

In dreams, it is said, we can move more freely into other realms and this certainly would be borne out by the many accounts of lucid visions seen by saint,

Above: ***The Goddess Kali.*** *A fragment from a nineteenth century manuscript. This dreadful goddess seems a strange choice for such swooning veneration as **Ramakrishna** (opposite) exhibited. But he was a unique religious genius who experimented with virtually all the spiritual paths, including Tantra and dreaming.*

been at the antithetical polarity to the Path of the Will. Yet that path does hold many delicious fascinations for me. My own guide would mercilessly poke fun at my penchant for esoteric garbage. The more psychic I got, the greater his amusement in knocking such notions firmly on my spiritual crown chakra. The Way of the Will is the way of the esoteric, and quite at the other end of the spectrum from such attitudes as those found in the Way of Tao, the way of the flow or what is more aptly described as the Watercourse Way.

The sorcerer and the shaman use *will*. Will is what sends the sorcerer through the barriers, up through the trap door of his or her own internal oubliette. It is what can send the reader into the other worlds of the dreaming self. It is, after all, the subject of most of the methods in this book.

And yet, having played with some of the extraordinary visionary phenomena available in these domains, having gained insights into the nature of reality and those around you, there comes a point where, far from freeing the participant, such talents and visions can become a burden. Such is the problem of the shaman. The normal everyday ego becomes blown up into a massive spiritual monster. Yet the more spiritually swollen it becomes, the more difficult it is to discern — most especially for the owner! The theory behind the path of will appears to be that the more crystalline the ego becomes, the easier it is to shatter. But that needs a master with a mighty hammer.

Even the great Indian mystic, Shri Ramakrishna, was so attached to his visualization and actualizations of the Goddess Kali that he got stuck at the third-eye stage. He would see her everywhere, in both his dreaming and his waking life. Her image was as alive and real as the physical world around him. His own master commanded him to drop the cherished vision, but Ramakrishna simply couldn't bear to destroy his beloved goddess. He needed help. The old master grabbed a splinter of broken glass from the street and deeply cut an incision on his forehead in the spot of the third eye, forcing him out of the ecstatic yet delusional state in order to face the reality of the situation. Painful and violent though such interventions may appear, they work. But few of us are fortunate to have such a master by our sides — one who has gone through the stages before us and knows the temptations to be encountered in the hinterlands of our minds.

So, having outlined some of the perils of this particular path, is there a way to experience lucid dreaming without the concomitant spiritual disease of psychic self-importance? If you study any of the major mystical and shamanic traditions, you will discover that there are many signposts which point out such dangers and suggest alternative routes. Invariably these methods are so mundane and ordinary that it is difficult to imagine they are spiritual at all, and they certainly would not appeal to the very ego that they are designed to supplant.

There is the case of the Zen monk, Hui-Neng, who, it is said, went to a master who asked him whether he wanted to know *about* truth or to *be* truth. When he chose the latter, the master sent him to the kitchens as a humble rice cleaner, a lowly status beneath even the most junior monks. He was told never to visit the master but just to clean rice for the community. After twelve years he had forgotten his spiritual quest altogether, but his mind had

relaxed and naturally, by itself, enlightenment happened. The striving monks of the community lacked what he had – non-striving.

And yet, paradoxically, even in the Will-less and surrendered way there must be a single-minded and persevering attitude. How to reconcile such seemingly opposite aims?

By *intending*.

Intending is the equivalent of Gurdjieff's oath to essence, and is that single-minded attitude to life which Carlos Castaneda's teacher, Don Juan insisted upon. "Intending" is a term actually coined by him, and whatever anyone might think of the questionable truth of Castaneda's account of his sorcerer's apprenticeship, the shamanic principles which lie at the root of his books are unquestionably authentic; and *intending* is the central pivot upon which they turn.

The single-minded intention becomes a focused attitude. This thought is sent into the deeper order of reality as a single burning thirst. The deeper order has a parallel in the scientific theories of the new physics, and we will shortly encounter this deeper reality, out of which the manifest world unfolds, in something known as the "implicate order." This is the very ground of all being, the blueprint of reality, out of which arises the manifest world of phenomena.

Usually we bombard this implicate order with a bewildered and confused chain of thoughts, often completely contradictory in nature. The result is an equally confused and bewildering life pattern unfolding in exchange. But if these thoughts are reduced to a single coherent pattern, like a laser beam, then the result will emerge in the same coherent way. In the worlds of the shaman and sage we are held responsible for what we put into the universe. They firmly believe the law that as we sow, so we reap. And however outlandish and preposterous it might seem, they insist that as we think, *so* our world actually changes to become that thought form..

From this you might conclude that there is will and *WILL*. Perhaps it would be easier to see will as raw energy, and one of the abiding hurdles facing the mystic, the shaman and the unwary reader who embarks upon any of these methods of inducing lucid dreams, is a basic lack of energy. In order to visualize at all, or to make an oath to essence, or to remain attentive, or intend to become conscious while asleep, one needs energy.

Superficially it would seem that a meditator, sitting silently, doing nothing, is the last person to need energy, any more than someone about to fall asleep. But that non-doing disguises a veritable eruption of energy arising beneath, just as we now know that the brain is more active in dreaming than in waking.

Now most of our energy is engaged in maintaining the world around us, and energy leeches away all the time. One Zen master, Ikkyu, used to call this world of desires the "Leaky Road." On it, we all manage to waste our energies chasing desires and maintaining the collective illusions about ourselves. It all leaks down the drain. But through various diligent practices both the shaman and the mystic manage to seal some of the unnecessary leakages, so there is sufficient energy to devote to meditation, or alert dreaming.

The worst hole in the energy fabric is the *ego*, that false sense of self which is the social mask of each individual entity. This illusory persona, which we are convinced is our real self, is the greatest energy drain, for it requires untiring attention for its self-created dramas and sense of self-importance. Most

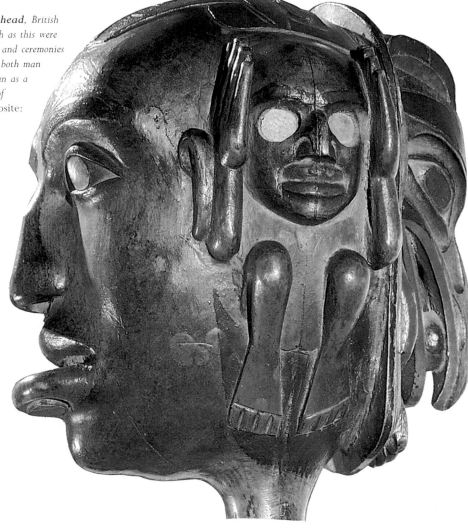

Rattle in the form of a head, *British Columbia. Ritual objects such as this were used in the shamanic dances and ceremonies of the Haida. This image is both man and bird, showing the shaman as a traveler between the realms of waking and dreaming.* Opposite: ***Dog totem*** *from the Sioux Native Americans.*

of the energy available is sucked down the ego tube to bolster its sense of worth, along with its endless thirst to be respected, loved and acknowledged. Without this constant drain we might have enough energy to break through the habitual perceptual prison which both surrounds us and creates the monstrous illusory self in the first place.

We will return to the narcissistic ego in the following chapter, for in dreams the ego often undergoes a strange metamorphosis.

The following methods chosen are either traditional or within the spirit of the shamanic approach.

SHAMANIC METHODS

A VISUALIZATION

FOR VISUALIZATIONS it is always useful to have the recording of a drum beat or a sound that is repetitive . Before sleep the participant relaxes in darkness, or with a blindfold, and visualizes passing through a long tunnel towards a light that is visible at the other end. Through the insistent drumbeat one feels propelled through the tunnel at greater and greater speed. As you enter the luminous haze you can call upon an ally, or guide, to assist in the exploration of the realm entered. This might be in the form of a mythic creature, an animal or a spirit. Take your time waiting for the ally to appear and do not be surprised at its form. Just allow it to take shape in your mind and do not be fearful if it appears in a frightening guise. In fact many shamans claim that the more ferocious the ally or the totem animal, the greater will be your vision quest. Allow the imagined event to unfold, and when you feel it is complete, make a point of bidding the ally farewell, thanking it for taking you into the realm and requesting it to join you in sleep.

Return along the tunnel and await sleep with the resolve that this sequence will be continued in a dream; that you will once again enact the sequence, but that this time, the moment you see the ally, you will immediately awaken within the dream.

If, later in the night, you manage to invoke a lucid dream, use exactly the same waking procedure in the dream. The power and reality will be of a radically different dimension from the earlier guided visualization when awake. So be alert and prepared, when a very real totem animal or ally appears, not to be any more fearful than when you were guiding a daydream. Avoid trying to control the dream past the point of meeting your guide; just follow the dream as attentively as you can, remaining a witness who remembers it is all a dream and yet who can marvel at the details and unexpected turn of events. Entering the "crack between worlds" or the rent in the inner veil, the world of spirits is an archetypal surprise. But remember it is a dream which you can change if the direction it takes is not one you enjoy.

Above: ***Mandan drum***, *Native American, North Dakota. Lucid dreamers encounter spirit guides in their vision quests who give advice, instructions, teach songs and new dances and give special talismans to the dream walkers. Motifs, like the four wind directions painted on this buffalo hide drum, are then executed as a means of recalling or even re-inducing the experience. Right: **Wooden mask**, Ninnivak Island, Greenland. Many shamans are as at home in the rich totemic realms of lucid dreaming as they are in waking life, and seldom make any distinctions over which is more real.*

LIGHT BODY

IN the lucid dream direct your attention to your body. Check what sort of body you possess. This can be done without any sense of being hurried. Take your time and if necessary look in a mirror. You may already see an energy body of light, but if you don't, you can easily intend one and it will manifest. How it appears is an entirely individual matter.

If you see it with a separate brilliant cluster of light and energy somewhere on the periphery of a central globe, bring your attention to that spot and see what happens.

Experiment with this new body, modeling it in the mirror or setting it apart from you as if it were a sculpture of light.

When you are satisfied with its form, attempt to use it, entering into its aura and seeing through its luminosity.

Note from what part of your new anatomy you can *see* and enjoy the surprise of what you can see.

CHAPTER 8

DREAMS OF WHOLENESS

....What is life?
A lie, a patch of shadow,
a fiction, fortune? an illusion?
All life is a dream
and dreams — oh mockery —
are themselves but a dream.

La Vida es Sueno (Life is a dream)
Calderon

WHILE WE MAY SIT BACK IN OUR ARMCHAIRS and ruminate upon the world of the shaman, or even tentatively try out a few shamanic techniques, few of us can really absorb such a perilous and vivid realm, tucked away as we are in our urban or suburban environments.

However dazzling our imaginations might be, we remain at best sofa shamans, and at worst knowledgeable raconteurs who probably don't even notice the moon and its cycles, and if asked couldn't even tell whether the moon waxes from the right or from the left.

How can the urban human feel the earth beneath the concrete highways, or the inner lifetides which sweep us through the seasons? Women at least fare better than men in this regard, for they carry within themselves, in their wombs and ovaries, those self-

same lifetides. Even so, most of us are distanced from the very sources of life that are integral to tribal communities.

Yet humankind is exceedingly resourceful. Many of us have managed to create artificial ways of being natural. Lacking the shared experiences of the tribe, we manage to create such devices as therapy groups and spiritual workshops. Missing the medicine-man and often rejecting the priests, we create psychologists, psychoanalysts, therapists and gurus.

To an increasing number of people there is a sense of a not belonging anywhere, of having lifestyles which only seem to have meaning within an artificially produced corporate pecking order. It is small wonder that so many modern urbanites rush along to their therapy tribe which will listen attentively to the problems of inner growth and encourage the desire to change for the better.

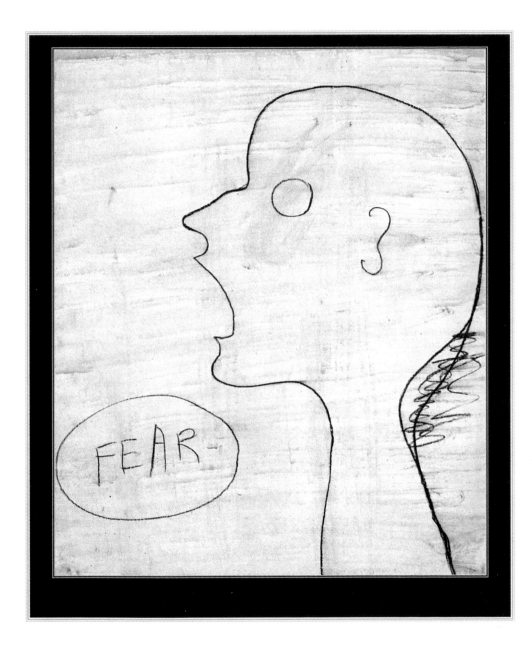

Drawing, by a fifty-year old patient suffering from schizophrenia. While the lucid dreamer might share some of the difficulties that the mentally disordered patient experiences in trying to differentiate reality from dream, conscious dreamers, by the very nature of lucidity itself, learn to meet their inner monsters safe in the knowledge that they are in a non-threatening situation and somewhere just asleep and safe in bed. Their schizophrenic counterparts are not so fortunate, as the borders for them are not so clear cut. It is said that the dividing line between a mystic and a madman is a hairsbreadth.

Seemingly there is an irresistible movement afoot to change ourselves, to transmute our all too human frailties into "higher selves" on more rarefied planes of awareness, or simply to get what we feel are our fragmented or multiple selves into at least a single, more manageable lump.

Even if we were to drop all pretensions of becoming transformed into a higher being, and to just accept ourselves, warts and all, there would always be a few deep-seated wounds that could be healed and fragments that could be made whole again.

In this strangely frenetic scene there is a simple self-help which is natural and available and free — lucid dreaming. It requires no guides, no psychological priesthood and no therapy. In it you are on your own, in your own.

Even the most virulent critics of the use of lucid dreams in therapy admit that they do have an undeniably potent therapeutic and psychological value. But it is still open to argument that, by consciously being able to edit the material which bobs up out of your unconscious realms in a lucid dream, you might dissipate a potential emotional charge. For the symbolic and archetypical imagery which presents itself in normal non-lucid dreams could bring about an insightful change to an unhealthy attitude or form of behavior, which lucid meddling might preclude.

To me, even with such valid reservations, it still seems preferable to be able to enter one's own dream scenarios and consciously face the demons and angels of the mind in order to re-define and re-integrate oneself, rather than leave it to some vague psychological "charge" which might or might not work. The very fact of lucidity implies new understanding, insight and metamorphosis.

During the last decade lucid dreaming has been seen to have a host of therapeutic possibilities. It is already used to combat recurring nightmares, especially in children who seem to be more able to slip into conscious dreaming than adults.

Over two hundred years ago the Scottish philosopher, Thomas Reid, was plagued by terrifying dreams. He was determined to be rid of them. He began to remind himself, as he fell asleep, that whatever happened during his sleep it would only be a dream, and that he was really in no danger at all. "After many fruitless endeavors to recollect this when danger appeared," he managed to become alert, "and often when I was sliding over a precipice into the abyss, recollected that it was a dream, and boldly jumped down." Such methods have become sophisticated with modern techniques and technologies. Now someone with sleep disorders who has recurrent dreams can learn to press a buzzer in sleep as the dream begins. A technician then signals back to remind the dreamer that they are capable of changing the dream's content.

The same effects can be triggered by simple hypnosis on receptive subjects. The patient can be given

a suggestion that triggers lucidity as the dream begins and then they can boldly face whatever is threatening them.

Instead of going into a detailed background of the human potential movement or the theories which lie behind the various therapies of inner growth, I propose to simply offer two guided visualizations. These will enable the reader to play an active and participatory role in unraveling, identifying and signifying the symbols and images found in the daydream.

Opposite: *Oh! How I dreamt of Things Impossible,* by *William Blake. This English mystic artist is known to have had the most vivid dreams, many of them appearing to have been lucid.*
Above: *Cabbage-Dress, by Morgenrot-Morgengran. The ability to change shape, becoming plant or animal, is a common feature in of lucid dreaming.*

Golconde, detail from a painting by René Magritte, 1953.

GUIDED VISUALIZATION 1

THE guided daydream is an extremely powerful technique which gives the subject a small taste of what lucid dreaming might be like. Used in conjunction with many of the other, simpler, methods of inducing lucidity, the subject should have few problems in breaking through the unconscious barrier. It does, however, require two friends who can help. It is ideal if all three take turns in the roles of leading, dreaming and taking notes in this mini dream workshop.

The dreamer should lie blindfold in a comfortable position on his, or her, back. The "guide" should gently rub the crown of the subject's head in a clockwise direction while the "recorder" massages the soles of each of the feet, rotating in a counter-clockwise direction. This soothes and relaxes the body in quite a miraculous way and should be done in silence for about three minutes. The guide then quietly instructs the subject to imagine the energy of the feet extending outwards about three inches. The dreamer should move as little as possible, merely indicating when this is accomplished by raising a finger. The guide then instructs that the energy should be brought back to normal. The same is done to the head, extending the energy three inches and then bringing it back to normal. This procedure is repeated, but each time the distance is increased, first to six inches, then to a foot and finally to a yard. On each occasion the energy is brought back to the normal perimeters of the body.

The subject is then instructed to expand the energy a yard all around the body, and then to extend it to the walls of the room. Once this has been felt, the subject is told to allow this energy to float up, through the ceiling to the very roof of the house or apartment. At this point, if the subject has successfully entered into the visualized condition, and when asked, confirms the experience to be authentic and convincing, the guide begins to direct his or her attention. If not, the guide continues the session but asks at intervals whether the visualizations are becoming clearer and more real. In actuality this intuitively becomes quite clear to the guide as the session proceeds.

It is important to understand that this is a two-way process, in which the questions force the participants to be aware of what they experience. The tendency is for subjects to drift off into a daydream, in which the attention is so identified and caught up in the imagery and thoughts that it simply gets lost, and there is no quality of alertness to what is happening. The guide is there solely to encourage a fully attentive awareness in the dreamer. When the subject actually manages to enter a lucid dream, the same type of attention will be necessary to prevent a slipping back into non-lucidity. It is exactly the same principle.

One question might be about what can be seen on the roof, or whether it is necessary to turn around or float upright. Details of the surrounding scenery thus elicited can, from this vantage point, be seen as a way to keep the subject building up the visualization until it appears to take on a dream life of its own.

Usually by now the subject is ready to go anywhere and do anything he or she would enjoy. The guide can suggest that they might like to fly to other places, familiar or unknown, or that they might even like to travel to the stars. Try to follow whatever feels best. Do not impose a direction but gently and firmly move the subject along with small suggestions, always verifying that it is what the dreamer might like to do. Ask what the subject is wearing and whether they like it, and what is on their feet. If they are wearing shoes, what do they look like or what period in history would they belong to.

It is often at this point that the dreamer has the first real surprise, for the feet might be those of a small child, or have black skin where the subject is white, or vice versa. When confronted with such a fascinating turn of events, as the visualization starts to grip, the daydreamer might show a certain reluctance to continue talking , and become petulant at what is seen as an intrusion. But the procedure ensures that he or she does not get lost in the dream and completely forget what is happening. So it is always good to make this understood before the visualization commences to avoid complications while in the actual session.

The purpose of the recorder is to take down everything being said. This can most easily done by tape. It is also helpful to record observations of emotional responses or excitement shown by agitation, smiling or REM. Each of the three participants can really gain by the experience, so do not become negligent if the dream imagery tends to be obscure or repetitive. Most probably it will be full of surprises and unexpected twists and turns.

Try to get the dreamer to determine the date or period of the scene before them, its precise location, and whether it is set in a rural landscape, a mountain region, a city or a town. Allow them to describe in detail the buildings, the trees, the clothes worn, the type of creatures or persons met and what their attitude is to the dreamer.

Ask simple questions, or suggest that the subject might like to move on or to inspect the scene from a different viewpoint or even through the eyes of one of the dream figures. Sometimes allowing the dreamer to enter into the figures in his landscape and look back at himself can bring gasps of surprise. For often the image of the dreamer is not at all what was expected.

The whole practice depends as much on the creativity, ingenuity and sensitivity of the guide as on the imagery of the dreamer. So it is important for the guide to appear connected and interested. A bored guide can spoil the entire session, for the daydreamer is in a very sensitive space and is almost supernaturally aware of the slightest emotional trace in the guide's attitude or voice. Sometimes the subject experiences what appears to be a past life, which can be very vivid and even threatening. If the subject is fearful, or is being faced with some monstrous image, the guide should gently and firmly remind the dreamer that he or she is not helpless and is actually in control: the monster can either be faced and accepted, and carefully examined in detail, or it can be banished from the daydream altogether. By facing the terror the dreamer often gains a powerful insight into his or her hidden fears — even though the point of the exercise is not to interpret the daydream, but to become aware of the process and to get used to interacting with dream material in a safe and sheltered environment.

At the end of the session it is important to guide the dreamer down to a soft and gentle landing. Just remind the participant of the steps back, down through the roof and into the body. Once back in the body, signal that you are going to count to ten and then let the dreamer open his or her eyes.

Figure in a Landscape, by Premgit, 1992.

Wood on the Downs, by Paul Nash.

GUIDED VISUALIZATION 2

THIS visualization is best done by two people, one guiding and the other with eyes closed, entering the daydream. Verbalization in the first part of this exercise is important, for it somehow grounds the dreamer and prevents an aimless drifting in which the dreamer gets lost and forgets everything. If you would like to try this alone with a pen and paper, then just write whatever you see, as clearly and in as much detail as you can, after reading each short instruction, until you are told to proceed on your own. It is best to do this before you go to bed, either by candle light or by a gentle illumination bright enough only for writing.

You are walking towards a small woodland. It is spring and the flowers in the fields and meadows around are vivid and vibrant with color and life. The woodland is on the side of a hill with a path leading from it to where you are standing. A gentle breeze brings a rich fragrance of new plants and herbs and the sun warms your back. In the distance you can see a high mountain glinting in the bright air.

Close your eyes and imagine the scene before you. When you have fixed it in your mind write down the major details. If you feel like looking again, do so and add this to your picture. Consider whether it is a familiar landscape or somewhere you have never been before. Are there animals, birds or even people in the landscape? Are you alone or with someone else?

You continue walking down the path into the wood itself and you observe all the new growth under the trees. Perhaps there are bluebells or primroses in the spaces under the trees. Maybe the light from the sun is dappling the ground, or are the trees so tall and thick that the wood is very dark? You walk along calmly in the knowledge that, because you know that you are really awake when doing this, nothing can threaten or really disturb you. Just enjoy the scene, whatever it is, as you move deeper into the wood or small forest.

Write about what you feel on entering this place. Whether it is friendly or disquieting. Whether you observe other human or animal life around you which is either reassuring or hostile. Remember you do not have to react to any threatening behavior simply because you are in complete control and can be invisible if it pleases you. When you begin to see light at the other end of the woods, as though the path continues beyond it, stop writing.

You are now emerging from the woods and you are surprised to see that you are quite some way up the mountain. You notice that in front of you there is the mouth of a cave and the path winds past it upwards towards the summit of the mountain. You feel drawn both to exploring the cave and to continuing up to the top, which does not seem as far as you had thought. In going closer to the cave mouth, you see steps descending into the rock, but you cannot at first see where they lead.

Choose which way you would like to go!

Describe the scene before you along with the feelings you have when having to make a choice about going into the mountain or climbing to the top. Then, in the most comfortable position you can find, either lying down or sitting in a meditative position, close your eyes and follow your choice. Do not criticize , analyze or in any way censor either yourself or others you might meet. Just be aware that you are deep within a daydream, wherever it might be, while remembering that physically you exist simultaneously in another place, time or world, in your home. Paradoxically, that body appears to be asleep, while you are awake and adventuring on the mountainside. Allow the episode to unfold without controlling or editing the events. You remain a witness to everything which happens. When you feel that the event is over or has lost its charge, return slowly to your body in your room. Be as aware as you can of the moment you leave the dream and of how you "wake up." Write down the whole scenario while it is fresh in your memory and then go to bed. As you fall asleep, recall how you began to fall into your visualization. Remind yourself when you wake up the next morning of how you also returned to your body after the guided daydream. This can give a real insight into the nature of the change from your waking to your dreaming states and vice versa.

As this is a deceptively easy yet powerful technique, try repeating the visualization with different outcomes, or even different scenarios. For instance, you could start on a city sidewalk heading for a particular house. You could check the weather, the amount of traffic, whether the shops were open and how many people were on the streets. If you entered a house or a building, you could go into the attic or the basement and begin the adventure at that point.

Alternatively you could start in another historical time altogether, either in the past or in a projected future. Likewise, a very powerful visualization is to be boating on a mysterious lake, and to choose between swimming or flying over the lake. Whichever scene you enjoy, give yourself the choice of going higher or deeper. The symbolism is completely unimportant. Witness the detail and complexity of both the plot and the scenery, the actors and the backdrops.

But above all, be aware of the changes in each state and of the maintenance of the awake and conscious dreamer. What you make of the dream is entirely up to you. It will be revealing whatever happens. You will find images which are a complete surprise and in every way unpredictable and ingenious. You will probably be amazed at just how creative and rich the dream material turns out to be. If you were to try to write such an event consciously you would fail miserably, and yet each of you will probably turn out a little masterpiece, with no effort at all, using this simple procedure.

If you choose to work with someone else, they

should merely take you through the first three stages in which you describe everything you are experiencing, and then leave you to complete the event in silence.

On returning you can share the dream with them if you choose.

Allow the dreamer to spot the symbolism and interpret it in their own way, without any pressure or interference from you.

Opposite: *The Easel,* by Micheline Boyadjian. This little painting eloquently suggests the dilemma of both visualizer and dreamer. Who is who — the inert body or the wandering mind? Above: *Placating Old Spirits,* by Albert Carl Willink. We are often helpless in our encounters with nightmarish situations in normal non-lucid dreams. In guided visualizations and lucid episodes such monsters can be exposed for what they really are, and the participant gain insights, integrity and the confidence to deal with them.

133

A CHANGE OF GESTALT

FRITZ PERLS, who must be one of the most per-ceptive psychotherapists of the century, approached dreams from a novel standpoint. He, like Freud before him, believed that the best road to the person's unconscious was through dreams, but he also sensed that by merely intellec-tually identifying the problem which the dream exposed one would seldom effect a cure. He felt that a person uncovered the inner dream symbolism better by re-enacting the dream and playing every role in it, since each role reflects an aspect of the self. His "gestalt ther-apy" methods are the foundation of the following technique. It can be done, as Perls would have done, upon waking from a non-lucid dream. Far more significantly, it can be practiced during its lucid coun-terpart. Let us examine how to use his method in a non-lucid dream first.

You have had a particularly strong dream which has a series of elements in it. Let us suppose that in the dream you are visiting a house, set in the woods. It is mysterious and slightly threatening. For some reason you think you are to meet someone there, but as you come to the front door you lose your confidence in this. On knocking, however, the door opens and there is an old fash-ioned English butler who welcomes you in a per-fectly friendly manner. You enter and he tells you that you are expected. You slowly walk up the main stairway which is very grand and marvellously dec-orated in art nouveau motifs. It glitters as if giving off tiny fireworks. As you arrive at the landing, you are dismayed to see that everywhere there is old

junk, trinkets and useless bric-a-brac. Everything is covered in a deep layer of dust and cobwebs. You pick your way across all this rubble, continuing along a corridor until you come to a closed doorway. You are fearful of opening it, not knowing what you might find beyond. Finally you pluck up enough courage to open the door and go inside. Once there, you know it to be the master bedroom in the front of the house.

In the middle of the room is a huge four-poster bed, heavily draped in grey billow-ing folds, and someone is lying on it. A book is lying by the side of the sleeping body. You quietly go to the bed and look at the book and instantly know that it contains the sacred secret that you have been seeking all your life. You check whether the sleeper isn't likely to awaken, so that you can read it. You are surprised to discover that the face is familiar but you can't quite remember where you have seen it before. You look up into a huge mirror on the wall and see your reflection. It is the same face as the sleeper! You awaken.

You now can enter what might be described as a psychic theater. You play the parts of each and every image in the dream. You become the house in its wooded grounds and sense its size, its history, the number of rooms. You feel whether it is happy or sad and what events have created this emotion. You look out at an approaching figure who is obviously a little afraid of what you might contain. You might even know what it is that the dream figure will find. You then in turn become the butler, the stairway, the bedroom, the secret book and the sleeping figure on the bed. You can discover what the sleeper is dreaming. Perhaps it is the same dream.

This active participation after the dream-event is typical of most modern therapy workshops, which have cloned or gone further than the originator of the technique. Such re-enactments of a dream scenario can be of tremendous help in uncovering inner conflicts, especially when they are played out in front of a group. Often such role-playing offers real insights into the nature of a patient's problems, and enacting them in retrospect can result in a release of tension and emotion which brings the warring fragments together into an integral and complete whole.

Now reconsider the dream as if you had been lucid during it. Let us suppose that the moment you see the house you become lucid and know you are in a dream. You know it is a dream house set in dream woods. You also know that you can banish it with a wave of your dream hand. (And this is where many psychologists fear a danger, for if the dreamer can wave it away, then the whole psychological lesson from the unconscious might be lost. It is equally possible, however, that if the need is great enough the lesson will be offered in a different dream script.) In this case, you feel the tension and charge of something that is waiting for you in the house and you are curious. But the fear disappears simply because you know that it is merely a dream and part of you.

When the butler says that you are expected, you might ask who expects you and this might give you greater insight into the situation. Imagine if he said "The Brain." This would alert you to what could be going on behind the scene. Climbing the ornate stairway you could inspect it far more closely than in a non-lucid dream, and if you entered the role of the stairway, you might know that it was actually a rep-

Opposite: **Fritz Perls** created the technique he named "gestalt therapy," in which the participant acted out each and every role in his dream, giving surprising insights into the deeper nature of the invented imagery. Above: **Femme à la Rose,** by Paul Delvaux, 1936. The theme of a house or a series of interiors is a favorite strategy of the dreaming self. The interior can represent the body or the inner self, which allows the lucid dreamer to explore his or her mansion extensively. Some such investigations have revealed deep insights into the health of both body and mind.

resentation of the brain stem and that you were about to enter your own cranium. Then each element might begin to fall into place, for on entering the front bedroom, you would instantly recognize it as being the frontal lobe and the grey folds over the bed as the intricate folds of the brain itself. The book on the bed might then be transformed into a precious lotus or a pineal gland, and instead of waking up you might have try to awaken your sleeping self on the bed instead.

The question which must arise in any one's mind having done this little exercise is, who or what is it that creates these scenarios, these dreams? Many of you might find, if you follow the guided methods, that the creativity of the visualization is far greater than what you would expect of your conscious inventiveness. If you then consider the full dreaming state, the question becomes even more mysterious. Sometimes the images are so alien and unknown that you could not possibly have drawn upon your own memories. So who or what dreams them? Is it the ego, the mind, the self, the brain's random firings, or what? In order to understand the nature of this question within the context of the holistic Human Growth and Potential movement, we must know what therapy attempts to do in the first place.

Most current workshops and therapies attempt to integrate the personality, either walking the Jungian royal road towards the individuation of the self, or the Perlsian road to integration. The problem is that in our modern and stressful world, we really don't know what a healthy and whole person is supposed to be like, or who the self – or Self – might be. The entire emphasis of early twentieth-century psychology has been pathological. Thus we have many dream psychologies of the sick but relatively few for the healthy.

This lopsidedness is compounded, paradoxically, by the fact that most current therapy aims at the holistic goal of a complete human being. Yet therapists are apparently caught in the dilemma created by the quasi-scientific background of the psychoanalytic field; for simple reasons of professional survival they have learned to remain as scientific as possible and have studiously avoided any taint of the religious or the spiritual within their concept of the complete and whole human. Thus we have a mighty hole in most holistic concepts. And that hole is one which becomes more and more evident when therapy is orientated towards psychological wholeness without including a religious or spiritual dimension.

If we consider the evidence of earlier or more "primitive" cultures than our own essentially materialistic and technologically based lifestyles, we discover that spirituality, religiousness and magic form the basis of life and that to speak of a whole person is to speak of a "holy" person. We witness a terrible loss of this spirituality within our own culture, and it is nowhere seen more clearly than in our ideas about the Self.

One of the funniest (no greater compliment can be paid) psychoanalysts of the century, the originator of the gestalt therapy we have just seen in action, and by default the creator of hundreds of clones across the breadth and depth of America and Europe, was Fritz Perls. Yet even this pinnacle of the trade came smack up against an insurmountable wall at the end of the therapy corridor, just as so many "groupies" do as they sign up for group after group in the hope that the final horizon of integration will be reached. Perls admitted at the end of his life as he continued to work away on his own personal pathology,

"When I concentrate on my schizophrenic layer, I can more and more stay alert and witness the thousand phenomena coming up. But then I either fall asleep or get so restless and excited that I often cannot tolerate that excitement and wander about lost in confusion without the anchorage of involvement."

Honest, yes; but as can be seen at the end of the

therapy, even at the point of death, there is always one more hole to be filled to complete the whole. He has this to say about the ego.

"Now we finally see emerge the picture of health, neurosis and psychosis. The extreme cases are rare and about everyone participates somewhat in all three possibilities.

In health we are in touch with the world and with our own self, that is, with reality.

In a psychosis we are out of touch with reality, and in touch with *maya*, a delusional system essentially centered around the ego, for instance the frequent symptoms of megalomania and worthlessness.

In neurosis a continual fight between ego and self, between delusion and reality, is taking place."

Now Perls' method is somehow to drain the delusional system or the ego and to put that energy at the disposal of the Self, so that the organism can grow and use its natural and full potential. For Perls, as an existentialist, which many therapists claim to be, the fundamental question is that of being a real, authentic and whole self. But what do they mean exactly when they speak of self?

"The Self presents the dream. The Self works to integrate and transform the dynamics within that have been evoked by how we have been living or not been living our lives.

It is the Self that presents the problems of the psyche in some healing context and asks for help from the conscious, or ego-directed, side of the personality.

It is the Self that questions and challenges our awareness, attitudes and choices by presenting other more healing possibilities to our consciousness. It does this through the dream, the dream that shocks, amazes and delights us with possibility."

These are the words of Strephon Kaplan Williams, in many ways Perls' therapeutic successor in the field of dream workshops, who combines two major approaches to dreaming. One is the Jungian journey towards individuation and wholeness, while the other is altering the dream state, based upon methods attributed to the Senoi tribes of Malaysia – the so called "dream people."

But this Self that he and many of his co-workers talk of is a tricky customer. And lucid dreaming forces a closer look at that particular individual than we normally allow.

The idea of self has actually been borrowed in part from the Hindu Vedantic scriptures. According to this source, the basic nature of a human being is that of ultimate wholeness, or *Atman*. It could equally be termed Buddha-nature, Tao or Christ-nature. It is a conflict-free awareness, blissful and free. It includes the egoic individuality, but is also the basic ground of all being; spaceless, timeless and ever-present. It cannot be divided for it is already whole. All separation is illusion. The wholeness of Self is pre-existent, indivisible, and cannot be modified.

Now this hardly matches the Self that Williams, Perls or even Jung appear to be talking about.

According to the Vedantic perennial philosophy, human beings face a double bind. On the one hand, we all want to be whole and we intuitively feel that wholeness and Oneness is the very ground of our being. However, the dilemma arises, that the very gaining of that transcendent Christ or Buddha consciousness entails the annihilation of what we know of as our separate selves, or egos. So we actually begin to fear our own Buddha-nature, and instead of recognizing it we create symbolic substitutes for it and the most misleading of these simulacrums is the ego. We substitute our egos for *Atman* and by doing so prevent the possibility of recognizing that we already are that which we seek.

This is why I personally think that many New Age therapists become frustrated when they never quite seem able to reach the horizon of individuation. This is the desert of endless horizons where most therapies eventually grind to a halt.

Da Free John has labeled our ideas of the self as "Narcissus." He looks beyond any therapy at creating a whole being when he says that self:

"... is the reduction of the world to the form of his own separate person.

The traditional paths see his salvation either within or without.

But there is no salvation for Narcissus.

Narcissus must die.

Salvation is Reality, which has nothing to do with Narcissus."

If we are truly seeking the reality which lies behind the dreams then we must go beyond the normal limits of the therapy chambers and explore the realms of the spirit.

"As long as he is Narcissus he must die.

There is only Reality, which is not Narcissus.

Therefore, salvation is Reality, which is understanding.

Understanding is the absence of Narcissus.

Where there is the absence of Narcissus there is only Reality."

If this sounds a little too serious and obscure, you may feel more at home with J. Krishnamurti as he simply pounds the ego with a blunt axe. Both of these mystics surely make us take a little more care when defining who's really *who*.

"So long as we live within the field of the mind there must be complications, there must be problems; that is all we know. Mind is

sensation, mind is the result of accumulated sensations and reactions and anything it touches is bound to create misery, confusion and endless problems. The mind is the real cause of our problems, the mind that is working mechanically night and day, consciously and unconsciously. The mind is the most superficial thing and we have spent generations, we spend our whole lives, cultivating the mind, making it more and more clever, more and more subtle, more and more cunning, more and more dishonest and crooked, all of which is apparent in every activity of our life. The very nature of our mind is to be dishonest, crooked, incapable of facing facts, and that is the thing which creates problems; that is the thing which is the problem itself."

Now from what we have learned in therapy, it would appear that it this is "crook" who is supposedly sending *honest* messages in dreams to the *dishonest* waking mind or self!

While it is accepted by both existential and religious therapists that the ego is bad and a false sense of self, the terminology is vague when it comes to the Self, itself. The point I am belaboring is, do not too quickly pick up attractive holistic jargon, because it is often misleading.

For one of the strangest lessons to be learned as you enter the realm of lucid dreamings is that the Self, whether it is capitalized or not, begins to appear to be just as much a dream as the ego. More beautiful perhaps, more gilded or full of radiating light, but still a dream. In a lucid dream, however, there is often a mysterious quality of unidentified and alert consciousness that for the moment we might call the "witness on the hill." It is this witnessing consciousness

which is the true goal of most mystery schools. Lucid dreaming has proved to be one of the simplest and most effective ways of allowing it naturally to arise.

Young Girl with Book, by Boris Zaborov. In a lucid dream it appears that we are less inclined to have a fixed sense of identity. It is easier to enter into the role of someone entirely different or return to childhood or an adolescent state.

WHOLESOME METHODS

MILD

THIS is the most effective method devised by Stephen LaBerge. MILD stands for Mnemonic Induction of Lucid Dreams and is simplicity itself. It is based upon our ability to use context to remember something. When I look at the knot in my handkerchief, I will remember to pay my car tax. We form a mental connection between what we want to do and the future circumstances in which we intend to do it. LaBerge goes on:

"The verbalization that I use to organize my intended effort is: 'Next time I'm dreaming, I want to remember to recognize I'm dreaming.' The 'when' and 'what' of the intended action must be clearly specified.

I generate this intention either immediately after awakening from an earlier REM period, or following a period of full wakefulness, as detailed below. An important point is that in order to produce the desired effect, it is necessary to do more than just mindlessly recite the phrase. You must really intend to have a lucid dream. Here is the recommended procedure spelled out step by step:

1. During the early morning, when you awaken spontaneously from a dream, go over the dream several times until you have memorized it.

2. Then, while lying in bed and returning to sleep, say to yourself, 'Next time I'm dreaming, I want to remember to recognize I'm dreaming.'

3. Visualize yourself as being back in the dream just rehearsed; only this time, see

yourself realizing that you are, in fact, dreaming.

4. Repeat steps two and three until you feel your intention is clearly fixed or you fall asleep."

LaBerge makes an interesting connection: the mental set involved in this practice is very like the one we adopt when we decide to awaken at a certain hour. The ability to set an internal alarm clock to wake up from our dreams can be as easily utilized to awaken in our dreams.

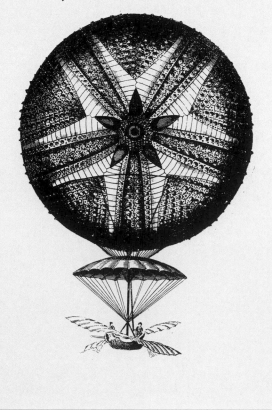

HAND VISUALIZATION

GEORGE Gurdjieff's technique predates by over seventy years the one described by Carlos Castaneda as being given to him by his Yaqui Indian teacher, Don Juan. It is very simple in essence. The object of your attention is irrelevant, just so long as it is familiar. In this case it is your hands. During the day make it a point to look at them frequently. Close your eyes and visualize them whenever you have a spare moment. While awaiting sleep, remember what you have been doing all day and re-visualize them. Take this image with you as you fall asleep and tell yourself that if you see them again you will be dreaming, and that you must become aware enough to awaken in your dream.

This is a simple habit-forming routine which admittedly takes time to take effect, but it is probably the most successful trigger mechanism of all. Gurdjieff's disciples record that it usually took about three to six months before there was any success, but it does work. By associating your hands with being in a dream, it also has the added effect of undermining your habitual assumptions of the waking state.

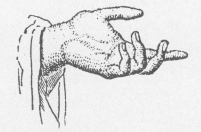

SELF-HYPNOSIS

IN the field of holistic therapy there must be dozens of methods of self-hypnosis. The simplest is to make yourself comfortable in whatever way best suits you. Starting at the feet, feel each muscle and every part of the feet and ankles tense up and then relax. Feel the tension/relaxation slowly spread up the body as if in rippling waves. Do this slowly, allowing each part of the body to become completely relaxed. When you get to the head, tell yourself to count down from ten to zero and that when you reach zero you will be in a light trance state. Know that you can come out of it by reversing the countdown from zero to ten.

Once in the trance state you can instruct yourself in the simplest terms possible that you will both recognize and remember your dreamings. You can tell yourself that at some time in the night you will dream of an object. It is anyway good to have a dream object by the bed to remind you of your resolve to dream lucidly. The moment you see the object in your dream, you will awaken within it. Keep the object in a special context and every time you look at it while awake tell yourself you are dreaming.

When you have given the instruction to your entranced consciousness, gently reinforce the command by simple repetition. Feel confident that your message has got through.

HYPNOSIS

You can of course go to a reputable hypnotist who can probably put you in a deeper trance than you are able to induce yourself. This will be far more effective. But be very sure of your intentions, and that you can communicate to the hypnotist exactly what it is you want to do. Not all hypnotists will have come across lucid dreaming. They will need to know precisely what you mean by waking up within your dream. It is best to enquire before you book an appointment whether they have had any experience in this field. Most modern practices are familiar with the procedures.

THE ROOM

This is a lucid dream scenario for the dreamer who is able to dream lucidly on command.

Decide to create a room which is set apart from all other realms. Preferably start with a door, to which only you possess the key. You open the door and will the creation of a room which is private and secret — for you alone. This is your temple, a sacred, quiet place where you can be yourself and are completely at ease. You notice you have collected a number of things. All your hopes and desires are here. The paintings and drawings around the room illustrate these desires and yearnings. Here you will find memories of your favorite people, or you can meet them here through a magical portal which is in one wall. All the *crème de la crème* of your memories are here in

some form. Just allow them to form slowly after you have created the whole room as your inner sanctum. When you leave the room you can lock the door to ensure that only you can enter.

Make a point of going back to this room every time you dream or you remember to do

so. Inspect the memories from time to time and check if any are changing or whether certain cherished persons have anything to say to you as they come through the portal. Maybe they pick up objects in the room. This special place is your check on being whole and healthy, your "state of play" room.

Girl in a Room, by Micheline Boyadjian, 1969. *The lucid room technique is very powerful as it gives you a base from which to operate. With regular use objects kept within the room assume a greater and greater substantiality. If you can keep an object in the room which you also have in your normal waking bedroom, this will act as a trigger for inducing lucid dreams.*

HEALING DREAMS

PERHAPS those who might benefit most from any lucid dream program would be those who are physically disabled in some manner or are bedridden. For anyone who is restricted in their ability to move around their environment, is infirm, blind, or has any other sense impaired, lucid dreaming can give an extraordinary sense of freedom. Within the conscious dream realms sight can be restored, youth regained, and the delight of renewed energy allow the waking disabled to once again run across the fields, feeling the power of their limbs. By offering such transformations, which appear so real and which can embrace all the senses, lucid dreaming can heal both the spirit and the body.

Anyone undergoing a bio-feedback program, in which, for instance, they are visualizing healthy cells replacing cancerous growths, can gain immeasurably by lucidly dreaming such a process. Just as a meditator can slip into the deepest of states while consciously dreaming, in ways which are very difficult while awake, so the patient who is trying to visualize healing often finds too many outward distractions which prevent entering the visualization deeply enough. Lucid dreaming avoids all distractions, for once the direction of the dream is established through an inner intention then the episode unfolds with an intensity which precludes any diversions.

One method which could prove of help to anyone physically disabled is to choose some activity which you regret you can no longer do. This might be anything from running fast under a warm sun across the beach into the sea, to making love. Choose something which will engage all your senses to the full, and at regular intervals during the day close your eyes and visualize whatever scenario you wish to enact. If you can find a postcard, a photograph or some object like a pebble which brings the whole beach alive in your mind, have it by you. Before going to sleep hold the image as clearly as you can and *intend* to consciously dream about it that night. If you give it your undivided and single-minded attention it will eventually happen. The neural connections need to be strengthened by repetition and persistence in order to build a pathway to lucidity.

Once the dream appears and you have enjoyed the sense of physical freedom and a new found health, you might take time to consciously examine your waking body to see if there is anything which you can do to help it heal in some way.

One way of doing this is to wait on the beach, feeling overflowing with energy which you would like to share. You walk towards someone on a bed which looks somewhat odd as it sits by the sea. You recognize yourself lying there and feel that you can, by running your hands across the body, diagnose the deepest physical malady. You gently stroke the part of the body which needs your overflowing energy, knowing as you do so that there is healing in the touch. Continue until the figure responds, but do not interfere with the process by willing the figure to rise or sprout an amputed limb. Allow your disabled doppleganger,

Purusa, "The Cosmic Principle," India.
Tantra starts with the body. It is used to symbolize the whole ordered cosmos. An understanding of your body, whether in health or pain, affords the deepest and most profound insights into the nature of reality. Sometimes a physical disability becomes an unexpected opportunity to explore your inner world, which you otherwise never might have done.

or physical self, to act on his or her own. You might find that the other "you" springs out of bed and rushes into the sea, or just stirs a little and smiles at you. Allow whatever happens and wait. If you can repeat this procedure through regular dreams of this nature you will have acquired the most powerful healing method possible, for you will have *intended* your own recovery, which cannot but enter the waking state. Although the preparation and persistence might be difficult, the rewards are truly overwhelming.

CHAPTER 9

DREAMS OF DEATH

To sleep: perchance to dream: ay, there's the rub;

For in that sleep of death what dreams may come

When we have shuffled off this mortal coil...

Hamlet,III,i,65, by William Shakespeare

IT IS TOLD that at the death of the false sense of self, it is like the snuffing out of a candle. This is one of the meanings of Buddha's term, *Nirvana*. What is extinguished, however, is not the self but those illusory imaginings with which we manage to entangle and embalm ourselves.

The sage knows that this world of illusions consists of the images seen in a dream of which we are the sole creators. Death is just one more dream, but one which the mystic no longer creates.

In the Buddhist *Dhammapada* it is said,

"He who regards the world with the same look as one regards a bubble, he indeed is capable of no longer seeing the realm of death....

Attention is the path that leads to freedom from death; lack of reflection leads to death. Those who

are attentive do not die. Those who lack attention are already as though they are dead."

For those of us who still supposedly live in the world of dreams and illusion, what can we expect at death and which part of us actually dies – the flesh-encapsulated ego, the Self or who? Is the creator of all these dreams amongst the first casualties?

As it is the Tibetans who, through insights gained in lucid dreaming, have systematized and catalogued the moments after death so carefully, we will briefly examine their ideas of the ego, for it is the leading actor in what they say happens at death.

In all of us there is a split between *I* and *Thou*; this is the basic separation of the ego which sees things in dualistic terms. The here of *me* and the there of *them*. Some South Sea Islanders even have no word for "I" but

Opposite: **Funeral papyrus** with images found in the Egyptian Book of the Dead. *The goddess Nut spans the earth with a star-studded body while a soul is being weighed on a scale.* Above: **Masonic floor cloth,** *1804. In the West it was the Freemasons who attempted to create an order dedicated to helping its members to transcend the limitations of the waking, material life. The image of the coffin symbolizes the death-like process involved, and the stairway suggests the ascent to awakening.*

"here." The ideal of happiness as far as the ego is concerned is to transfer all the territory of "them" into "here" and "mine." The trouble is that the struggle to achieve this ultimately illusory state creates an even higher wall between one's internal and external space.

The ego constantly sends out patrols from its self-created fortress to determine whether it can expand its territory or whether there are threats to be avoided. The information brought back by the patrols becomes what the Tibetans see as the three fundamental poisons. That which can enhance the ego and increase its territories is the *attraction of passion;* that which reacts to threatening forces outside is *aggression;* and all things which can neither enhance nor threaten are treated in *ignorance.* Out of these three – *passion, aggression* and *ignorance* – arise a whole complex series of plots and sub-plots which keep the ego totally absorbed. The basic three are joined by *pride* and *discrimination.*

The very concept of ego is false in the first place, but, according to Buddhism, out of that false idea arises a karmic chain. This chain can be seen as fold upon fold of fantasy which encrusts the being and which even carries over from lifetime to lifetime. The chain can only be interrupted by meditation, by conscious and lucid dreaming which is practiced long enough to see the true situation, or by a moment in death when the whole illusion can be seen in a flash of illumination.

Right: ***Funeral robe*** *from the tomb of Hsin-Chui, Han period c.193-145 BC. The robe is divided into three sections of the underworld, earth and heaven.* Opposite: ***Death voyage,*** *woodcarving, New Guinea. The Malanggan of New Ireland carve canoes representing the journey across the great divide. To them the experience of a tunnel with a light at its end might be reinterpreted as sunset across the ocean.*

AN EXPERIENCE OF DYING

OF COURSE, anything said about death can only be founded upon belief. We simply won't know until we experience it, notwithstanding the assertions of priests, of great religious texts, or the tales of enlightened beings assuring us that death is this or that. Perhaps the nearest we can get to knowing about the state is through out-of-body and near-death-experiences. However, even when someone "returns" after being pronounced clinically dead, it doesn't necessarily mean that they have died. After all they have returned to tell their tales, and anyway the brain is known to continue quite a feverish activity up to thirty minutes after a person's heart has stopped.

In a study of over eight-hundred deathbed visions reported in both India and the United States, Osis and Haraldson found that the imagery experienced is startlingly similar to that described in the eighth-century *Tibetan Book of the Dead*, the *Egyptian Book of the Dead* which precedes it by over three millennia, or the accounts found in ancient Hindu texts like the *Yoga Sutras*, and in medieval European literature before the Inquisition and the Age of Reason temporarily squashed such outpourings.

The major features are, first, that the newly "deceased" appears to float above his or her body, aware of what is happening. There is usually a magnetic attrac-

What is found is that the reports of those who have experienced leaving the physical body are more than suspiciously similar to accounts of lucid dreaming.

Another surprise is that near-death-experiences appear to be far more widespread than suspected. It has been found that more than one person in twenty in both America and Europe has apparently had some form of experience of "dying" and of being revived and returning to the normal everyday state. From the considerable data collected on the subject two remarkable things emerge. One is the sheer consistency of viewpoint, and the other is that if they actually are lucid dreams then the phenomenon is far more common than has been believed.

tion towards a tunnel or passageway.

In my own case, I almost died from hepatitis in India, agreed by those who have suffered it to be the most "spiritual" disease if ever there was one. At one point I started to be sucked down a dark passageway. The end could be seen, bathed in a warm and joyous light. But across the tunnel stretched a fine red line, pulsing like a laser. There was an instinctive feeling that on crossing that line there could be no going back. The temptation was great to have done with the appalling sickness, but somehow I turned back, with much regret, feeling that there was still just too much unfinished business.

Those who manage to get to the end of the tunnel

149

Tree of the Cosmos; *illustration by Dionysus Freher of the teachings of Boehme. The Western taboo-like fear of death contrasts sharply with Eastern concepts of rebirth. But there were rare individuals such as Boehme who proposed a wider and less fearful vision. At the top of the diagram is the essential unity of the Godhead, which gives rise to the dualism of Eternity and Nature, which in turn, through a divine spark or lightning flash, give rise to our Solar World.*

almost invariably find themselves in a realm of dazzling, brilliant light. Eventually the would-be-deceased is met by friends or relatives or some sort of friendly guide. The world around slowly takes on shape and form; it is usually paradisaical, consistent with what might be expected of the person's cultural background

From all the evidence available, both from recent research and from accounts as far back as the two-thousand year old *Yoga Sutras* of the Indian sage Patanjali, deathbed accounts and near-death-experiences are not hallucinatory or delusional, but appear to be journeys to radically different, extra-dimensional, realms of reality.

According to the impeccably hard-headed business president of the Gallup Poll, researchers, who had been gathering and evaluating near-death encounters for a national survey, uncovered "trends that point toward a super parallel universe of some sort."

Beyond encountering a realm which seems to be composed of dazzling light and what is often described as "higher vibrations," the near-death experiencers often refer to "cosmic music"– a music of the spheres which is not so much melody, or even sound as such, but more like a combination of frequencies. The experiencer also finds that, like Christ's description of Heaven, in which "There shall be time no longer," space, time, and location are all irrelevant.

When the brain-mind encounters higher frequencies of light and energy at the point of death, it continues to operate as it has always done by translating such frequencies into a known phenomenal world of flowers, trees, meadows and people. Beyond that conditioned vision lies the realm where thought is light and light is thought.

In experiments in which subjects are hypnotized to regress to between-life states, it has been discovered that patients reported all the classic imagery of the near-death experience, including the passage through a tunnel, across water or over a bridge, encountering long dead relatives and friends, and meeting with the light-filled guides.

One of the other classic features to be found in the near-death-experience is that of the instantaneous life review – the drowning man who sees his life pass by in a flash. Those who have managed to return from death, or have been hypnotized into a supposed remembrance of other lives, report that every moment is played back, complete in its entirety, from the important to the most trivial. They all stress that it only takes an instant and yet every emotion and feeling, every sense and intellectual memory accompanies those brief playbacks. We will later find that this life review can be seen as a sort of hologram, storing a phenomenal amount of information. At the point of death the *focus of attention,* which we encountered in the dreams of power, apparently slips away from the physical energy body and its cherished fixed spot, and in doing so, scans the entire parade of one's life, simultaneously comprehending the whole and each tiniest part. This information is often reported to come in clusters or chunks.

The instructions in the *Tibetan Book of the Dead* are simply to let go of everything and to accept death as the crescendo of life. It gives clear and detailed descriptions of what the deceased might be experiencing at various stages along the way. But in essence the text is a continuous reminder that what one is so attached to, and what one is letting go of bit by bit, was only the stuff of dreams.

Some of the schools of mysticism from which the *Tibetan Book of the Dead* arose say there are three basic stages in death and rebirth.

First is the recognition of the dreamlike illusion of the phenomenal world and of the one who projects this illusion. Then comes a gap in which there is no dream but only a luminous reality. Finally there is the re-entry into a womb.

For anyone who dies consciously, who experiences the gap of purity, and enters the womb in full awareness, will be born alert and aware and will attain enlightenment in that life time.

THE techniques found within *The Tibetan Book of the Dead* are really only of real use if practiced by a lama who knows the whole tradition and who is trusted completely by the dying person. If a moment of doubt enters then the whole death time is wasted.

The shamans of Malaysia have similar methods in which they enter a lucid dream state during which they claim to accompany the deceased on his or her journey into the death lands. We can see that the Tibetan methods arose from what was essentially a similar shamanistic tradition; in this case the Bön, which long pre-dates Buddhism. However, there was a marvellous marriage between these ancient ways and Buddhism created by Padma Sambhava in the latter part of the eighth century. He was the major influence in the conversion of the Tibetans to Buddhism for, rather than denying the earlier, more magical, native beliefs, he embraced their sorcerers' ways as well as Dzogchen, Bön and Tantra. This extraordinary feat brought about a miraculous synthesis in the whole Tibetan way of life, in which meditation, sorcery and dreaming seem to have found a perfect expression, unsurpassed by any other culture.

The Dzogchen teachings, the most ancient school of meditation in Tibet, originally arose in Orgyen, northwest India and around Mount Kailash, the center of the ancient Bonpo tradition. The founder of Dzogchen transmitted it to Padma Sambhava who took it to Tibet. These traditions were the source of the *Book of the Dead*. The original and essential teaching claims that we are fundamentally enlightened, our beingness is "luminous conscious awareness."

We don't have to search for enlightenment for we already are in that state of grace, and have only forgotten this by identifying with the phenomenal world of memories and events. All we need is for our luminosity and vision to be re-awakened, and the primordial and essentially natural state of illumination is there, as it has always been there. Nothing has to be transformed, only illuminated. And lucid dreaming is considered one of the foundational tools with which to realize this.

Tibetan Dream Yoga is in fact a kind of dress rehearsal before the final curtain. The adept learns to become conscious of his or her dreams and of the natural luminosity of the sleep gap state. In being able to control the illusions of that realm, the sleeper can over-

Above: ***Mandala of Samantabhadra***, *"Supreme Buddha," Tibet.* Opposite: ***Wheel of Life and Death***, *Tibet. The cyclic pattern in this wheel of Samsara, of birth, death, and rebirth, is a constant undercurrent in Tibetan Buddhist thought. The whole activity is understood as nothing more than an elaborate dream.*

Opposite: **Death on a Pale Horse,** *by Albert P.Ryder, 1847-1917. The artist was a self-confessed recluse, mystic, and dreamer. This image of death charging around a race track reinforces the idea of life and death being an unending circuit, in which we continue, lap after lap, to dream and yet fail to recognize that we do.*

come the strange dream-like occurrences at death where the mind creates many phantoms both benign and otherwise.

The Book itself is strangely not really based upon death at all. It could as well be called the book of re-birth and would probably best be described as "The Tibetan Book of *Dreams*." Originally arising from the pre-Buddhist Bön traditions of Tibet, the death practices were concerned with the psychic force left behind by the deceased. *The Book of the Dead* goes further than acting upon the traces; it deals with the bardo, the gap or interval which happens at the point of death. But the bardo is equally part and parcel of our whole situation when dealing with the phenomenal world. It is where we can encounter the entire illusionary fabric which we have managed to maintain in life. This illusionary matrix is encountered once again at death. The Tibetan Bud-dhists maintain that we create the entire fabric of our universes. At death we are presented with this fact in what appear as six stages. These correspond to the six psychological and illusory realms of Hell, the Hungry Ghosts, the Animal, the Human, the Jealous Gods, and the Gods. We either recognize these apparitions for what they are – our projections – or we become iden-tified with them and have once again to join the wheel of illusionary life.

What appears more relevant to any Westerner is the bardo. Originally the Tibetan "bar" meant in between and "do" an island or a mark. Thus, although the bardo is more often translated as an "in between" or a "gap," it is also like an island or a period between *confusion* and *confusion about to be transformed into wisdom,* or insanity about to be transformed into sanity. It is the gap between a past situation and one about to begin.

The bardo experience is that of a luminosity which appears to be the very ground of one's being and it is only the witnessing consciousness, which is undisturbed by identification, that can see it for what is truly is. All other phenomenal experiences are a dream.

The Taoist sage, Chuang-tzu wrote 2,500 years ago:

"How do I know that the dead do not regret that they ever prayed for life? We drink wine in our dreams, and at dawn shed tears; we shed tears in our dreams, and at dawn go hunting. While we dream we do not know we are dreaming, and in the middle of a dream interpret a dream within it; not until we awake do we know we were dream-ing. Only at the ultimate awakening shall we know that this is the ultimate dream."

PRACTICE OF THE LIGHT

THE method is a meditation used by the Dzogchen sect as part of the "Practice of the Natural Light." This abbreviated version, of an original given by the contemporary master, Namkhai Norbu Rinpoche, could give the practitioner a taste of both lucid dreaming and the luminosity which is called the Clear Light which arises at the moment of falling asleep.

Concentrate upon a white Tibetan syllable **A** at the center of your body. This corresponds to the sound *AHHHH.* If you prefer a Western "A" then use that. If this is difficult to visualize, write it on a piece of paper or use the example on this page. Stare at the image, then close your eyes and a  white after image will form on your retina.

The idea is to try to fix the image as a presence in your mind as clearly and as sharply as you can. You will find it helpful by imagining a second image coming forth from the first **A.** This can be continued until you have a chain of **As** appearing out of one another, and slowly reaching the crown of the head. Try to keep this **A** present as you fall asleep and you will find that a charged state of alert and clear awareness is carried naturally into your dreaming state.

The Tibetans are not really concerned with the lucid dreaming which arises out of these practices as such and merely consider it a secondary effect. Their primary goal is to become conscious of the full presence of the natural light at the point of sleep.

The natural light is the basic luminosity of being. If this light, curiously called the "son," has been recognized during one's lifetime, then at death the practitioner will be able to merge with the "mother" light. This mother Clear Light is considered by the Dzogchen to be that natural, innate luminosity as it appears in the after death state.

This dream technique is most beautiful for those interested in the bardo states, for it encapsulates the whole after death experience.

There are six bardos or gaps and all these can be explored through lucid dreams.

The first is that of the ordinary waking state of consciousness. The second is that of the dream time as we sleep. The third bardo is that of meditation, which covers the entire spectrum to realization. The fourth is that of the dying process as the five elements of our body dissolve into one another.

The fifth is the bardo of reality, which actually is the arising of hallucinations and apparitions. (*It is in this bardo that the practice of lucid dreaming is so enlightening. The images have the same dream-like reality found in conscious dreaming and the practitioner can recognize them as illusion. If you can maintain an alertly aware and unidentified attitude at this point and recognize the imagery as being a manifestation of your mind, then enlightenment, say the Tibetans, is assured.*)

The sixth and final bardo is that of the rebirth of the individual into what the Tibetan Buddhist sees as the wheel of *Samsara* or the roundabout of the illusory world, of birth and death and rebirth.

Mansions of the Dead, *by Paul Nash, 1932.*

CHAPTER 10

DREAMS OF AWAKENING

I am not the one who, finding himself awake,

does not know who he is.

I am not the one who, finding himself

in dreams and visions,

thinks he has returned to his deeper self.

Da Free John

TO MANY MYSTICS, the individual's primary responsibility in life is seen as the attainment of a realization that our dreamworld does not differ from our waking reality: both are, in truth, an illusion. So what happens on the "Royal Road to Reality," and a true awakening?

In the ancient text of the *Mandukya Upanishad,* as greatly revered by many of the Tibetan Buddhist traditions as it is in the original Hindu, there is an outline of the four states of consciousness within a sound.

A U M, the primal sound, is made up of the three letters and the subsequent sound of OM. These four elements signify the four levels of consciousness.

The sound A is the *waking* and outwardly cognitive state. It is the consensus reality, what is agreed collectively as a description of what is real. Also called the Common-to-all-Men.

U is the *dreaming* state, the reality of the personal spiritual life, which is also called the Brilliant.

M is the *deep sleep* , the consciousness of undifferentiated unity. It is a blissful sleep in which there are no dreams and is called *Prajna*

The sound of these three in unison, OM, is said to be the fourth, *Turiya,* about which nothing can really be said. It is the ultimate and ungraspable mystery of Universal Consciousness.

The quintessential message, whether it is given by the Hindu teacher, Sankara, or the Tibetan saint, Milarepa, is that in order to pass through the three states of consciousness of *waking, dreaming* and *dreamless sleep* towards the fourth and final state, *turiya,* one must journey in complete lucidity.

Through various yogic techniques the practitioner gradually becomes lucid in each state in full and alert

---

Mandala OH-HRM, *Jaina painting, Rajasthan, nineteenth century. This represents OM, the original, all-pervading and inclusive sound and the symbol of the Supreme One.*

The Potala Palace rises on the Red Hill in Lhasa. Photograph by Pat Fok. Tibet has given rise to the extraordinary religious synthesis of the sorcerer and the sage.

The Indian eighth-century mystic and Buddhist, Padma Sambhava, brought together the Tantric Buddhist teachings and the earlier shamanic based knowledge of Bön which was indigenous to Tibet to create a unique religious viewpoint. No other culture has been so engrossed with the concepts of Tantric Buddhism, has so many

enlightened masters, or is so concerned with lucid dreaming and its practice as a means of gaining greater insights into the nature of death and the final awakening from what they believe to be the world of illusion.

The invasion of Tibet and the subsequent tragic destruction of that culture has had the unlooked-for effect of spreading Tibetan culture, through its spiritual exiles, throughout the Western world, bringing first-hand word of such great teachings as those of Milarepa.

awareness, and then he or she simply wakes up.

The systematic and scientific methodology for becoming awake and aware reached an extraordinary peak during the twelfth century in Tibet, as is exemplified by the life of the most famous of Tibet's many masters, Milarepa. The particular school which he founded was in essence the condensation of many traditions, including the shamanic Bön and the Dzogchen, the teachings of which Garab Dorje transmitted to Padma Sambhava through such enlightened Indian and Tibetan men as Naropa, Tilopa, Nagarjuna, Marpa and the Tantric master, Saraha.

In the *Chos-drug*, or six doctrines, which outline the steps on the Tibetan way to enlightenment, we find:

1. *Vital Warmth*: the control of body functions.

2. *The Illusory Body*: the realization of the illusory nature of the body and all phenomena.

3. *Dreams*: the insight that as dreams are illusory, so are all phenomenal experiences in both dreaming and waking states.

4 *The Clear Light*: the state of natural light which is the awareness of being without the intrusion of the mind.

5 *The Bardo*: the gap which is an intermediary state encountered at the point of death and rebirth. And finally

6. *Transference:* rebirth.

Milarepa brings heart to many would-be lucid dreamers. He had been a great sorcerer, a powerful shaman, before he turned towards a path of greater truths. He had a superb master called Marpa, and yet even after years of hardship and perseverance he still could not reach even the first level, which is the normal initiate's easiest hurdle. All over Tibet there were young yogis who had easily mastered the Vital Warmth, which is a yogic control over bodily functions, but not 'Mila.' It was only after eight years of solitary meditation, and constant rituals of purification, that he managed to finally reach the third level – Dreams.

"By night, in my dreams, I could traverse the summit of Mount Meru to its base – and saw everything clearly as I went. Likewise in my dreams I could multiply myself into hundreds of personalities, all endowed with the same powers as myself. Each of my multiplied forms could traverse space and go to some Buddha Heaven, listen to the teachings there, and then come back and teach the Dharma to many persons. I could also transform my physical body into a mass of blazing fire, or into an expanse of flowing or calm water. Seeing that I had obtained infinite phenomenal powers even though it be but in my dreams, I was filled with happiness and encouragement."

But this was only the start of his journey, for to the Yogi, the Tantrica or the mystic, lucid dreaming remains only for the beginners. At best it is a secondary phenomenon, however spectacular it might seem.

In the dream trances of the shaman, on the other hand, the dream is used as a device to integrate and heal either the dreamer or his, or her, peoples. It is an end within itself. The mystic, however, uses the lucid dream only as a first step to full awakening from what we know as our waking world, which they call only another dream. And attentive awareness or lucidity is the key.

But, as far as I can see, the reason why many masters are so pleased when a disciple either manages to awaken in a dream through persistence, or just stumbles upon the happening by chance, is that awakening is already beginning to happen. For in the very act of lucid dreaming, one is beginning to stir in the greater sleep, simply by being alert and lucid.

When you assume an aware and witnessing attitude, knowing all the while that what is being enacted before you is a dream, this will then become a way of perceiving your waking experiences in the same light. With the arousal of the lucid witness, the ego begins to take a back seat, for that false self is also is seen as a mirage, as insubstantial as the rest. Where there is only the witness, there is the real awakening. The trouble is that

the ego can't be there to appreciate it.

The master of Tao, Lieh-tzu said:

"The spirit chances on it, and we dream; the
body encounters it and it happens.
Hence by day we imagine and by night dream
what spirit and body chance upon.
That is why when someone's spirit is
concentrated, imagination and dreaming diminish
of themselves.
What those who trust the time when they are
awake do not explain, and those who trust in
dreams do not fathom, is the arrival
and passing of the transformation of
things.
It is no empty saying that the True
Men of old forgot themselves when
awake and did not dream when they
slept!"

According to Lieh-tzu, there are eight
proofs of being awake and six tests of dreaming. The proofs are 1. events, 2. actions, 3. gain,
4. loss, 5. sorrow, 6. joy, 7. birth, and 8. death
. The six tests are more in the nature of classes
or categories of dreaming, which are given as:
1. normal, 2. alarm, 3. thinking, 4. memory,
5. rejoicing and 6. fear.

This seems all pretty ordinary stuff in comparison with Milarepa's exotic experiences, but
for the man of Tao there was no need to distinguish
between dream and wakefulness, so the whole subject
was not regarded with the obsessive fascination of the
Indians and the Tibetans.

The Buddhist does seem to take the assumption that
our waking, illusory world is one of suffering and grief
a little too seriously for many tastes. To sit in a freez-
ing cave, alone for eight years, living as a beggar, eating
only stinging nettles and turning bright green because

of that diet, as Milarepa did, in order to leave this
world of suffering behind, appears somewhat counter-
productive. It hardly appeals to all and everyone.

But his solitary tale embraces only one methodology
and is, in any terms, pretty rare. There is another
school of Tibetan Tantricas who at least share their
caves, living together in both physical and spiritual
union, and even sharing the same dreams.

Opposite and above: **Mohammed's Night Journey,** *from a
fifteenth-century miniature. In a sacred dream Mohammed is said to
have traveled on the back of the legendary beast, the "Buraq," while
visiting all the holy sites and meeting with the earlier prophets and
holy men.
He then ascended through the cosmos, learning the greater mysteries
and visiting the various heavenly spheres and the levels of hell
(opposite). The Prophet is reported to have said: "My eyes slept
while my heart is awake."*

THE ONE HUNDRED AND TWELVE

WESTERN ISLAMIC traditions establish spiritual credence for many of the visionary states of their mystics by identifying a mid-way realm between the material world and the world of the imagination; between waking and dreaming. *Alam al-mithral* is said to be a realm where the figures and images have a real existence of their own. The great Sufi mystic, ibn-'Arabi, says of it that the power of active and lucid imagination developed in him to the point "that it presents my mystic beloved to me visually in a bodily, objective, extra-mental figure, just as the Angel Gabriel appeared bodily to the eyes of the Prophet."

But the best way of describing a dream of awaking is to give a way of directly experiencing it.

Dreams of Awaking are radically different from lucid dreaming. Although the state of lucidity remains a prerequisite, these states cannot strictly even be called dreams, for they exist in the gap between the states of waking and sleeping, as the following techniques show.

These techniques come from the Indian *Vigyan Bhairava Tantra,* in which Shiva answers the questions posed, on our behalf, by his beloved Devi. It is also known as "The hundred and twelve" since there are 112 meditation techniques given. Supposedly this is a finite number, and Hindu Tantricas insist that these meditations cannot be improved upon. The origins of the texts go back over five thousand years and yet the methods are as relevant today as they were then.

Devi seems to ask very philosophic questions, like "What is your Reality, my Lord?" Shiva does not answer any of them in philosophic terms, but rather describes a technique which will give the seeker a direct experiential taste of that reality. He doesn't give the questioner second-hand knowledge *about* reality, but drives the experiential nail into the seeker to enable him or her to to plunge in. The questioner will then know through his or her own experience. This is not a belief system, some second-hand idea, but direct communion which has been imparted through the use of a method. And "method" is one of the meanings of *Tantra.*

After an introductory passage these Hindu Tantric *Sutras* open with a series of simple techniques which have a direct bearing upon our initial experiments with waking dreams. The first technique is to induce lucid dreaming, and in the seventh sutra the seeker is instructed as follows:

With intangible breath in the center of the forehead
~ as this reaches the heart at the moment of sleep
~ have direction over dreams and over death itself.

Above: **Rama and Sita**, *Rajasthan, eighteenth-century. Indian deities invariably have balancing consorts; Shiva and Paravati, or Vishnu and Lakshmi are such couplings. The relationship between the male deities and their* shaktis *is such that the male Purusha, being the principle of witnessing consciousness, observes the world which has been created by his female consort, Prakriti.* Right: **Scroll** *showing the third eye and the Sahasrara chakra, Nepal, seventeenth century.*

However this method by itself is not complete and needs some understanding of the fifth sutra before it, which reads:

Attention between the eyebrows!
Let mind be before thought.
Let form fill with breath essence to the top of the head
and there shower with light.

Now this sounds far more incomprehensible and "spiritual" than it proves in practice. We must remember that this is a translation from centuries ago and in modern language would read more like a simple motor bike manual or cooking recipe. It is essentially pragmatic. Let us examine the first method which can lead into the dream work.

Attention between the eyebrows is a simple direction to focus upon the third eye, or what we now understand to be the pineal gland. Modern science has not really fathomed what its function might be. It appears to be dormant in the adult unless activated in some way. If you close your eyes and focus between the brows, you will feel a strange pull, as if you are exerting a whole new range of muscles. Some feel it as a strain, but if you persevere this slight headache will slowly disappear to be replaced by a powerful sense of attraction. The spot is quite magnetic and greedy for attention, as if it has been starved of it too long. This attention stirs the otherwise dormant gland into life. While this is happening, it is extremely difficult to be aware of any other part of the body or focus on any of the thoughts which you normally have. Rather, thoughts seem to be separate entities with lives of their own dancing across

Desert Dream, *by Malcolm Godwin. The creative possibilities once one can direct the course and shape of one's dreams are endless and frankly exhilarating. Dreaming the impossible is just one of the delights in store for anyone who persists in lucid practice.*

your inner screen. Even after only a few minutes of this meditation, the subject seems to have gained a distance between what we might call the witnessing-self and the thoughts.

It is said that of all meditation techniques this is the most natural way to dissociate yourself from the chattering mind. But it can also be one of the most diverting for the unsuspecting inner traveler. For the third eye is a powerful focus of the imagination. And by this is meant not just the usual daydream or idle fantasy — there are too many instances of the most extraordinary happenings around those whose third eyes have become open for this to be the case. Imagination is a real force which can produce what we might once have called miracles.

Hypnosis also creates a focus at the third eye. Imagination and actualization are not two a-causal states but one and the same. With the third eye there is no distinction between dream and reality.

Hindu mystics claim that the third eye is the center of the divine dream and that whatever is dreamed there will become actualized. This was the problem that Ramakrishna faced when he became so single-minded in his love of the goddess, Kali, that he actualized her, and it took the violent action of his master to dissipate the image.

Because of this danger would-be seekers should purge themselves of all impurities of the mind, otherwise the actualizations could be disastrous.

It is still difficult to convince sane and rational Westerners that what one dreams of will become real and substantial, but we will be examining evidence of such

Masonic apron, given by General George Washington to a member of his staff in 1770. It bears a diagram of almost universal appeal but which nevertheless shows the Western approach, through reason and symbolism, to enlightenment. Between the columns with the sun and the moon above them, showing the paired duality of the known universe, is the central, balancing column of human consciousness which appears as a temple of four stories. Within this edifice the individual can gain access to the divinity. Many lucid dreamers report dreams containing symbols of columns, eyes, temples and figures of light, which suggest that our archetypes are as common as Carl Jung maintained.

claims in a later chapter. At this point, however, all that is necessary is to follow the sutra.

Let mind be before thought. Simply watch the thoughts while keeping attention between the eyebrows. You will feel your two closed eyes rolling back in your head and become fixed on the invisible third eye. Keep awareness in that simple act and let the thoughts come and go as if at a great distance.

Let form fill with breath essence to the top of the head. This is breathing not just air but *prana*, that mysterious invisible force which Indian yogis claim is fundamental to all vital life energy. Ignore the scientific arguments about whether anything has been discovered which corresponds to this mysterious power. Here we are dealing with raw psychic imagination, so let it flower. Imagine, without any intense effort involved, that this essence of breathing, the prana, is filling your entire head and showering from the top of your head like a soft fountain. Let this shower of light cover you and allow a sense of being cleansed and being reborn.

This whole technique, which is a truly beautiful experience even if you do not achieve instant *samadhi* or enlightenment, will prepare you for the seventh sutra which is directly concerned with dreaming. But keep it all easy. There is no need to take any of this esoteric or mystical stuff too seriously. Your spiritual ego might have some investment in this but the moment you catch yourself becoming long faced and fanatically intent, remember that those two very qualities will create an indestructible barrier to your efforts. With this firmly but lightly in mind, let us journey onwards.

The seventh sutra:

With intangible breath in the center of the forehead
~as this reaches the heart at the moment of sleep
~have direction over dreams and death itself.

We have already explored the first instruction so we join the sutra at the moment of sleep. The really

Buddha, *Sri Lanka. This huge carving portrays the Buddha asleep to the world of illusions. One notable litmus test of authenticity for any enlightened being is that they do not dream. It is said that once awake, always awake and that their sleep has the same quality as their waking life.*

important part here is to allow the sense of prana which you first experienced at the third eye (being the easiest point to start from) now to start to flow from your heart into your whole body. Allow this to happen while you fall into sleep, and you will discover that you will become conscious in your sleep and *have direction over your dreams*... This is as true for awaking in the dream as it is for determining what type of dream you will have as you fall asleep.

It is emphasized by Hindu mystics that, if one becomes a master of dreaming, then not only can one direct the course of the dreams but one can cease to dream altogether. This brings us to ... *over death itself.* For when the dreaming ceases, one enters a sleep that is like death. The mystics insist that sleep is a short death and death a long sleep. And when you can direct your dreams, you are on the first step to being able to direct your waking life, for the stuff of dreams is also the imaginative source of the waking self.

FALLING BETWEEN WORLDS

The next meditation technique of Shiva is very specific. It is concerned with the process of awakening rather than dreaming, but uses sleep as its starting point.

At the point of sleep,
When the sleep has not yet come
and external wakefulness vanishes,
At this point Being is revealed.

We are now venturing on very sacred and, for many, very dangerous territory. This is neither a technique for the idly curious nor for those who only have a tenuous grip on reality.

How many of us have experienced a sudden sense of falling, just as we drop off to sleep? For some, this falling can continue for what seems an eternity, before they sit bolt upright in bed still feeling the adrenaline racing through their system.

The Sufi mystics even have a preparatory stage before anyone attempts a technique such as this. It is called "Falling into the Darkest Well."

Imagine falling down a well which has no bottom while you are blindfolded. You just fall and fall endlessly, going deeper into the darkness. There is an infinite and eternal void into which you plunge. Once past the sheer terror of the experience, you begin to feel a calm and silence which grows deeper and deeper. It has a great beauty, leaving all attachments, all that is familiar and habitual. Obviously at any moment you can open your eyes or remove the blindfold, but somewhere in your inner being the process of falling continues. This, however, is only a preparation for the main device.

At the point of sleep, when the sleep has not yet come. This is a threshold, a crossroads where one is neither asleep nor awake. At this point the process changes, making a radical leap from one state to another. There is a gap between the two states and it is said that in that gap you can glimpse your real Being – that truth of who and what you are. This is known as stirring in one's sleep, for at such times you are really awake, and what you experience is both radical and transforming.

According to the Tibetans the mind enters a state of dreams. But the Dzogchen practitioner, for instance, attempts now to become aware of the state of natural light so that when dreams arise he, or she, is lucidly aware that they are still dreaming while dreaming. Here is the essence of Tibetan dreamwork, as opposed to shamanistic vision quests or Western laboratory experiments.

The Indian tradition, with which we started this account, gives a very simple methodology. While going to sleep just relax and wait. Feel every sensation as you drift into sleep. Don't attempt to do anything about it, just wait and watch. Try to remain alert and aware. The actual moment when you change from waking to sleep is tenuous, subtle, a minute gap – but it is there. Another of the "hundred and twelve" speaks of watching the gap between one breath and another. It is precisely the same process. The gap where one can gain a glimpse of reality is so miniscule, it is gone before you notice. Some practitioners optimistically say that it takes at least three months to catch a glimpse of what they talk about. I am inclined to be more generous in my estimates. Thirty years is still a breeze, but it is really up to the person's intensity of commitment. If you give your whole and total being to the task, it has been known to happen in the first moment. Regrettably, to be as total as that is somewhat rare.

But there comes a point when you become aware that you are neither awake nor asleep. This often is said to be a very fearful space, for you suddenly find yourself in a void, in the vast and abiding emptiness of an eternal abyss. It is, as some describe, like having ice cold and boiling water poured over you at the same time.

As a small child this used to happen to me. Every time I was pulled towards this void there would be an overwhelming sense of bliss, and at the same moment an unspeakable terror which would yank me back to the normal world. My bemused father did not know what to make of it all, so he told me to stop it lest I go mad. So, by the time I was seven the experiences began to fade. How many children suffer similarly at the well-meaning hands of their parents? It is likely that many of us experience such heightened states as children, but because they do not fit into a socially acceptable norm, our parents ensure that such events are suppressed.

Certainly the void is not for the fainthearted or the dilettante. Yet when you fall into the "well between worlds," when you are neither awake nor dreaming, you feel *real*. And that experience of falling into another, radically different dimension is one sign of an imminent awakening.

Jyoti, or the principle of light. Light is the manifestation of radiating energy, and the phenomenal world is the reflection of forms created by that light. (Based upon a Tantric image.)

CHUANG-TZU PARADOX

THE IDEA that all and everything is really an illusion is still a fundamental belief which flows through the whole of Far Eastern culture. Nothing we experience can be truly verified. There is really no way of judging whether what we see or hear is an illusory dream or not.

Chuang-tzu was a Taoist master in China during the fourth century BC. He awoke one morning with a puzzle for his disciples. That night he had dreamed that he had been a beautiful butterfly, but on awaking a question arose. Was it Chuang-tzu who had been dreaming he was a butterfly or was it a butterfly dreaming he was Chuang-tzu waking up?

We have no way of telling whether he was testing his disciples' awareness of how to distinguish the reality of dreams and waking, but the essence of this little anecdote, of the blurred distinction between reality and dream, is one which has captured more minds than those of the Taoists.

This blurring of reality and dream was one of the themes posed by Socrates. In Plato's *Theaetetus* the Greek sage asks, "At this precise moment what proof could you give should anyone ask us whether we are asleep and our thoughts are a dream, or whether we are awake and discussing with each other in a waking state?" Theaetetus agrees that they could both be dreaming. Pleased his friend had got the point, Socrates declares, "See, it is even open to dispute whether we are awake or in a dream."

For less obviously sophisticated peoples the paradox seems irrelevant. Among the San tribes of the Kalahari desert such a problem has no meaning. The question of which is dream and which reality is subsumed in their understanding of the "Great Dream which dreams us."

The Indian debate over the illusory nature of the phenomenal world, led by the Hindu mystical philosopher, Shankara, has often faltered upon the awkward question of pain. Curiously we find that pain is the yardstick of reality, even for a yogi.

A Yogi while living in Deal,
Declared "Although pain is not real,
As the point of this pin,
Pricks into my skin
I don't like what I think that I feel."

And yet it is to be remembered that actual, physical pain rarely appears in dreams, even lucid ones, except when we already have some physiological problem in our waking life.

Let us try Chuang-tzu again.

"Those who dream of a banquet at night may, in the next morning, wail and weep. Those who dream of wailing and weeping may, in the morning, go out and hunt. When they dream, they do not know that they are dreaming. In their dream,

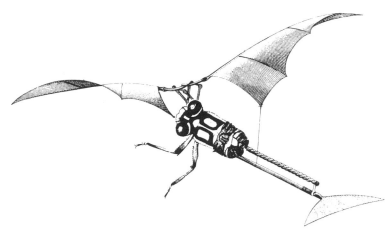

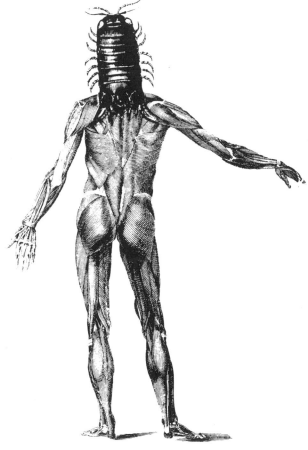

while the fools think that they are awake; that they know. With nice discriminations, they make distinctions between princes and grooms. How stupid! Confucius and you are both in a dream. When I say that you are in a dream, I am also in a dream."(*Chuang-tzu,* trans. Fung Yu-lan)

This is the world of *maya* or illusion. The word in India has a different connotation from what we understand in the West. Illusion is not so much unreal as simply impossible to differentiate. We cannot determine what is real and what is not. Nothing is certain, we are confused and everything is so much in flux that not even one's own witnessing self appears to be real.

So far we have been examining the lucid realms of the sorcerer, sybil, shaman, therapist, and sage. But what do we know of the actual, factual, scientific and objective reality of either our waking or dreaming states?

The mystic can insist as much as he, or she, cares that our waking world is but a dream, but what do our scientists say to such a claim? We will shortly explore the realm of the new physics and of neurophysiology in order to know whether modern scientists are likely to agree.

they may even interpret dreams. Only when they are awake, they begin to know that they dreamed. By and by comes the great awakening, and then we shall find out that life itself is a great dream. Mean-

FALSE AWAKENINGS

ANY READERS who have managed by this point to have had a few lucid dreams will probably also know of the false awakenings and will know the difficulty of recognizing them for what they are. You appear to awaken and go about your morning business only to discover that you are still dreaming. It is a curious quirk of the process that the more one has lucid dreams the more one experiences these unreal wakings. There seem few satisfactory explanations for this phenomenon. Maybe it happens because dreamers already believe that they are awake, or that the expectancy of really waking up as the lucid dream fades, triggers the effect.

Whatever the cause there are a variety of methods of overcoming these false awakenings and which allow the dreamer to continue dreaming with undiminished consciousness and alert attention. All have one factor in common – the sensation of rapid or vivid movement. Some lucid dreamers favor whirling or spinning like a top, while others prefer to throw themselves backwards into an abyss or off a cliff.

The two methods which most appeal to me are simply flying and performing the most spectacular aerobatics, or creating a hanging veil or a door through which you charge at full tilt.

I have read somewhere that there is indirect evidence that there might be a connection between the vestibular apparatus (the balancing mechanism of the inner ear) and the production of bursts of REM during dreaming. If there is some link, then this might account for vivid dream movements fooling the brain into stimulating more REM sleep and thus more lucid dreaming.

COUNTING DREAM SHEEP

THIS IS A VARIATION on a very old method which was once used to fall asleep. While waiting for sleep imagine watching sheep jump over a low fence. Really take time and trouble to visualize each sheep and how they jump. But keep a very close count as each jumps over the hurdle. Keep in mind that they are only dream sheep, phantoms created by your own visualization. So as you count remind yourself, "One sheep that I am dreaming, two sheep that I am dreaming..." This helps one to retain an alert attention whilst remembering that it is all dream stuff.

This technique is actually designed to become lucid within the non-REM, first stage of sleep. But these sleep-onset dreams seldom last for more than a few seconds at most and are often interlinked with hypnagogic imagery. However the method also seems to work in the later stages of the sleep cycle near dawn.

This is especially suitable for those who sleep easily and rapidly and who experience hypnagogic imagery.

DREAMBODY PROJECTION

This is very simple and yet extremely effective for some dreamers. As you are drifting off into sleep imagine that a projection of your resting body rises through the ceiling and up through the roof. It can travel anywhere you wish but it is important that this body is far away and doing something totally different from your prone and almost sleeping one. If you can identify with this projected body, then when you dream you will find less difficulty in becoming aware that you are in it.

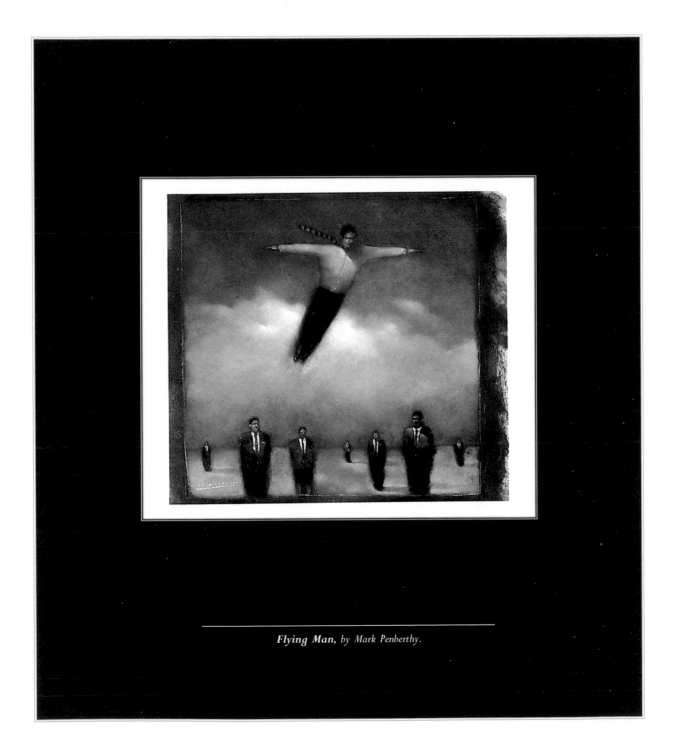

Flying Man, by Mark Penberthy.

THE METHODS OF A TIBETAN MASTER

ATISHA, Thrice Great, was born in India almost a thousand years ago. Called thrice great because of the extraordinary fact that he was, simultaneously, the disciple of three enlightened masters, he traveled from the Indian Himalayas to Tibet. And it was in this rich meditative soil that he was able to impart his great teaching, The Seven Points of Mind Training.

We will only be concerned with one sutra from this work, which opens a whole sequence of meditations that can flower into a final awakening of consciousness. At first glance it might appear so absurdly simple as not really to be a meditation at all.

Think that all phenomena are like dreams.

Do not be fooled by this seemingly simplistic technique; it is one of the most powerful and condensed methods ever devised.

When Atisha talks of "phenomena" he is indicating all and everything, the great and the small. It includes the mundane and the spiritual, from movements of the bowel to movements of energy arising in each of the chakras. As long as there is an experiencer and something to be experienced Atisha calls it a dream. While all phenomena that can be witnessed are a dream, the witnessing consciousness, the seer, is not.

If you really enter this method and experience everything around you as a dream, as insubstantial and unreal as any nightly dream in sleep, there will come a point when you begin to question whether you are also a dream. If the object is a dream and unreal, then what about the subject who dreams the object? One of the first insights to occur with this method is that your false sense of self, the ego, begins to evaporate, for it is part of the whole illusion you have been living. It requires constant energy to maintain its sense of self-importance, and by accepting that everything is a dream that energy is no longer available for the ego and it begins to dissolve.

Paradoxically, in the midst of maintaining that everything is a dream, a new sense of reality arises. However, we are concerned at present with one of the secondary spin-offs from this meditation – that of the lucid dream. For in continuously thinking that everything is a dream during the day, that mind-set begins to appear in your nightly dreams, and suddenly you will start to experience yourself both deeply asleep and yet fully awake at the same moment.

As far as Atisha was concerned, this new insight transforms the day-time life, for once one is conscious, the dream is seen for what it is – an illusion. Awareness and Dreaming cannot exist side by side. Once both the object and the subject lose their reality, a new witnessing self arises which reflects just what is. This is the true awakening.

But let us not get too carried away by such spiritual glories before they occur. For the modest moment, let us simply enter into the technique, setting aside maybe two hours a day to really focus the energy upon this device. *Treat all phenomena as dreams.* As far as inducing lucid dreams goes, it is one of the most successful methods ever devized.

Allegory, by Joseph. M. Gandy. This nineteenth-century painting
of the world's religions expresses the romantic and exotic view of the
realms of the spirit. Such popular fantasies have little to do with
the reality which might lie at the source of any religion, and Atisha
cut at the roots of our fabulous imaginings of the spiritual
dimension when he asserted that all phenomena, including that of
the spirit, are a dream.

Part III

A Waking Dream

Chapter 11
Dreams of Reality

Chapter 12
The Reality of Dreams

Chapter 13
The Dream Maker Awakens

Ittal, *from the house of Tissano, Ganjam District, Orissa, India.*
This pictogram is by a female shaman and depicts her spirit/dream
husband with his friends. The two figures at the bottom right
represent the shamaness's spirit children whom she sees in her dreams.

CHAPTER 11

DREAMS OF REALITY

If modern physics is to be believed, the dreams we call waking perceptions have only a very little more resemblance to objective reality than the fantastic dreams of sleep.

Bertrand Russell

SO FAR WE HAVE SEEN how, throughout history, both the sage and the sorcerer have always asserted that the world we accept as solid and stable is nothing more than a dream. Now scientists are putting forward theories that confirm this vision, and nowhere is the radical change of perspective, that paradigm shift which challenges all our preconceived notions of the nature of reality, advancing so fast as in the fundamental discipline of physics.It is important to understand that the theories we will examine are not scientific findings carved in stone. Rather, they are intriguing and fascinating possibilities that deserve open-minded consideration. Most are at the cutting-edge of controversy, and yet no one would question the credentials of the scientists who put them forward.

The particular hypotheses which magnetize our attention, as far as the nature of lucid dreaming and waking are concerned, are:

1.The innovative neurophysiological theories, pioneered by Karl Pribram, of a *holograph-like* universe in which the brain appears to act as both a laser beam and a holographic plate at one and the same moment.

2.General theories about the nature of reality based upon quantum mechanics and the study of subatomic phenomena, in which consciousness appears to have a fundamental influence upon the physical world.

3. New concepts of an *implicate* and an *explicate* order as being the foundation of a vast *holomovement,* which has been proposed by the physicist David Bohm.

4. The nature of *morphic or habit fields* advanced by the biochemist, Rupert Sheldrake.

A Carnival Evening, by Henri Rousseau. Is the world an absolute and solid reality or is it a unique, ever fluctuating fantasy created afresh by each one of us? The new physics suggests it is more illusory than we could ever have imagined.

These four theories together point towards a holograph-like universe of fields, in which the observer is no longer seen as a separate witness, standing outside events, but as an inseparable part of the whole. This is a radical shift in how we have always viewed the role of the observer.

Science, by definition, has always been the study of phenomena based upon impartial observation, experiment and measurement. What the new physics clearly implies, and has shown to be true at subatomic levels, is that there can be no such thing as a purely objective viewpoint. The scientist has now to be seen as an active participator, in a new "subjective role." How has this new idea arisen, what does it imply and why should it be of particular interest to the would-be lucid dreamer?

We appear just to have passed through what might be called the Golden Age of scientific method. We are surrounded by the fruits of a traditional way of viewing the universe, from space shuttles to dishwashers, soap powders to artificial intelligence. And as long as science keeps to relatively big things like jumbo jets and planets, technicians can predict how matter and energy will work, in what seems a relatively stable and solid world, almost a hundred percent of the time. However, it is at the foundational levels of the energy spectrum that things are not quite what we have always believed them to be. For as soon as the scientist tries to predict, or even observe, the behavior of the most fundamental and smallest of things, existence presents a very different and bizarre face — more like a surrealist dream.

Such "things" as electrons which make up our

Si c'était, by Yves Tanguy, 1939. The artist captures strange morphological entities in an otherwise formless expanse. What is the reality of the external universe "out there" when it appears to be the product of our minds creating their habitual outlines?

seemingly so-solid universe apparently can even change "faces" as soon as they notice they are being watched, just as if they are coyly conscious of an invasion of their privacy. Not only do they appear to change their shape and behavior from waves to particles the moment anyone takes a peek at them, but when the observer tries to take a measurement of their size, location and speed, they suddenly don't seem to exist in space or time at all. No one can pin them down to a specific location. Far from being the solid and fundamental stuff of the universe, these tiniest building blocks of the material world exhibit a skittish reluctance to even be there at all. And to add to the scientist's frustration of not being able to pin anything down long enough to observe it, there appears to be no deterministic process by which *effect* invariably follows a *cause*.

At the present time, the scientist working at the level of quanta can only measure and predict the behavior of the tiniest denizens of the sub-atomic world in terms of what seems to happen during an overwhelming majority of the time. And it is this radical shift from an essentially *causal* model of the universe to a *statistical* one that creates some of the confusion within the scientific community.

However, the disquiet felt at discovering that the universe is far less substantial than once supposed still doesn't shake the bedrock of science to its core. What does is that the objective role of the observer is now being seriously questioned, to the extent that the very act of observing a phenomenon is believed to change its behavior.

It would also appear that consciousness is the prime suspect in the search for the creator of our solid and familiar realm of matter. Because, up until now, the observer has always been assumed to be outside what was being observed, consciousness has never entered into any scientific equation. But at the deepest levels of matter this traditional way of looking at the phenomenal universe is proving, at best misleading, and more often invalid, which means that

all our accepted and seemingly stable physical laws have to be completely overhauled. If the classical observer can no longer be locked away behind glass screens, to observe the universe without affecting it, it means that the role of the scientist is promptly and irrevocably transformed into that of a participator in the whole enterprise, and he or she starts to act suspiciously like a mystic.

It is this discovery and its theoretical implications that is so crucial to any understanding of our own dream world and of the possible identity and location of who or whatever manages to create such extraordinarily authentic dream realms.

Opposite: ***Castle in the Pyrenees***, *by René Magritte, 1961. In the light of the new physics we can no longer assume that, simply because we have become familiar with and accustomed to rocks being solid and substantial, that they are, actually, solid at all.*
Above: ***Meditation***, *by Ludwig Schwarzer, 1971. The problem with most languages, especially those in the West, is that they are predominantly built upon nouns. Nothing fixes a happening in perpetual rock as much as does a noun. Nouns transfix a living process into an inert and unchanging thing. This largely determines how most of us then perceive the world we inhabit. We see a rock as solid simply because we have a word for it.*

THE GREAT THOUGHT

IN this newly viewed, *contingent*, universe, which is predictable only within statistical limits, we leave the snug safety of a machine-like, deterministic and causal reality and appear to be rolling headlong towards the paradigm of a non-mechanistic, non-material cosmos. As the astronomer, Sir James Jeans, remarked way back in 1932:

"The universe begins to look more like a great thought than a great machine. Mind no longer appears as an accidental intruder into the realm of matter; we are beginning to suspect that we ought rather to hail it as the creator and governor of the realm of matter."

Well over half a century later his words have even more import, for many experimental findings and a whole new range of discoveries and research seem to have confirmed his prophetic predictions.

So the "golden age" of science, which reached its peak in the three decades after World War II, looks as if it is having an almost religious crisis of faith. The revolutionary ideas which jostle the older dogmas might be summarized as: the discovery that the universe is not the causal and deterministic affair we thought it was and consequently has to be viewed as a more holistic and interconnected phenomenon and, secondly, that consciousness cannot stand outside this physical cosmos, for it is consciousness that seems to actually have created it. Matter and consciousness are increasingly recognized as a continuum or a field. The mind and the universe appear to be as one — a vast, interconnected, multi-dimensional energy field within fields; all these nesting fields appear to resonate with each other, giving rise to interference patterns by their differing frequencies. And it is these interference patterns that appear to create what we have come to know of as the phenomenal or material universe.

There have been two distinct and conflicting theoretical breakthroughs in this century, being the theory of relativity and that of quantum mechanics.

In relativity, the universe is seen as a series of events with a unified time structure in which the object is secondary, being an expression of a long causal chain of processes.

In quantum physics, on the other hand, the universe is seen as a series of objects, waves or particles, with a unified logical structure. The process is

Above: *The Future of Statues,* by *René Magritte.*
Opposite: ***Waves over a breakwater.*** *To define a wave we must freeze time into a past, a present and a future, while in reality waves are continually appearing and disappearing as one, ever present happening. Our methods of thinking tend to fix our experience into a collection of labels which don't really exist, and yet we react to them as if they do.*

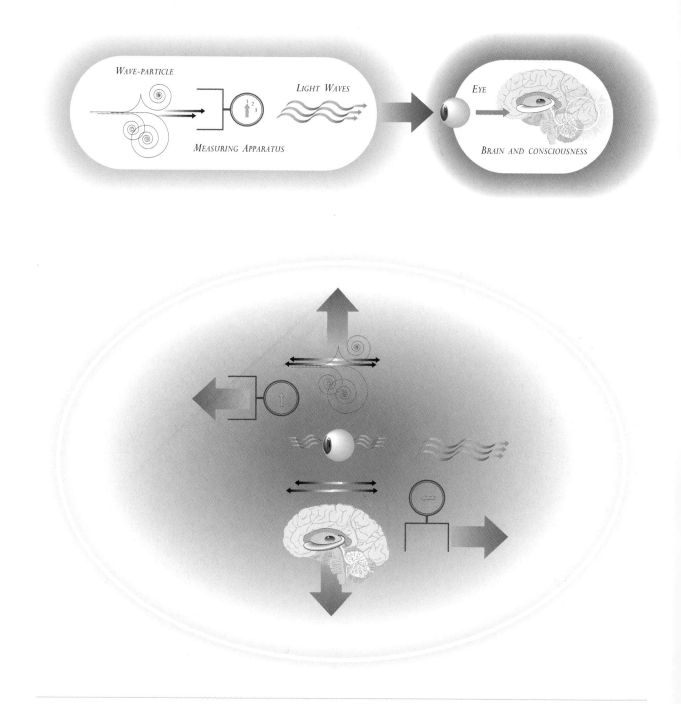

Top: *The classical concept of how an observer measures the behavior of a particle. Essentially existence is seen as two separate realities — a world "out there" and an observer "in here."*

Bottom: *The new physics suggests that one cannot separate the observer and the observed. Consciousness is seen as both the source and the creator of the phenomenal world.*

secondary and is seen more as a mapping of objects through their various conditions. So the essential question a scientist of today must ask is whether the phenomenal world consists of *beings* or *becomings*.

In the West it is suspected that we have been programmed, through the very nature of our lineal languages, to experience our world in terms of *cause* and *effect* — like a *noun* acting on, or being acted on, by a *verb*. Within that contextual linguistic framework we also experience a past, a present and a future. Yet mystics of all persuasions, from time immemorial, have hammered into us that nothing happens in either the past or the future. Both are non-existent, for there is only the here-now, *this* very moment which can be real. Everything happens in an eternal now. Tomorrow never arrives anymore than you ever reach the horizon.

In the classical Newtonian universe time is an absolute, a background against which events play in linear sequences of cause and effect. Time to Newton was not a construct. In the functioning of our everyday lives the "classical approximation" works perfectly well. Unmanned spacecraft can land on Mars with perfect precision using Newtonian principles. It is only when we consider the implications of sub-atomic behavior, or view reality through the eyes of a lucid dreamer, or a mystic, that such approximations come unstuck. No longer can we assume the view that every event — be it ever so solid, or ephemeral, or past, present or future — occupies a particular location within space-time. In the world of quanta there appears to be no time, no before and no after, so questions as to *when*, or *where*, by default, have no meaning. Does this all begin to sound like a dream?

DREAM PRACTICE

This is a variation of an Eastern technique known as *tratak*. Before going to sleep set up a mirror in such a way that you can sit comfortably in front of it for about a half-an-hour. Place a lighted candle nearby so that your face is illuminated well. Stare steadily at your reflected image without blinking (eyedrops help this). You will find that there is a curious connection between thoughts and blinking and this technique allows clearer witnessing without the constant clutter of distracting thoughts. The face in the mirror will start changing quite dramatically like a series of undulating and fluid masks. Many practitioners believe these represent past lives. Be that as it may; we are only concerned with the fact that the face you are identified with is not, in reality, a fixed event. *Intend* to dream that night of looking in a mirror at your dream self. Watch the changing faces a while before wishing to see your real face. Try to have no preconceived ideas which might influence the outcome. Meditators claim that in waking life the image in the mirror disappears altogether. In lucid dreams prepared to be even more surprised. After this practice you may feel an exhuberant sense of wholeness and fulfilment in your subsequent waking life. But ask the real question behind the enterprise. Just who was observing you? Mystics claim this is the witnessing consciousness which is seen as the embracing reality in the second diagram opposite.

THE HOLOGRAM

I believe in the future transmutation
of those two seemingly contradictory states,
dream and reality,
into a sort of absolute reality,
a surreality so to speak.

André Breton

THE original idea that the universe has remarkable similarities to a holographic process really evolved from questions of how and where memories were stored in the brain. Early research into the workings of the brain had revealed that we appear to store, in some miraculous fashion, virtually everything that has ever happened in our lives, from the most trivial moments to those of utmost importance. Under hypnosis, or having certain areas of the brain stimulated by electrical charges, patients were able to vividly recall detailed memories of events completely forgotten by the conscious mind. The question which puzzled neurophysiologists was simply where could we have stored so much information? There had to be limits to the "shelf space" available determined by the size of the brain itself. It quite simply didn't seem physically possible to fit a lifetime of memories into the size of our craniums. Some other explanation had to be true. One model did seem to fit most of the criteria.

Holography is fundamentally a phenomenon of interference patterns. Just as a handful of stones thrown into a calm pond creates many concentric waves all rippling through one another creating inter-ference patterns, so holography is an interference pattern of light.

Any wave pattern, be it from water, radio waves or light, can create interference patterns. However the very purity of laser light creates especially well defined patterns, and holograms are formed when a single laser beam is split in two. One beam is bounced off the object to be photographed while the other crosses its reflected light, creating an interference pattern which is then recorded on light sensitive film *(shown opposite)*. The image on the film appears to be rather like a reconstruction of those ripples from the pebbles thrown into a pond, and yet when the light of another laser beam is shone through the film a *three-dimensional* image of the original object appears. One can move around this uncannily real image just as though it were the original, even seeing the faces hidden from a full frontal view.

What particularly impressed one neurophysicist, Karl Pribram, was the holographic film's remarkable ability to retain information even when it is cut into many pieces. Although the three-dimensional image does get hazier and more vague, even the tiniest fragment of the original film will still project the

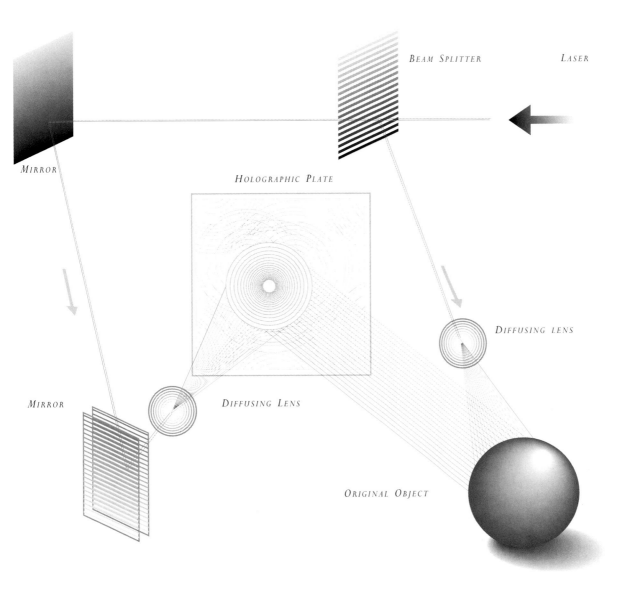

BEAM SPLITTER   LASER

MIRROR

HOLOGRAPHIC PLATE

DIFFUSING LENS

MIRROR   DIFFUSING LENS

ORIGINAL OBJECT

A hologram is created when the light from a single laser is split into two separate beams. One beam is then bounced off the object to be recorded, or holographed. The second beam is then directed in such a way as to collide with the reflected light of the first and the resulting interference pattern which is produced is recorded on the light-sensitive emulsion of a film. Unlike a normal photographic film, however, every part of the holographic film contains all the information of the whole image. So if a holographic film is torn into pieces, each fragment can be used to reconstruct the image with only a certain loss of sharpness.

whole object. So unlike any other recording device, such as a photographic film, or a CD, every smallest part of a holographic film contains *all* the information recorded in the whole.

Scientists working on the nature of memory have discovered that, within the brain, the neurons' tree-like branches fire electrical messages at one another, which most likely set up just the very kind of interference patterns to be found in holograms. These would then create a perpetually moving and multidimensional holograph within the brain-field, believed to constitute the miraculous complexity of our minds and to create our ideas of the world around us.

The holographic view suggests that reality is really a *frequency domain,* and our brain an encoder that converts these frequencies into what we see as the phenomenal world of appearances. "Frequency domain" is a term created by Karl Pribram to describe the interference patterns that possibly compose the deeper order of reality. As the brain apparently edits out anything which doesn't fit our preconceived notions of what our waking world is supposed to be like "out there," we tend to get fixed in our ways of viewing the world. Mystics, psychics, psychotics, shamans and lucid dreamers all seem to share the unusual ability to cancel the editing program and thus to experience glimpses of the original frequency domain in all its splendor.

So here is a possible model of how we store so many memories in the absurdly tiny space of our brainpans. Holographs have a phenomenal capacity for storing information. Not only can an enormous amount be stored on a single film, but if the angle at which the lasers strike the film is altered, even fractionally, it is possible to record another set of images upon the same surface. All that is necessary to retrieve these multiple images is to illuminate the film at the original angle the photograph was taken.

Pribram suggested that an analogous process might be happening within the brain and that a similar action takes place when we forget or recall experiences, or when we associate memories which have little immediate connection with one another.

This particular feature of the whole holographic paradigm is fundamental to our understanding of both the dreaming exercises and of the habitual, almost addictive, *fixing* of our waking perceptions into a single, stable and unchanging world view. For just as a piece of film, when tilted in the illumination of a laser beam, reveals an array of changing images, so, when our internal equivalent of either the film or the beam shifts, we recall or forget both personal and collective memories. And it could be this ability to move our *focus of attention,* especially during dreams and trances, throughout the vast holographic library of existence, that accounts for such a radically different vision from that in our habitual, waking condition.

To understand these often obscure and difficult ideas more clearly we must turn our attention to how we manage to construct our perceptions of the waking world in the first place.

Sunlight on an outgoing tide. The light catching the constantly moving waves and interweaving ripples reminds us of the frequency domain model of the brain. That model, too, is not static. The waves created by the multitude of synchronous firings of the neural network which makes up the brain create interference patterns which are in continual motion, in time and in space.

PERCEPTIONS OF THE WAKING WORLD

WHEN we experience what we believe to be "outside reality," what we actually experience is sensory input – an image carried to the surface of our retinas by light, or a sound carried by air to our eardrums – which is then interpreted by the various nerve receptors in our brain. We do not perceive the image as actually being on the light-sensitive cones of our retinas, or the sound on the vibrating drum, at all. Indeed, to do so requires a act of awareness of which few of us are capable. Instead, we see the image as being outside our brain, and similarly the information from our other senses as being out-

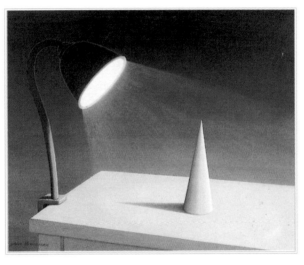

side ourselves. So when we think we feel the solidity of a rock, the reality of the situation is not so much a case of being "out there," but rather a complex set of neuro-physiological processes happening within our brains.

How then does our grey matter distinguish between internal and external reality, between what is illusory and what is actual? And just *who* is trying to fool whom when they get mixed up?

This is where a hologram is such a beautiful analogy, for it is an illusion *par excellence*, and extremely difficult to distinguish from the actual and substan-

tive original. It has every appearance of existing in space, but is as ephemeral as a rainbow when you try to touch it or examine it with instruments. A hologram is a virtual reality appearing *where it is not,* in much the same manner as the image which appears to be behind the surface of the mirror, or a mirage is seen in the hot desert air. The film of the hologram is the actual location of the image, just as the silvering behind the glass of the mirror is the location of the reflected image, or the rain droplets the location of the rainbow spectrum.

It would appear, from recent research, that our brains and all our senses could actually be operating as complex frequency analyzers which convert and encode all the patterns received into a system of wave forms, in much the same way that a hologram converts interference patterns back into an image of the original scene. Which brings us to the question, what if the "picture" in our brains of what we believe to be reality is not a picture at all but a kind of hologram?

Opposite: **Euclidean Walks,** by René Magritte. Above: **Out of Things Alive,** by Jeroen Henneman.

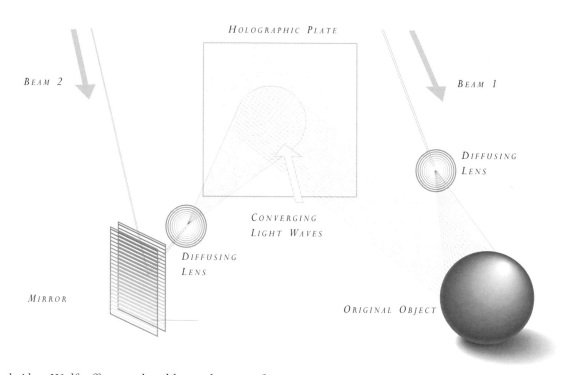

BEAM 2

HOLOGRAPHIC PLATE

BEAM 1

DIFFUSING LENS

CONVERGING LIGHT WAVES

DIFFUSING LENS

MIRROR

ORIGINAL OBJECT

Fred Alan Wolf offers a plausible explanation for lucid dreaming within the context of the holographic model. He points out that the holographic film actually generates two images as seen in the diagram above. The virtual image that appears behind the film has no substance, location or extension in space any more than a reflection of the moon in water. It appears through diverging light. But in *front* of the film another, actual, and factual, image comes into focus which does possess extension in space. This is not normally visible unless something like dust particles are dropped through it. Unlike the virtual image this is not an illusion but a real and spatially factual converging of light waves. Wolf suggests that, while all dreams are inner holograms, our normal dreams are only virtual images on the back of the inner brain film. The sheer vibrancy and reality of lucid dreaming might be explained by the brains' possible ability to create real images. Wolf then goes one step further, for he believes that if the dream observer

Above: **Converging light waves** in front of the film which possess extension into space, as opposed to the virtual image which is projected behind the film.

steps into where the waves focus, "that viewer will be bathed in the scene, and the scene coming to a focus will 'contain' him." As a sporadic lucid dreamer himself he can confirm that there does not seem to be very much difference between the experience of the world "outside" and of the world within our heads.

It must be stressed at this point that while the holographic paradigm is fast gaining support among neuro-physiologists as a model of how our brain, or our perceptions, might work, it remains a highly controversial proposition within the field. However, there are a number of other scientists, in very different disciplines, who have come up with similar conclusions about the nature of reality. And in each case, our habitual assumptions and perceptions of reality are shown to rest upon very shaky foundations indeed.

THE NEW PHYSICS

Those who believe in existence
are stupid like cattle.
But those who believe in non-existence
are even worse.

The Royal Songs of Saraha, Tibet 12th century.

I N an earlier chapter we examined physiological models of the working of the brain and how they might account for some of our dreaming processes. Most physically based theories, predictably, loudly chorus songs of praise for the extraordinary talents of the bio-computer we all possess. And so they should. They sing of things like brain stems, neural firings and bombardings of the forebrain. We feel such things are of the real and substantial stuff of nature which can be understood, for they fit within our accustomed mind-sets.

Now, in stark contrast, we once more venture into altogether different territory to explore further evidence which suggests that our current understanding of a solid, comforting, down-to-earth reality is truly nothing more than an elaborate dream. And as the true nature of dreaming reality is our immediate concern we must briefly examine these new ideas.

The first dilemma facing us is that the bizarre concepts of the new physics simply cannot be measured by the traditional scientific standards we are used to, because, by default, these are the self-same scientific models which have proved no longer to be adequate. The major hurdle to any understanding of the radical shift which has occurred in physics during the past sixty years is that the very tenet of science – that of being as objective and as impartial as possible when examining phenomena – is being fundamentally questioned. The new physics simply suggests that the observer is not separate from what he or she observes. Because of this, consciousness apparently can not only alter matter but might be the very foundation of matter.

It was over sixty years ago that Werner Heisenberg set in motion an idea which has gradually seeped into the deepest foundations of mechanistic classical physics. In 1927 he announced his revolutionary *uncertainty principle,* according to which it is impossible to simultaneously measure the position and velocity of a sub-atomic particle. He believed that this uncertainty arose because of the unavoidable disturbance of the object by the very process of measurement. Since those days this idea has grown, and consequent quantum experiments suggest that consciousness actually does appear to change the state of matter.

The Nobel Prize winning physicist, Eugene Wigner asserted, thirty years after Heisenberg, that without explicit reference to consciousness scientists could not adequately describe the processes found within quantum mechanics. He proposed that the relationship between consciousness and what is known as objective reality should be radically re-examined. Since then a number of eminent physicists, like J. Scarfatti, John Wheeler and Hugh Everett, have taken up that cause.

Scarfatti, in suggesting that matter may not be independent of consciousness, goes one step further and proposes that it is the gravitational field which is responsible for the interaction of consciousness and matter. He believes that living systems are organized by "biogravitons" (variants of the gravitron, a hypothetical particle which is believed to be, in some way, responsible for the structure of matter). These biogravitons might be controlled and influenced by the collective or individual consciousness, and it is these which interact with the fields that govern the shape and structure of the material and manifest universe. In effect he is suggesting a field of consciousness which interacts with other fields, much as Wheeler has proposed that the universe is created by the participating observers.

Few scientists, even those in the field of quantum mechanics, care to firmly grasp the nettle of what this implies, and as far as popular imagination is concerned the question remains completely speculative and "off the screen."

Nevertheless, no one can escape the pervading new message which suggests that consciousness plays an active and indivisible role in what we know of as the physical universe. Like the lucid dreamer in sleep, it even appears that we can alter the material universe while being awake and change its script simply by *willing* it to change. However, even though the old viewpoint of a reassuringly solid universe has been shown to be illusory, in the face of such radical and disquieting ideas we still cling tightly to what at least seems to be the sanity of that familiar view.

The picture of the physical world which is emerging from the quantum experiments is so surrealistic and dreamlike that few can easily live with its implications. And if some scientists do manage the conceptual quantum leap, they are more likely to find themselves deep in the world of the mystic than in the hitherto deterministic and empirical province of science. The new physics seems to be doing nothing less than creating a new mystical science, of a kind which has never existed before in the West — what might even be called a "religion" of human consciousness, or a "psychology" of the cosmos as a *consciousness acting upon itself*. And in redefining the role of the scientist what better description could we get for dreaming, and lucid dreaming in particular, than *consciousness acting upon itself*?

Adam, True to Measure, by Rudolf Hauser, 1973. *The problem in measuring sub-atomic particles is that the instruments used to measure them are also composed of them. If the particle has an indefinite velocity and an indeterminate location then so has the instrument. Such paradoxes abound in the field.*

UNCOMFORTABLE HYPOTHESES

A QUESTION which any layman, like myself, might ask is, how does all this theorizing actually affect our normal view of the universe and reality. If there truly is a revolution in the understanding of the nature of consciousness and matter, then why does it appear to be passing by so quietly and virtually unnoticed by the general public?

Let us first list some of the major discoveries of quantum physics in the last half century to see what such findings might imply about our understanding of reality. In doing so we will discover that the list is more like a description of the lucid dreamer's world than of the waking one.

1) Consciousness appears to alter the physical universe. The observer can no longer be seen to be standing outside what is being observed without altering it.

2) Increasingly it has been found that our description of the world and how we think it works is confused with how it actually works. In other words, we so encapsulate ourselves within our world of ideas *about the world* that we fail to *see* the world as it actually is. Concepts and words only stand for reality; they are not reality. This dilemma is thrown into high relief when a quantum physicist attempts to analyze the external phenomena of the world "out there" only to find that all that is being analyzed is "a concept for the world out there."

3) The assurance that there is a past, a present and a future running in one linear direction does not appear to operate at all at sub-atomic levels. Indeed, some scientists seriously speculate that

there are even zones where time does not exist at all.

4) Just as time does not run in one direction at sub-atomic levels, so we discover that cause and effect also have no meaning; the normal world of energy, objects and space seems to exhibit causal relationships only by some curious statistical coincidence. In other words, while we believe cause is followed by effect, or future always follows past, this sequence could appear that way because of our belief that it happens that way.

5) If consciousness is seen to affect the physical nature of existence, the implications are that there might be no one single reality at all. Rather, it could be that there are multiple universes, continually bifurcating and splitting off at critical junctures. In what increasingly look like science and fantasy fiction scenarios, we might find that in one universe World War II never happened, while in another it was lost by the Allies. Some physicists go as far as suggesting that our consciousness edits out those events which do not fit the consensus idea of reality.

6) Western science has until now been at considerable pains to be as objective as possible, shielding all experiments from any subjective corruption by the observer. It is now proposed, by an increasing number of scientists, that consciousness, rather than being a phenomenon to exclude from proper experiments, might actually turn out to be the *only phenomenon that exists*. Reality proves to be more a *no-thing-ness* than a *some-thing-ness*, and about as substantial as a passing cloud.

Rumor, by Joop Moesman, 1935. *Mysticism and modern science appear to agree that we live in a cosmos which dreams itself. The familiar nature of our waking world turns out to be little more than a collective and social habit, in which riding naked on a bicycle is unusual. But it is still a dream.*

7) Consciousness can be understood as a field similar to that of gravity. Two or more fields could resonate with each another as a continuum. Mind and matter can then be seen as merely waves in the same ocean.

None of these hypotheses are in any way new. Ancient yogic and tantric texts from India — which were the mystical equivalent of quantum mechanics in their day, and were just as rigorous

and precise in their observations as those of modern physics today — make no distinction between consciousness and reality. Instead they define three states, or stages of consciousness. The first is dualistic with the emphasis on 'This,' where the reality of the object is seen as separate from the self. The second emphasizes the total subjectivity of the 'I,' and the third stage is one in which neither object nor observer, neither the 'This' nor the 'I,' is present.

By now the reader must wonder, once again, what all this has to do with lucid dreams. What emerges from this brief summary is that according to both modern science and ancient mysticism, the cosmos begins to look *as if it dreams itself.* Increasingly it appears that we ourselves are a dream and perhaps suspect that those we dream of might even be dreaming us. But because we seek stability and sameness, we slip easily into habitual patterns through repetition and an unconscious, and essentially unaware, sleepiness. Now science seems to be offering a basis for a new awareness of consciousness itself, comparable to that of the mysticism of the past. And when one is alert and conscious of being conscious, one is lucid. It is a small step to see that the implications of lucidity within dreams can be extended into the waking universe. In other words we are as capable of changing our waking reality as we are of the scenarios of our lucid dreams. Those who have learned to dream with awareness begin to discover that the worlds are unexpectedly similar, and intending something in waking reality can have precisely the same effect as it does in dreaming.

It happens!

IMPLICATE AND EXPLICATE ORDER

As SCIENTISTS divide matter into tinier and tinier pieces, we have already seen that those pieces, to all appearances, cease to behave like matter at all. In fact as soon as a physicist gets down to the level of an electron he or she discovers that it can appear as either a particle or a wave. Either way it has no dimension that can be measured. It simply is like no-*thing* we know of. Sub-atomic phenomena exhibit this schizophrenic behavior of being both a wave and a particle at one and the same moment, depending upon whether someone is looking at them or not. From what is known, and from some very weird experiments in which the scientists tried not to look, while looking at them all the same, the coy particle changed its posture to that of a wave. It seems that when unobserved the sub-atomic world apparently prefers to act like a wave, but as soon as anyone takes a peek it does a rapid change. These "now you see me, now you don't," sometimes waves, sometimes particles, are what we know of as *quanta*.

But not only do quanta have no dimension and the disquieting predisposition to be two personalities at the same time, they also have no location. Perhaps, more accurately, it should be said that location ceases to exist at this level, and all points in space are equal to all other points. Such disturbing properties made scientists look for

some radically new overview, and the eminent physicist, David Bohm, suggested a model which shows the universe to be a vast holographic movement, in which our known and seemingly stable universe is really a kind of illusion, like a holographic image. This manifest reality he called the *unfolded* or *explicate* order. Underlying this manifest and seemingly substantial order, however, and giving rise to it, is another, yet deeper principle, the *implicate* or *enfolded* order, in which everything is enfolded into everything (see opposite). And the totality of the universe is the result of the endless enfolding and unfolding of these orders, taking place almost as though they are breathing in and out.

In such a totality of flux, or holomovement, it is meaningless to conceive of the universe as composed of separate parts. There is just one seamless whole, even though there is an apparent

---

Above: ***David Bohm.*** Opposite: ***A model for the explicate and implicate orders.*** *One of David Bohm's favorite models used to demonstrate his theory is that of a dye being dropped in glycerin which is held between two rotating glass cylinders (see fig.1). As one of the cylinders is rotated (fig.2) the dye begins to spread until the original drop disappears in a homogenous mixture within the medium of the glycerin (fig.3). However, if the direction of the rotation is then reversed (as in fig. 4) the drop of dye reappears exactly as it was (fig. 6). Bohm suggests that existence enfolds and unfolds in a similar way.*

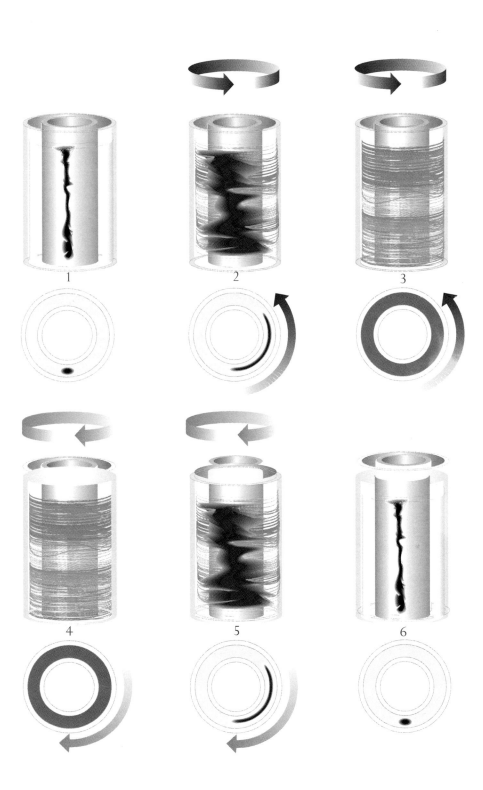

separation of relative sub-totalities at the virtual or explicate level. And it is our insistence on the separate nature of "things" and on fragmenting and dividing the explicate world, that creates problems, both in science and in our lives.

Here Bohm's ideas coincide with the discoveries of the mystics of all ages. Indeed he appears to be one of the first of a new breed of mystical scientist. Virtually every mystical tradition insists upon the illusory nature of the everyday world, the unity and wholeness of all things and the ever-flowing, eternal present of all and everything.

The Islamic Sufis have long used a mystical diagram of a cross to express this. In it the horizontal axis denotes the world of time and space, of apparent location and substance existing in a line between past and future. This can be seen as the explicate order of the universe. Bisecting this linear plane *at the present moment* is the vertical part of the cross representing the eternal, timeless and implicate order. Stand at the threshold of the two orders and one is in the ever living present moment, witnessing the endless unfolding procession of the explicate order as it passes from past to future. At this point there is pure consciousness watching in the virtual world of illusion and yet not being identified with it. *A glimpse of this threshold can be had by gaining of lucidity within dreams.*

Bohm's model suggests that consciousness, being part of the seamless whole, can be seen as a more subtle form of matter, present in varying degrees of enfolding and unfolding. This also indicates that it is meaningless to attempt to categorize the universe into living and non-living "things," for all are inseparably interwoven. When we divide things in our minds we are deluding ourselves, but the delusion becomes a way of life, the origins of *maya,* that Eastern belief that the phenomenal world is but a dream.

Sosan, the third Zen Patriarch, and one of the great men of Tao, was about as succinct as you can get. The very simplicity of what he said almost two thousand five hundred years ago pre-figures the present understanding that duality has no place within the new holographic paradigm.

"The Great Way is not difficult for those who have no preferences.

When love and hate are both absent everything becomes clear and undisguised.

Make the smallest distinction, however, and Heaven and Earth are set infinitely apart.

If you wish to see the truth then hold no opinion for or against.

The struggle of what one likes and what one dislikes is the disease of the mind."

His *Verses on a Faith Mind* anticipate the essential difference between the classical idea of the scientist who divides the world into smaller and smaller parts in order to see how the machine works, and Bohm's vision of an indivisible reality which includes consciousness, light, matter and anti-matter in one vast and seamless whole.

"In this world of suchness there is neither self nor other-than-self.

To come directly into harmony with this reality just simply say when doubts arise, 'Not two.'

In this 'not two' nothing is separate, nothing is excluded.

No matter when or where, enlightenment means entering this truth.

And this truth is beyond extension or diminution in time or space: in a single thought is ten thousand years."

If we are to believe this old man of Tao, or what an increasing number of scientists appear to be saying now, it is as if our brains are holograms enfolded within a hologram, *ad infinitum*, each brain constructing what it believes to be objective reality by interpreting frequencies from a deeper order of existence outside space and time.

If this is so then the objective world is not the absolute reality we believe it to be. Reality appears to be an oceanic vastness of interfering frequences which our brains then decode into relatively fixed ideas of what it *is supposed to be*. This doesn't necessarily mean that rivers aren't rivers and rocks aren't rocks, but it does mean that what we see is only that which our brains construct. Without that de-coder, perhaps we might experience it as an interference pattern. Both are real or not real. Sosan again:

"To deny the reality of things is to miss their reality;

to assert the emptiness of things is again to miss their reality.

The more you talk and think about it, the further astray you wander from the truth."

Opposite: ***Zen Hotei Crossing a Stream,*** *by Kanô Tanyû, Japan.* Above: ***Patriarch and Tiger,*** *Japan, thirteenth century. The mind of this old man of Tao, like the patriarch, Sosan, is so clear of any distinction of safe or dangerous that he can contentedly fall asleep using a sleeping tiger as a pillow.*

THE PRIMAL WEB AND THE HAIRS OF SHIVA

IF we pay attention to the accounts of psychics and shamans, there are many descriptions of what a less filtered vision of the reality of the interference patterns might be like. Virtually all of them in some way describe their inner universe as one of light. Some tell of filaments or infinitely fine strands of light-consciousness interweaving like a vast multi-dimensional spider's web. People are often seen as pulsating clusters, globes or eggs of different colored light.

Accounts vary, but one common feature appears to be that in trance, lucid dreaming or in altered states of waking, the visionary often finds that the images of light slowly give way to become more recognizable "things" – as though the mind, because it cannot comprehend the world in this new, light-filled and chaotic way, reverts to what it knows, or thinks it knows. For this universe of energy appears as chaos to any minds conditioned to seeing the world as comfortably solid and recognizable.

I once remember, in India, experiencing a similar state, but I was terrified. Everything was in such an insane flux that all I longed for, even though I am English to the core, was an image of Holland, which obviously I felt to be the ultimate in waking normality. So instead of just witnessing what was really happening, I blew it, desperately holding on to a visualization of the ordered Dutch highway signs, the baker's shops, and the canals, to keep me from going completely insane.

In visions of what might be the primal state of reality, or what Bohm calls the implicate order, many eye-witness reports suggest that human beings appear translucent and vibrant, consisting of fibers of light, enmeshing the whole body in a web of fine threads rather like a floating egg. From this egg of energy, luminous bristles and long tenuous fibers reach out in all directions. In India these are known as the Hairs of Shiva. At a point on the outer energy bubble, variously seen above the upper back, the right-hand side of the heart, or at the third eye, lies what appears to be a junction box where all the fibers of the world meet or are channelled. In Carlos Castanedas' terms this is the *assemblage point*. In the descriptions of the Indian Vedanta this point is at the heart, while in Indian Tantra it is the third eye. Each tradition considers this to be the unique location of the conscious attention of each entity.

So the mind, when confronted with such incomprehensible information, rapidly transforms that experience into an image of the known or semi-known, with often bizarre consequences.

In the *Tibetan Book of the Dead* one of the first moments of death is described as being a confrontation with the basic luminosity. "*Now the pure luminosity of the dharmata is shining before you; recognize it.*" The mind is perceived as having both male and female aspects. The male aspect is seen as a sparkling, pure and vibrant luminosity while the indivisible female nature is one of pure emptiness. "*This mind of yours is inseparable luminosity and emptiness in the form of a great mass of light, it has no birth or death, therefore it is the Buddha of Immortal Light.*"

But even at this pure level the mind will attempt to make something familiar out of it. Those subjects who have undergone a near-death

The Pleasure Principle, by René Magritte.

experience in which they have encountered an overwhelmingly brilliant luminosity often recall that they thought someone had shone a powerful flashlight into their eyes, or that they were caught in the headlights of a truck. We have already seen that in subsequent stages of the bardo state, the deceased experiences sounds, colored lights and rays of light and can become full of terror and fear. At this point the bardo guide must remind them to recognize "now that I have reached this crucial point I will not fear the peaceful and wrathful ones, *my own projections.*" As one proceeds in the bardo state, one can become more and more identified with the utterly real illusions thrown up by one's mind.

The *Tibetan Book of the Dead,* or as it is more correctly known, "*The Great Liberation Through Hearing In the Bardo,*" is an amazing description of the holographic model. The deceased becomes increasingly identified with the often violent and confused projections of what the Tibetans call *karma,* or what we might, in the context of the hologram, call a fixation of attention with habitual viewpoints, fears, attitudes, guilt and all the other social beliefs and conditioning programs forced upon us from childhood onwards.

If the deceased has already had some experience of lucid dreaming, then much of the imagery will

Left: **Bindhu**, *painting from Rajasthan, eighteenth century. Tantra conceives the universe as either the most minute point or the all encompassing whole. The Bindhu is the fundamental point out of which inner and outer space take their origin and in which they*

again become one. Above: ***The Freiburg Room,*** *by Peter Dreher, 1978. That we tend to see distinct and separate objects within external space, in color or in monotone, is increasingly understood to be the result of a collective and habitual program rather than reality.*

be familiar, and recognition of it all as purely dream stuff will be of inestimable value in helping to dissociate his or her self from the projections and in turning the attention to the basic luminosity instead.

As we turn from science towards mysticism, many of the ancient statements take on new meaning for they are almost identical with those holographic ideas of today. Swami Vivekananda, in *Jnana Yoga,* echoes age-old Hindu texts when he says that, "Time, space and causation are like the glass through which the absolute is seen," and that we mistake the glass for the universe. He goes on to say that from this image we gather that there is no time, space or causation in the universe and that what we call causation begins after "the degeneration of the absolute into the phenomenal and not before." Such a statement is uncannily like Bohm's implicate-explicate orders.

Of all the Indian texts those of Tantra are most clearly seen as anticipating modern quantum mechanics. The Hindu concepts of *nada* and *bindu* are virtually identical to the quantum physicists' idea that matter can be both wave and particle. According to ancient Tantric texts, when Brahma creates matter a vibration or wave *(nada)* is set in motion. But when matter is viewed as separate from consciousness, it is seen as many points *(bindhu).*

INTENDING, WE CREATE THE WORLD

Most of us are completely unaware of the power of our thoughts and present an almost unbroken babble of conflicting and incoherent ideas. This acts as a sustained and confusing bombardment of the implicate order from which all of us arise. However, the moment one focuses such thoughts, makes an oath to essence to that essential being at the center, or *intends* to have something happen, then the thoughts are coherent and no longer confuse the creative, deeper layers of the implicate order. And it is out of these layers that the explicate unfolds. A single-minded intention reaps a single-minded harvest.

According to both Bohm and the Tibetans, once an *intention* is made, the explicate rolls out as smoothly as if on greased wheels. If a person takes time out to visualize in substantial terms what they really want to make of their lives, then they are able consciously to manifest the events that happen to them. *This is precisely the same process we find in a lucid dream*, when the dreamer wills or intends the general outcome and yet is often surprised at the specific or peripheral details of how the dream unfolds. In our waking states we can establish the general impetus and direction of our lives by simply *intending* them that way, and allowing the details of how it happens to flow naturally. This is at the very heart of the single-minded approach to invoking lucid dreaming. All that has to be done is for you to *intend* to dream consciously and to send a clear and uneqivocal message to the implicate order that this is to happen, and it will.

David Bohm clearly echoes this when he says that, " Every action starts from an *intention* in the implicate order." This intention or act of creative imagination sets in motion the form which eventually appears in the explicate level. In the implicate order, in the deeper levels of reality and of the blueprint of the raw stuff of the universe, imagination and reality are one. So images in the mind can ultimately manifest as realities in the body.

This is evidenced by the miraculous cures of patients who undergo imaging and bio-feedback therapy. If a patient with terminal cancer, by visualizing a ray of light which destroys the cancer cells and at the same time heals and builds healthy replacement cells, can totally reverse the action of the disease, this does suggest that our minds have a direct and inseparable link with matter. There are too many well-documented cases of so-called miraculous cures to dismiss such claims.

When patients believe they are being cured, then a completely useless pill will have the desired effect, and yet when the same patient has lost hope even the most potent drug will have no effect whatsoever. It has been discovered in a number of experiments with *placebos* (harmless pills without any curative properties whatever) that most of the cures sold over pharmacy counters work simply because the customer believes they will work. Taking an asprin for a headache is as much an act of faith as taking a drug. When the mind is tricked into believing something, we are somehow able to bypass our normal scepticism, our discrimination between what is factual and what is fictional. By sending a clear message of healing down the line into the implicate order, we manage to manifest that healing in the phenomenal world. Hypnosis is yet another powerful way that the mind can be given

Landscape from a Dream, by Paul Nash.

an *intention* to heal or to perceive the factual differently.

And if you want any spiritual authority on this subject consider that Gautama, the Buddha once said,

" We are what we think. All that we are arises through our thoughts.

With our thoughts we create the world."

'The greatest wizard," writes Jorge Luis Borges, in *Other Inquisitions,*

"...would be the one who bewitched himself to the point of accepting his own phantasmagorias as autonomous apparitions. Wouldn't that be our case? I surmise it is so. We (that indivisible divinity that operates in us) have dreamed the world. We have dreamed it enduring, mysterious, visible, omnipresent in space and stable in time; but we have consented to tenuous and eternal intervals of illogicalness in its architecture that we might know it is false."

Perhaps Borges is just hopeful about leaving a few clues strewn about where we might trip over them. The major wall to climb in order to see beyond the dream is *habit,* or in more scientific terminology, the morphic, or morphological field.

MORPHIC FIELDS

THE third theory, which we will all too briefly touch upon, is that proposed by the English scientist, Rupert Sheldrake.

He suggests that memory is *inherent* in nature. That it is cumulative, and through repetition the nature of things, from atoms to elephants, becomes increasingly habitual. Sheldrake suggests that, "Things are as they are because they were as they were."

According to his *hypothesis of formative causation*, the nature of everything depends upon fields, which he terms morphic fields. Like other fields in science these habit fields, like those of gravity, "are non-material regions of influence extending in space and continuing in time." As the memory within these fields is cumulative, things and ideas become increasingly habitual through repetition. When such repetition has occurred over billions of years, as it has over such an event as a hydrogen atom, the nature of this habit is so ingrained that it is effectively changeless and eternal.

So matter can be seen as a kind of habit, repetitively being created from out of the implicate order. Matter in this way is an almost neurotic memory pattern, chronically fixed and stuck in the otherwise constantly changing flux of reality. The very laws of the universe appear to be fixed in the holomovement in the same way as our habits and beliefs are fixed at our points of attention.

I personally feel that this hypothesis perfectly describes our own state of perception. Through the repetition of countless generations of human beings, we have built up a cherished environment which is so habitual that it has taken on the guise of being eternal, fixed and solid.

Morphic fields, however, take time to build up sufficient memory to impose a shape or habitual form. Experiments have shown that when scientists attempt to create crystals from a new substance, it takes an inordinate length of time. But once one batch has been created, it appears to become progressively easier to create the crystals even when the laboratory experiments are in totally different geographical locations. Once

something has been created, whether it is a new organism, or a new idea, a habit field also comes into being. The more times the new thing is repeated, the greater the effectiveness of the habit field, the easier it will be to create again. It appears there might be a threshold point at which the habit field suddenly clicks on for everyone, whether it is an idea, a molecule or a full blown organism

In this respect we might well wonder about

Opposite: *The Big Table*, 1962. Above: ***Souvenir of a Journey***, *1955. Both by René Magritte. We appear to be habitually set in our ideas about a fixed reality. But Rupert Sheldrake proposes the novel hypothesis that reality has even more habitual ideas about us.*

213

Street Scene, by A.C.Willink, 1934. The deserted city is a theme which many conscious dreamers find they awake into as they move from a non-lucid state to one of lucidity. On close inspection of the buildings and the street, most lucid dreamers are amazed at the perfect and minute detail of the dream world. Shadows are cast perfectly, reflections seen in windows adjust to the slightest movement, and on concentrating, the surface of the road can be felt beneath the feet. From where do we build these extraordinary replicas of the waking world? Are our memories prodigious beyond belief, or we do actually enter a parallel or separate reality?

lucid dreaming, for up until only a decade ago it was very much reserved for a chosen few. It is as though the memories which had built up over the centuries reached the threshold point and suddenly everyone is attempting to dream lucidly, and it apparently is getting easier all the time as the lucid-dream-field grows in intensity and habit and interacts with other fields.

Sheldrake himself has encountered considerable resistance from the established scientific community. One prestigious publication suggested that his book, *A New Science of Life,* was only fit for burning. But this is a perfect demonstration of what might be expected from habit fields, for they are especially fixed around ideas. Traditions are some of the most difficult habits to change. When you try to change someone's cherished belief, it has been observed that they begin to act like an addict. However, we are all addicted and habituated to our beliefs, and are likely to behave irrationally when someone attempts to take away our particular dogma-drug.

Virtually all great discoveries and new ideas, like Sheldrake's own, are at first met with the most passionate of denials. Many of the scientists who have put forward the theories we are at present examining have had to suffer vilification from their established peers. It is a paradox that while beliefs are the foundation of our perceptions of the world, they are not really ours at all but always someone else's. When you discover and experience something on your own then it is not a belief, it is a *knowing*. To the blind, the shape of the sun coming up in the morning has to be taken as a belief, for they cannot verify it with their own experience. To those with sight it is a simple experiential knowing. We don't often say we believe the sun appears on the horizon. We *know* it does!

But as far as questions of ultimate reality are concerned, we are on far shakier ground. Even though we all have learned at school that the sun does not actually rise and set, but that our planet revolves around it, few of us can actually *feel* that. In this we remain not so very different from anyone a millennium ago, who believed the earth was flat. Our perceptions are fooled as far as, so called, scientific fact is concerned.

Consider then the quantum leap we must make in order to grasp the concept that the universe around us is not solid at all, but merely appears that way because we have been programmed to perceive it the same way as our forebears and that by repetition it has stuck.

How then can we make the jump to see existence as a "multiverse" of parallel worlds like some vast holographic movement in a spaceless and timeless eternity, which is what appears to be the possible truth of our condition? Physicists might tell us that reality is a vast network of conscious energy, and that when we bump into what appears to be a very solid chair, it no more exists than a dream. But can we truly feel that? Our programming would never let us. Our underlying habit field is far too strong. And yet when a mystic or a shaman defies all physical laws by leisurely walking across fire, or sitting, happy as a sandboy, naked in temperatures of twenty degrees below zero, melting the snow with the heat of his body, we manage to ignore such unexplained mysteries simply because they do not fit with our beliefs.

HABITUAL AND FLUXING

STRICTLY speaking we are not really born into an actual world at all. We are born into something that we make into an actual world through accepting the habits of the society we find ourselves in. And here we at last return to dreams, for exactly the same can be said of them. Our external environment, as we collectively perceive it, is probably our own creation. We do not really observe the physical world but participate in the creation of what we think is "out there." We find what we want to find.

The paradigm of the new physics appears to imply that we have dreamed a world which is relatively stable and enduring, and one which could be said to follow certain natural laws of matter, space and time. It is a perfect morphological field, or rather a set of fields, ranging from the habit of a protein molecule to the even greater habit of a galaxy. But, essentially our world is still just a habitual dream. The world we inhabit is a world we *habit-in*.

All we really have is a description or program of the world, learned by having its dimensions, characteristics and parameters drummed into us from birth, which after a while we take for granted. This is the habitual field which is the illusory reality. It is the way our consciousness has learned to cope with the sheer abundance of a multi-dimensional existence. For the aim of conditioning our consciousness is primarily a social one, which ensures we all see the same single reality. To grasp this, it is only necessary to see what we do to those who do not see like most of us. The Indian mystic, Meher Baba, traveled throughout his continent gathering together men and women whom he called "masts." By all normal standards they were crazy, schizophrenic, anti-social bums or bag ladies. Yet Meher Baba could detect that many were very close to being enlightened, but caught in the dilemma of seeing and feeling in radically different ways to those around them.

Our usual, single, monochrome view of reality can best be termed the *monotonal*. It is fixed and unyielding and will do everything in its power to ensure that everything fits the habitual single world view.

But there is another reality which we might term *fluxing*. Unlike the fixed monotonal, it is a multi-dimensional, omnijective and catalytic reality, which is simultaneously many things and events. Our faculties have been so well trained by the monotonal, that even when we are confronted by an experience which basically challenges all our assumptions of the world – like teleportation, miraculous daytime visions, or any other para-normal or supra-normal happenings – those faculties refuse to step outside the habitual pattern. So they either reshape the image to fit the pattern or, if it is too outrageous, simply ignore it altogether.

If energy fields and auras were part of our monotonal conditioning, all of us would learn to see them, which only a few, rare individuals do at present. What we believe to be reality is, in actuality, learned, and the fact that most of us do not see auras or people as globes of pulsating light does not mean that they do not exist, but that they do not exist in our monotonal. In the fluxing

Blue Sky, by Wassily Kandinsky, 1940.

senses that there might be other realities out there and so to relax their chronic control. But our habitual is stiffened in its resolve to fix the world view by our unconscious use of language. Nouns fix objects like pins through a butterfly collection. The butterflies are dead and so are the objects. A mystic master admonishes his disciples to beware of nouns altogether. *Living* is a verb, not a fixed noun like *life. Knowing* is a verb, it is existential and experiential, whereas *knowledge* is a dead thing from somewhere other than yourself. It is a record of someone else's *knowing* and never your own. We imprison ourselves in a word-dominated world, a semantic environment built out of local cultural beliefs. This is the reality which we have learned. But when we dream, that waking, verbal dominance is overwhelmed by the earlier mammalian blueprint of REM sleep which was designed to enhance memory. That imprinting was essentially non-verbal, being of the senses. Perhaps this is yet another reason lucid dreaming appears to be a heightened reality.

To experience the fluxing implied by the new sciences, we must enter the dream. We have already encountered Atisha's meditation in which he exhorts the disciple to treat all phenomena as dreams. A Tibetan text, the *Madhyamika,* asserts that the world is only an illusory dream. And we have already met the Tibetan spiritual discipline of *Mi-lam,* the Yoga of the Dream State.

The Hindus, the Jainas, the mystic Sufis of Islam, the Kabbalists of Judaism, the Zoroastrians and the esoteric branches of Christianity, all agree that the material world is a dream, an illusion. Control of one's dreams in each of these traditions and the subsequent realization of the dreamlike nature of reality appears to have been a foundational device, one of the major secret teachings which is common to all.

all things are possible in the most improbable of alternative realities within a vast multiverse.

The best way of seeing the fluxing is as a dream. You will remember that when asked what he was, Buddha replied, "I am awake." So it is hardly surprising that it is the Buddhists who devised the Yoga of the Dream State, in which the adept must consciously learn to control the dream state and in so doing to realize the nature of the waking and dream experience. It is fundamental to most Buddhist traditions that the world of things is as illusory as are our dreams.

The dream trick is to convince your habitual

THE FOUR DEMONS

ACCORDING to the eleventh-century Tibetan sybil, Machig Lapdron, any practitioner of *Chod* (a visualization-actualization technique) must face four dream demons who are functions of the false self, the ego. This remarkable teaching perfectly describes the habitual prisons we have created for ourselves.

The first is the "Demon that Blocks the Senses." When we see something, immediately a series of processes are set in motion. Thoughts and memories about that object, or subject, come rushing into the mind. There are associations, words and concepts, desires for it, and judgements on it. The moment this happens, the true perception of it is overwhelmed and we are lost in fixation or attachment to the thing perceived. In other words, a habit.

The second is the "Demon which Cannot Be Controlled." This is the unending procession of thoughts which follow one another without a break. The mind wanders aimlessly from one thought to the next and our awareness is completely lost in their distraction: the second habitual field.

The third is the "Demon of Pleasure." This appears when we find something pleasurable and do everything to prolong it. The desire then becomes an attachment and a habitual attitude and creates a barrier to any clarity.

The fourth is the "Demon of the Ego," which programs the way we see the world in terms of separation of the "self" and the "other." This

creates a barrier to awareness and to an understanding of the essential oneness of existence. Perhaps this is the worst habit of all, and certainly the most difficult to break

So what of our monotonal favored reality? We also make of it whatever we imagine it to be. In an infinite regress of reflections, our minds mirror the cosmos which reflects our minds. Only

all of the time. By simply watching them pass yet not identifying with them, not chasing after a thought which catches our attention, but rather just allowing it to go on its way, the meditator discovers that there are gaps appearing in the otherwise uninterrupted flow. In seeing this, an understanding arises and with it a cessation of mental formations. That which is outside of the birth of these mental forms is Reality.

Milarepa again:

"By leaving the mind in its natural state, without causing it to assume form (ideas, mentations, ways of perceiving) the first dawnings of Knowledge appear. By keeping the mind relaxed, flowing like the peaceful water of a river, Reality is reflected therein."

Now science is offering an insight as profound as that of Milarepa. It appears to be creating the foundations for a new mystical science based upon what might be termed the "psychology" of human consciousness. This development is quite apart from any established dogmas or creeds, religious orders or belief systems. And the foundation stone of this new "religiousness" looks to be the same as that of mystics like this twelfth-century Tibetan – that the manifest world we are in is but a dream, dreaming itself.

meditation and lucid dreaming seemingly can change this. Both tend to undermine the walls of our habitual and fixed monotonal world view. Meditation, especially, breaks the links between thoughts.

Normally, thoughts stream past our consciousness like an unending wall. We cannot see past them for they occupy all our attention,

Opposite: **Hermit with the Gods**, sixteenth century, Mogul, India. The tradition of Indian hermits was rigorously embraced by the Tibetans, replacing a generally benevolent Hindu pantheon with a fierce demonic counterpart befitting the harsh physical conditions. Above: **Tankha**, nineteenth century, Tibet.

SUMMONING THE DEMON

As we have been examining the raising of demons it seems useful to look at any methods of dealing with them in a lucid dream. There usually comes a point in dreaming when we must face our worst fears. In a lucid dream the reality of this can so shock the dreamer that he or she comes to believe in the particular monster and invariably falls from any state of alertness, usually waking from the dream immediately. However real the horror may appear at the time, it remains a dream, and this understanding is usually enough to dispel any fear. But sometimes the dreamer is not so convinced when facing down a twenty-foot demonic presence. At such times the thought goes through anyone's head that perhaps they have entered some hellish separate reality, a parallel realm in which one can really get hurt. The principle to understand with all such apparitions is the simple equation that their substantiality is in direct proportion to your belief. So first of all remember that it is a dream image and probably some unacceptable aspect of yourself. Love, laughter and light seem to be the best weapons against such entities. Keeping a sense of humor in a dream is perhaps the most precious talisman you can possibly take with you to the other realm. But the same could be said for the waking world as well. Loving the beast is another strategy often tried by dreamers. Embracing the monster and accepting it usually brings an immense sense of relief, as if you have been repressing a part of yourself and creating your own Minotaur in the center of your private labyrinth. Often it is reported by lucid dreamers that in embracing the monster the dreamer discovers the unacceptable part of themselves. Talk

to it, asking it who it is — its name is often revealing. Ask it why it is trying to threaten you or what it is trying to do and how you can help it.

If you are of a particularly courageous and foolhardy disposition you can summon up your worst fears in a lucid dream. However, this can be almost as fearsome as the experiences of the dancer of Chod if the dreamer is not prepared for the reality of the summoned. Your pet demons will appear only too easily by themselves, and will be far more true if they happen by themselves. Summoned entities in lucid dreams often bear a curious mark of empty artificiality, quite regardless of whether they are the embodiments of good or of evil.

And yet a nudge in the right direction can yield real insights. Summoning your favorite person, your worst enemy or a wise old man or woman, can reveal unexpected delights of real wisdom, humor and compassion. If you can remember in the midst of all this activity to do a reality check on whomever you have summoned or intended, you will be able to discern revealing differences between the original and your dream replica. And there is always a very real chance that you might somehow have invoked the actual person from their own dreams. Personally, I have shared dreams with others on a number of occasions, and yet I can not really confirm that what both of us experienced was the same thing or whether it was just wishful thinking.

Opposite: **Lotus flowers and Crane**, *hanging scroll, eleventh century, China. In lucid practices scrutinize the dream scene down to the minutest detail. You will be rewarded for such attention.*

A SENSE OF PLACE.

Most of us have a favorite spot, whether it is in an open landscape, the sea, a river or the city. If it is possible go there and imbibe the place as deeply as you can. Soak up every visual detail, every nuance of smell, taste, touch and sound. Ask yourself while you are doing so whether you are dreaming.

On going to bed keep some memento of the place – a photo, a sketch or postcard or some simple artifact which encapsulates the atmosphere for you. Intend to revisit the spot in your dreams and upon seeing it to remember that you are dreaming. With persistence, this method is usually very effective. Once you manage to revisit the site and become lucid while doing so, do a reality check on all and everything which catches your attention. Do not be distracted but really look carefully at the details, noting differences you

might remember from the original. Many who experience this are convinced that they are looking at the scene in an out-of-body state. Check yourself, your clothes or lack of them, or your completely incorporeal body. Take one detail and examine it intensely. Just see how real it is. There is often a surprise waiting in store.

DREAMING DERVISH

One question which arises for any lucid dreamer is how to remain lucid. It is sometimes difficult to remain alert and at some point all dreamers find themselves slipping away into unconsciousness, either prior to entering the sleep mode again or just when they are about to wake up. At such moments a sudden burst of activity can help push you into another lucid scenario. Many lucid experimenters find that spinning or whirling is a very effective way of staying alert. Whirling has been one of the most powerful meditation techniques used by the Sufis, the mystical arm of Islam, to awaken the disciple. The best known practitioners are the whirling dervishes of the Mevlevi Order, named after the great Sufi master and poet Mevlana Jalal-ud-din Rumi. Whirling has the effect of heightening lucidity in the waking world and strangely seems to have the same effect in the dreaming realm as well. Yet almost any powerful movement in the dreaming state has the effect of keeping the lucid dreamer alert. My own rather clumsy style is to fall backwards while flying. What it lacks in elegance it makes up for in effectiveness, and as it appears to be spontaneous, there is not much I can do about it anyway.

CHAPTER 12

THE REALITY OF DREAMS

Confucius and you are both dreams,

and I who say you are a dream

am a dream myself.

This is a paradox.

Tomorrow a wise man may explain it.

Chuang-tzu

THERE WAS A MAN OF CHENG who killed a deer and, fearing someone might find it, hid it in a ditch until he was ready to go home. But when he came back later he could not find the animal. He concluded he must have been dreaming.

A passer-by heard him muttering to himself about the affair and, acting upon what he heard, found the deer. When he returned home he told his wife: "Just now a woodcutter dreamed he had caught a deer, but did not know where it was. Now I have found it. His dream was a true one."

" Isn't it rather that you dreamed you saw a woodcutter catch the deer? Since you have really got the deer, isn't it your dream that was true?"

"All I know is that I have got it. What do I care which of us was dreaming?"

When the woodcutter got home he had a true dream of the place where he had hidden the deer, and of the man who found it. Next morning, guided

by his dream, he confronted the man and then went to law to contest his right to the deer.

The Justice said: "If in the first place you really caught the deer, you are wrong to say that you were dreaming. If you really were dreaming, then you are wrong to say it actually happened. The other man contests your right to it. His wife says that he recognized it in his dream as another man's deer, yet denies the existence of the man who caught it. All I know is that we have a deer, so I suggest you divide it between you."

When reported to the Lord of Cheng, he commented: "Alas! Is the Justice dreaming he has divided someone's deer?"

The Prime Minister was consulted, who said: "It is beyond me to distinguish dreaming from non-dreaming. Only the Yellow Emperor or Confucius could have told you and they are dead. For the present we may as well trust the decision of the Justice."

On a Warm Summer Afternoon, by Adelchi-Riccardo
Mantovani. The war between good and evil is less defined in the
dreaming realm. In a lucid dream, even the darkest of fallen angels
can suddenly turn into a creature of light, as dreamers confront
their deepest fears only to discover that demons are often facets of
themselves which have just not been allowed free expression.

223

This Taoist tale, from the *Book of Lieh-tzu*, written well over two thousand years ago, illustrates the paradoxical nature of dream and waking realities. This is a humorous account but consider the implications of another Eastern story, from the life of Buddha.

One of Buddha's greatest disciples was Sariputta. As his meditations deepened many strange visions started to occur. He saw angels, devas, demons, heaven and hell. They were so real, so perfectly actualized that he told Buddha, who said they were only dreams. "No, no," said the disciple, "they really are *real*. These are not phantoms at all. They are as real as you or I at this moment." Buddha then told him that when one's attention is at the third eye, dreams can become real just as the real becomes a dream.

This is a true dilemma for both yogi and lucid dreamer, for the problem is how to distinguish which is which. Both seem so authentic. However outlandish this may seem to most of us, it can be the experience of someone who is focused at the third eye. This is the basis for many strange *siddhic* powers manifested by Eastern yogis and saints. Of course, if you are not already grounded in your being, when it happens you experience great confusion.

The Badminton Game, by David Inshaw, 1973.
The painting shows two women, with whom the artist was in love, playing badminton. He says of it that everything had been taken from near his house "and rearranged into its right place. I changed everything I used in the picture in order to increase the mystery and wonder I felt all around me in this magic place." He could be describing the way we create in lucid dreams. And in dreaming all places are magical.

In contrast to the previous page the photograph relies on the mechanical, fixed-point perspective that we have become so used to. And yet this view of reality has only come into being since the artists of the fourteenth century created the first camera obscuras and began to understand how to reproduce the effects technically.

Since that time we have been fixed in this way of seeing, which only takes into account a reality seen through one eye, looking through a static frame. Even moving pictures and television are essentially the same. Yet we accept photographic images as reality, forgetting that they are just another illusion.

It is precisely this same bewilderment which is felt by the lucid dreamer who finds it increasingly difficult to differentiate between dreaming and waking reality.

At this stage, if the reader has followed all the methods successfully, he or she will already be confronting an inner world whose frontiers go far beyond their imaginings, and some of the territories have a reality which is disturbingly substantial. Are these realms within our heads, and just the result of our over active and creative bio-computer? Or is there some other explanation, like the action of the third eye, for the sheer outlandishness, reality and power of some of the worlds you will have visited?

Perhaps the answer lies in some of the theories which the new physics has invoked. Having just examined the possibility of a holographic or holo-moving universe, we might explore what that fully implies. For a hologram, like the spatial actuality of a rainbow, is an illusion, or a virtual reality, the very stuff out of which our dreams would appear to be made. So it seems possible that the dreamer, the visionary or the psychotic have access to the entire holographic realm, and by moving their laserbeam-like focus of attention, what Don Juan calls the *assemblage point,* change the realities they perceive.

By this time the non-lucid dreaming reader may well have stretched his or her credulity to the limit and be considering the whole theory an illusory and preposterous dream anyway. It is a perfectly valid question to ask, whether the whole appearance of *waking while dreaming* and *dreaming while waking* are all delusional and mystical mind trips which have a simple explanation within a simple universe? Maybe the fabulous worlds of the mystics are themselves supra-delusional after all.

We might ask if there is truly any solid evidence, apart from their lofty claims, for what mystics have discovered about our seemingly solid and reassuringly stable world – that it is only one more dream.

Apparently, from what we have learned from the scientists so far, the mystics may be right to suppose that the universe we have learned to recognize is more a virtual reality than the real thing.

But as we are concerned with the essential state of the dream, the nature of reality and of wakefulness, it is perhaps necessary to define what we mean by such terms before rushing blithely on.

Dream *n.* mental activity, usually in the form of an imagined series of events, occurring during certain phases of sleep. To suffer delusions; be unrealistic: Unreal.

Real *n.* existing or occurring in the physical world; not imaginary, ficticious, dream-like or theoretical: actual.

Reality *n.* the state of things as they are or as they appear to be, rather than as one might wish them to be.

Wake *vb.*(often foll. by *up*) to rouse or become roused from sleep; to become conscious or aware.

These abbreviated dictionary terms must confirm any unease we might have over the inadequacy of words – that definitions of the most profound and fundamental roots of life tend to be somewhat less than satisfying. Here we find the real is explained by what it is not – dreams. Dreams are defined by what they are not – the real. And by wakefulness it is implied that this is the only conscious activity, which lucid dreaming shows to be patently untrue.

In our normal waking lives, however, we might accept these dictionary definitions as a rough approximation; but if we were to ask anyone who had just been aroused from a lucid or conscious dream to define the four concepts, he or she would be at a complete loss. For one thing the subject might have dreamed that they had awoken twice already within their dreams, only to realize that they had merely dropped into yet another dream. For such a person it would be hard to judge whether this was yet another dream from which to awaken. Many would say that the so-called dream state was far more substantial and alive than the world into which they had awoken. And there would be little evidence that the world in which they now found themselves was any less a dream than the preceding ones.

So this, in essence, is the dilemma facing the lucid dreamer. It is at the very heart of the worlds of the shaman, the psychic, the mystic and the schizophrenic. Any innocent dream bystander who has experienced the golden brick of lucidity descending into his or her dream world will acknowledge that the experience is both wondrous and shattering. For it brings into question the whole nature of what is real and what is imagination. Boundaries no longer appear clear cut and simple, and insanity seems to beckon a curled finger around every corner.

So, summarized, the scenario of our phenomenal experience begins to look something like this:

At birth we are neither more nor less than a witnessing consciousness. As the brain acquires memories, so we are involuntarily sold an entire social programming package which codifies what is being experienced into collectively agreed patterns. There is a crucial moment in every child's life when the witnessing consciousness becomes identified with one of these memory traces. Identifying with just one of these previously coded traces, the witness effectively opens a floodgate and is engulfed by all the memories within the brain, including the pre-programmed idea of a separate self. The brain which creates this situation is the true Dream Machine, for what it does is to create an inner environment which is constantly playing with ideas both about what it finds around it and about who it is.

What is fascinating about the mind is that if it does not have any perceptions of the "outside" to process, it begins to create its own reality which it then believes in. Experimenters who have been immersed in sensory deprivation tanks will attest to a heightened inner reality as their brains begin to hallucinate and build complete inner universes. The subject often has difficulty in distinguishing between the real world and the illusion. And this all happens because of neural energy being released within our craniums. That there should be such confusion is in part due to the fact that the ratio of sensitivity to change, within the brain and within the external sensory receptors, is about 100,000 to one in favor of the internal, neurological network. In simple statistical terms, what happens within the neuro-networks of the physical mind means that the brain is thousands of times more receptive to changes within the internal environment than it is to changes in the external one. We are better equipped, cell for cell, neuron for neuron, to perceive our inner worlds, than we are to receive our outer one. When we consider that the universe "out there," which we see, can also be understood as patterns of neural energy firing off "in here," within the confines of our skulls, then the story of the Sufi saint Rabi'ya takes on a new meaning.

Rabi'ya was noted for her detachment from the external world around her. She was so intoxicated with her inner visions that she even shut her win-

Sita-Tara, *Tankha from Tibet, nineteenth century. This is the primal shakti figure who is the creatrix of the thousand and one things of the phenomenal universe. In Indian cosmology, while the male consort is the witnessing consciousness, it is the female who actualizes the manifest world.*

dows in Spring, lost in contemplation of her inner world. When another Sufi called out to her to watch the most glorious sunset she replied that, on the contrary, it was he who should come inside and view a far richer glory.

Neither Rabi'ya nor the Sufi can claim exclusive rights to the truth, but we tend to overlook the power of our internal reality when confronted with what we believe to be the external world of events.

A passage from the ancient *Upanishads* shows the authors' understanding of this state even three thousand years ago.

"When one goes to sleep, he takes along material of this all-containing world, himself tears it apart, himself builds it up and dreams by his own brightness, by his own light."

It has recently been suggested by neurophysiologists that certain higher brain functions might well utilize an optical system whose processes are dependent upon a form of bio-luminescence or a discharge of light within the cells, and that it is this to which the Upanishadic authors refer as they continue:

"Then this person becomes self-illuminated. There are no chariots there, no spans, no roads. But he projects from himself chariots, spans, roads. There are no blisses there, no pleasures, delights. There are no water tanks there, no lotus-pools, no streams. Yet he projects from himself water tanks, lotus-ponds, streams. For he is the creator."

The Dance of Chod

CERTAIN Tibetan sects like the Kargyupa believe the entire universe to be the product of mind, created by the collective stuff of the thoughts of all beings. Some dream yogins, like Sariputta in India, even manage to create illusionistic entities which gradually take on what appear to be an independent existence. An eye-witness account by Alexandra David-Neel, in the earlier half of this century, tells of certain adepts conjuring up demons and an image of themselves. The demons, or *tolpas,* then proceed to tear the illusory adept to pieces, as a dangerously symbolic enactment of the destruction of the ego. Understandably this practice is not without its perils, for many yogis, having created these monsters, can come to believe in their existence, which in turn gives the phantoms even more life. Alexandra was horrified to learn that yogis

were frequently found murdered by their own creations.

Far fetched as this may sound, this intrepid Frenchwoman managed, through persistent use of visualization techniques similar to those found in this book, to create a relatively harmless phantom of a monk who appeared to follow her on her travels. Many others witnessed him around the caravans, apparently living a completely independent existence, and Alexandra actually felt him — on occasion he was substantial enough to touch. However, when his creatrix attempted to dispel her creation, it took longer to do than when she conjured him up.

For readers who might be fascinated with this practice and the visualization techniques involved, and would like to try out what is called the Dance of Chod, it would be well to point out that not

Opposite: *Alexandra David-Neel* with Buddhist nuns in Tibet.
Right: *Lama dancer's apron*, nineteenth century, Tibet.

only is it likely to be suicidal for an untutored, curious Westerner to meddle with such methods, but that the Tibetan *chodpas* take at least five years training in special schools, or with established practitioners, before they are ready to meet these demons, let alone allow them to rend the novice's dream-body apart.

We find a similar account in Castanedas' books on the teachings of the mysterious Don Juan. In his account the tolpa is called the *nagual*. Irrespective of whether anyone believes in the factual existence of such a splendid figure, the warnings of the enigmatic teacher to his student-sorcerer appear authentic enough. Don Juan warns Castaneda that no one could survive an encounter with such a nagual without prior training. He insists that the goal of a sorcerer's training is to "prepare his *tonal* [the habitual gestalt] not to crap out. A most difficult accomplishment. A warrior must be taught to be impeccable and thoroughly empty before he could even conceive witnessing a *nagual*."

Just how real are these tolpas or naguals and what

becomes of them? Alexandra relates what a Tibetan *gomchen*, or sage, had to say on the subject:

"May it not be that like children born of our flesh, these children of our mind separate their lives from ours, escape our control, and play parts of their own?"

The closing words of the *Vajracchedika Prajna-paramita*, reputedly written by the renowned second-century sage, Nagarjuna, read, "Like images seen in a dream, thus we must regard all things."

The great Tibetan yogi, Milarepa, was Nagarjuna's true spiritual successor through the line of his own teacher, Marpa. Milarepa had been a powerful sorcerer of great fame until he began to pursue truth rather than power. One day, on returning to the cave which was his lodging, he saw,

"...a number of demons who were engaged in wantonly destroying his little store of food and books. He admonished them to no effect; then he endeavoured to reason with them: 'I have made you no offerings,' he said. 'Do not be angry with me, I do not always forget to do this, I had not any intention of offending you.' But neither threats nor arguments produced any effect upon the demons who went on with their work of destruction. Then Milarepa, who had meanwhile realized the situation more clearly, apostrophized himself: 'O Mila, was it really worth while to have spent so many years in meditation and still

believe in the existence of demons? Do you not know that they are a product of your own creation and exist only within your mind?' Then, addressing the demons, he said, 'Do then what ever you want to do.' At once the demon shapes vanished."

So by the very act of giving attention, and therefore energy, to these simulacra we feed their substance and their apparent reality. Ignore them and they dissipate.

The twelfth-century Sufis have a Persian word for the stuff of thoughts, *alam al-mithal*. These mystics held that reality is a series of planes of being, or *Hadarat*. That which is closest to ours, but on a deeper level, has the original blueprint of our manifest reality in which the stuff of our thoughts gain substance. They believed that as we think, so we create. If we send a concentrated thought form into this realm, it will manifest as a substantial reality in our universe. Here we find another remarkable parallel to the concept of the implicate order which is constantly enfolding and unfolding our conscious thoughts. The Sufis, having their spiritual feet firmly on the path of love and prayer, rather understandably locate the control of this thought stuff at the heart chakra.

When these twelfth-century Sufis visited the land where spirits and the great teachers dwell they called it the "country of the hidden Imam," what one Sufi called "the land of no-where." They believed it to

have been created by the minds of many people from the subtle matter of thoughts. It had its own substance and corporeality. It was this apparent reality which prompted the Sufis to believe that *thought is inseparable from perception and shapes the very fabric of our lives.* The afterlife was seen as the creative matrix which, like Bohm's implicate order, gives rise to, or unfolds, the manifest universe.

At the point of death, many reports claim, it is like entering into one's mind. This surely suggests that reality is within us and not somewhere else. Appar-

ently that after-world the Sufis called *Na-Koja-Abad,* the land of "no-where," turns out to be the land of an eternal "now-here" instead.

Just as primitive humans sensed that we possess

Opposite: *Alexandra David-Neel with Nepalese servant. In 1923 this extraordinary Frenchwoman was the first Western woman to enter the sacred city of Lhasa. She had disguised herself as a pilgrim. She learned the language, studied with a hermit for a year 13,000 feet up in the Himalayas and earned the yellow robes of a Buddhist Abbess.* Above: **Masks of demons,** *worn by Buddhist dancers. These masks depict the demons of the dreaming worlds.*

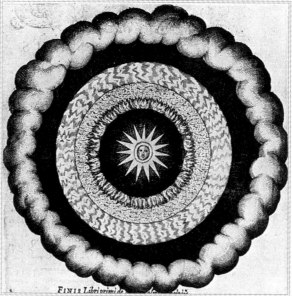

two bodies – a physical body and a soul – it is increasingly apparent that we have at least two separate realities. One, in which our bodies appear to be solid and possess location in both space and time – our normal everyday waking selves. And another, which appears to be a dazzling cluster of energy which seemingly has no location in either space or time.

We tend to identify with our brains, as the locus of our awareness and attention, and yet what we know now of the human energy field is that it often responds to stimuli long before these are recognized by the brain or we are conscious of them. Thus it would appear that, in speaking of the brain-mind, we are once again looking at the wrong thing. Perhaps we have overrated the brain entirely and it remains just a good bio-computer. The mind, however, unlike the proposition in the physiological activation/synthesis model we examined earlier, *does not seem located in the brain but in the energy field*. If this is so, it gives even greater credence to Castanedas' contention that it is within the energy field that the focus of our attention, or what he calls the *assemblage point*, is actually located. The central character in his books, the Yaqui sorcerer, Don Juan, claims that it is because this assemblage point has become so

chronically fixed at the same location within the field, that we are unable to see reality as it truly is.

Instead, we have collectively fixed our viewpoint of what the world is and how it works by means of social indoctrination, cultural conditioning and descriptive programming. The whole purpose of both the shamanic teacher and the spiritual master is to break down these lifelong patterns in order for the disciple to momentarily glimpse another reality. And this requires a massive demolition of all our preconceived ideas of who and what we are.

My own far from merciful master, Osho, said that he was not giving anything to his disciples at all. Far from it. He was merely taking away what we believed we possessed, but didn't, and returning to us what we already had, but believed we hadn't. And it was this utter confusion that made us so desperate in our search for what we already were – enlightened.

The confusion we all experience, of being One with the universe and yet forgetting that it is the ground of our being, is simply due to our programming and the absurd beliefs we have managed to pick up in our search for who we really are. Beliefs are always second-hand, someone else's ideas, or the collective sum of ideas of any social group.

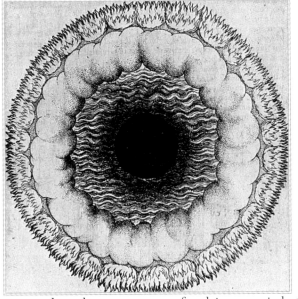

They are *never* one's own. They are imposed upon us at an early stage, tricking the brain into creating superb interior holograms of the idea. Thus we never quite know which is reality and which the virtual reality. And this is the *maya* or dream world which the Hindus and the Buddhists speak of.

Lucid dreaming allows one to explore the nature of this maya simply because, by its very nature, lucidity brings with it the understanding that what is being witnessed is only a dream, however real it might appear. Bring the same unidentified lucidity to bear upon the waking world, and the ultimate awakening is not far away. There is an old Zen saying that,

"In the beginning rivers are rivers
   and mountains are mountains.
In the middle rivers are no longer rivers
   and mountains are no longer mountains.
At the end rivers are once again rivers,
   and mountains are again mountains."

This is the royal and lucid road one travels towards awakening. When we are totally within the waking dream none of us even suspect that there might be any reality other than the one we are accustomed to see, hear, feel and taste. But once we begin to question the nature of the universe we inhabit, that world starts to appear far less substantial than we ever imagined it to be. The reason this is so is because we are all caught in the delusional state of 'imagining it to be' something it is not. The real world has become so confused in our minds that it is almost impossible to determine whether it is real or not. Upon awakening from this projected and imagined universe, we will discover that we can witness once again the river as a river and the mountain as a mountain, but this time with an open and uncluttered perception. The view is radically different, yet the reality of the river and the mountain is unchanged.

Opposite:*The Appearance of the Cosmos.* Above: **The Formation of the Material Elements.** *Two plates by De Bry illustrating a seventeenth-century treatise, by the English Hermetic philosopher, Robert Fludd, on the creation of phenomenal existence. The first image shows the cosmos as an inner vision of God, while the second shows the material world coming into existence from that inner idea. In lucid dreaming each of us is our own God, but it appears increasingly evident that our everyday world is also a collective, yet no less godly, construct, for which we are no less responsible.*

CHAPTER 13

THE DREAM MAKER AWAKENS

The breeze at dawn has secrets to tell you.

Don't go back to sleep.

You must ask for what you really want.

Don't go back to sleep.

People are going back and forth across the

doorsill

where the two worlds touch.

The door is round and open.

Don't go back to sleep.

Jalal-ud-din Rumi (*Sufi master*)

I
T SEEMS A CURIOUS QUESTION TO ASK, in a volume dedicated to dreaming, what it might be like to stop dreaming altogether and be awake. And yet this is the paradox inherent in lucid dreaming and one of the themes of this last chapter.

There appears to be a real confusion in the minds of many of our new metaphysical generation. In our ideas of what enlightenment, and being ultimately awake, must be like, we seem to be caught somewhere between the fabulous and psychedelic worlds of drug-induced states, psychic imagination, the spirit world of the shamans, or that radically different state of no-mind enjoyed by the sage.

As our everyday, explicate, universe might just be the construct of our collective and individual imaginations, we must wonder what the raw stuff of the implicate order could be like, and whether this is the ground of all being into which, we are told, we will finally awaken.

One way of approaching this is to look at how we might have fallen asleep in the first place.

In an exquisite looking-glass image of the Creation myth, the Uitoto Indians of Colombia say that the Word begot the Father. But all was phantasm. The Father touched illusion but nothing really existed.

236

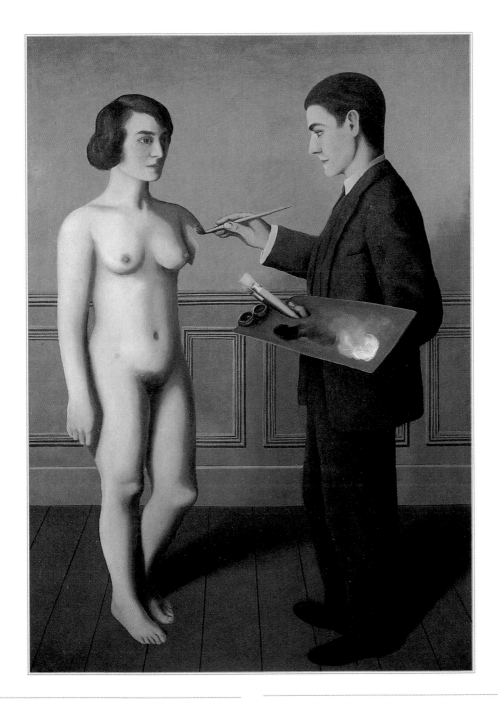

Attempting the Impossible, by René Magritte, 1928. It is impossible to tell whether the painter, here, is also the painted. This seems to be the predicament facing us all. We appear to create the world around us within our brains, including ourselves. But what happens when we cease to dream either the sleeping or the waking universe? When we stop dreaming what remains "out there?"

The Holy Fire, by Alex Gray. *Consciousness of separateness and the impact of the Divine upon the human personality. The modern metaphysical movement with its particular New Age style of imagery tends to gravitate towards a romantic view of enlightenment. One awakened man, U.G. Krishnamurti, had a balancing effect when he pointed out that most of us, if we really knew what enlightenment entailed, wouldn't touch it with a barge pole. From what we have heard, it is a truly radical annihilation of the cherished idea of oneself. Many modern seekers seem more attracted to a heightened, illuminated and more powerful sense of self, which appears to be at the opposite pole to a real awakening. That is rather like believing your reflection in the mirror is the one which can wake up.*

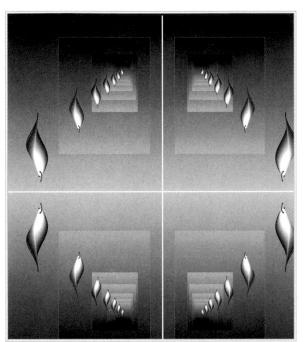

Even the name of the father is "he who is, or has a dream, Nai-mu-ena." Only through dreaming can he sustain the mirage of his body while he ponders his predicament. For nothing existed to support his visions.

Finally he attached the illusion to the thread of a dream and kept it there by the aid of his breath. He plumbed to reach the foundations of the appearance but there was nothing, for no thing really existed.

"He then tied the empty illusion to the dream thread and pressed the magical substance upon it. Then by the aid of his dream he held it like a wisp of raw cotton.

Then he seized the bottom of the mirage, and by stamping on it repeatedly, finally sat down upon his dreamed earth."

After examining the evidence so far, it does seem likely that we ourselves are trapped, like Nai-mu-ena, within a holographic-like description of a fixed universe which we have devised and perpetuated. We are boundless, but have become strangely encapsulated in a virtual image with boundaries that we have largely created. *We are imprisoned within our own description of the universe.*

The scientist appears to suspect, while the mystic has always claimed, that our present environment is created by the totality of all collective consciousness, each of our own included. But it has become a monstrous habit field, chronically fixed in a familiar pattern, simply because we have fixed it there.

The Empress Wu, in the seventh century, had a similar problem She could not understand the Buddhist concept that the universe was interconnected like a vast network of jewels which reflected one another.

Her own universe did not seem to. So the master, Fa-Tsang, devised a beautiful demonstration of what turns out to be a very similar version of our present-day holographic model. Fa-Tsang held a candle in the center of a room completely filled with mirrors. "This," he told the Empress, "represents the relation of the One to the Many."

He then placed a crystal at the center and said that this reflected the Many to the One. He then added that this was only a partial truth, for the whole model would have to be moving to really show what dynamism was involved. Here we have an echo rolling down the centuries towards our freshly minted ideas.

D R E A M   S E L F ~ T H E   H E A R T   O F   T H E   M A T T E R

Ramana Maharshi, whom many consider the greatest spiritual master of this century.

How does any of this help us in discovering what we had set out to explore at the beginning of this volume – the identity and location of the creator or creatrix of our dreams? Who or what is it that dreams, either in the sleeping or waking states? Are we any closer in the search for the elusive Dream Maker? Let us tread softly through the next pages, for we are close to the goal but in order to open that final door we must have a closer look at the "Self."

One of the most beautiful enlightened beings of the earlier part of this century was the Indian mystic, Ramana Maharshi. His later work was linked to the Indian Vedanta, to that perennial philosophy which sees the center of the self, "to which the mind in sleep retires from its activity in the brain as the Heart." This is neither the physical heart nor the heart chakra, but is located to the right of the chest.

The core of his teachings are to be found in a short work called *Sri Romana Gita.* In Canto Five, the science of the heart, he describes the heart as *Hridayam,* "that into which all things subside at the end."

He then asserts a concept that would impeccably fit the scientists' view of a holographic universe.

"The body is an epitome of the entire universe and the Heart is the epitome of the entire body.

Therefore the Heart is the epitome of the entire universe."

While his style may be somewhat difficult for the Western reader, his condensed words well repay careful attention. He continues:

" *The universe is none other than the mind, and the mind none other than the Heart. Thus the entire story of the universe ends with the Heart.*

The Heart exists in the body even as the sun exists in the universe. The mind exists in Sahasrara as the orb of the moon in the universe.

As the sun lights up the moon even so this Heart imparts light to the mind.

A mortal, not established in the Heart, perceives only the mind, just as the light is perceived in the moon in the absence of the sun.

Not perceiving that the source of the light is one's own real Self, and perceiving the objects through the mind as apart from himself, the ignorant one is deluded.

The Enlightened One inhering in the Heart, sees the light of the mind merged in the light of the Heart, like the light of the moon in the daylight."

If we are in any doubt that this could as well be a description of a holographic reality, Ramana continues:

The notion that the Seer is different from the seen abides in the mind. For those that ever abide in the Heart, the Seer is the same as the Seen."

Here the concept of the Heart, or "that into which all things reside at the end," indicates the nature of reality as a perpetually present consciousness. This is the witness, the source of the light and all levels of being. It appears to reside in an area to the right of the chest. If we were to transpose this imagery into Bohm's holomovement, then the Heart would be the location of the implicate order in each and every one of us and perhaps the locus of the Dream Maker.

"Not perceiving that the source of the light is one's own real Self, and perceiving the objects through the mind as apart from himself, the ignorant one is deluded."

The ignorant are dreaming. This surely is the simplest description of the dreaming self that we are ever likely to encounter. It also describes the selfsame state of natural luminosity found within the Tibetan bardo. This is that light which is seen at the point of death and is really one's own. Because we perceive the objects through the mind, as being apart from ourselves, we dream both our sleeping and waking lives.

Such a mystical explanation might not make much sense to most readers, or those who are just beginning to explore dreams lucidly. However beautiful, it still seems a little remote from our everyday, or every night, experiences. For instance, is the dreamer identical to the person we seem to be within the dream? Or is the lucid dreamer the one who is lying in bed, apparently asleep? After all, the brain is sleeping in what we understand as the waking and external reality. That brain does not even exist in our internal dream reality.

We usually witness the events in a dream through a main character. At times we look through his or her eyes. In other moments we see the character as if in the third person, while sometimes we find a curious combination of the two. But we only *dream* we are that person; it is only a simulacrum, a representation of us.

In lucid dreams we can actively choose to be either actor or audience, participator or observer, although most such dreams are in the first person. We can choose to be identified with the dream persona who is part and parcel of the dream world or with the dream observer who is not. It is the combination of simultaneously being both actor and audience that is the most characteristic quality of lucidity – being within the dream and yet not part of it. This is precisely the quality one finds in a mystic, or an enlightened one. "Being in the world but not of the world" remains a favorite description of the sage in many traditions.

So lucid dreaming appears to be a fragile balance between being an identified participant and a detached observer. Any moment dreamers become too identified with their dream roles they fall back into the non-lucid state, losing the alert awareness that they are dreaming. In order to sustain lucidity, or to invoke it in the first place, it seems necessary to be an identified participant, center stage. Yet, at the same time a degree of detachment is required in order to remain alert and not to get lost in the role-playing. Becoming lucid has these twin levels of awareness, although their combination often brings bewilderment and paradox. Believing you have just woken up as your normal waking self, only to recognize that you are in fact still asleep is an example of how confusing it can be.

While the dreamer is fully lucid, the dream ego is not usually mistaken for the real thing – that real person lying asleep while all these dream events are happening somewhere else. However, in the early stages of learning how to dream lucidly, the dream ego can often be mistaken for the true self. From many of the accounts of long-term lucid dreamers, the period in which the dreamer plays with his, or her, new found powers, is surprisingly short. As Stephen LaBerge points out with impeccable authority, backed up by over a thousand lucid dreams in his log book, at first, lucid dreams are interpreted as "...my dream. But the dream ego is not the dreamer; rather than dreaming, it is being dreamed. The unenlightened but semi-lucid dream ego falsely believes itself to be the only reality, of which all other dream figures are mere projections."

Dreamers who can do anything they like, with whomever they like, fulfilling every secret wish and passion, seem very quickly to get bored and begin to look around with a more critical and interested eye, being especially drawn to the dream ego, only to discover that it is just another dream figure. And they then discover that the dream maker is not part of the dream at all, but the sleeping self.

The self-image they had in the dream is radically reviewed and it is found that the dream ego is more like a suit of clothes than a self. As the identification with the dream ego gradually falls away, the lucid dreamer can change "clothes" as often as needed, never mistaking such a self-image for the self. To the mystics this stage has particular significance, for it mirrors the mistakes we all make in identifying with the false sense of self – the ego – in the waking state. But in dreams it is far easier to become unidentified with the dream ego. The dreamer does not need to struggle to break free of it. This is the great gift of the lucid state – to be able to cease to identify with the events, or the actors, and yet participate to the full and not spare the stamps.

The Dream Maker. It would appear, from what we have learned so far, that the brain is a vast neural network in which the cells are constantly competing with one another for connections. This network is continually updating its strategies and reinforces those neural highways which best fit its reward/value system. In dreaming, alternative strategies are routinely tested, connecting pathways which sometimes are extremely bizarre. Some of these pathways off the beaten track remain just possibilities to be tested against what is learned on subsequent days. Those paths which are then used again become reinforced and widened, while those which have proved useless simply disappear. This Darwinian process of neural selection creates the dreams through which we create memories and learn best moves. It is possible that the Dream Maker is the expression of this total and manifest activity of the explicate order. Consciousness, however, is an expression of the implicate order, the underlying first cause of existence out of which the explicate unfolds. Each of us appears to be a wave in that vast ocean, which becomes identified with the memories of the evolutionary neural net. It is only when consciousness becomes alert to this true situation and dis-identifies with the constant flow of memories generated by the neural network, that dreaming ceases, both in waking and in sleeping states. Enlightened beings simply don't seem to dream at all.

LEAVING THE LUGGAGE

MANY long-time lucid dreamers have experiences which seem to go far beyond their waking level of consciousness, and they often claim that transcendental states are gained while being lucid. Certainly, as the ego-associated desires are consumed in complete wish-fulfilling dreams, so these passions appear quickly to reach a satiation point. The experienced lucid dreamer becomes less concerned with deliberate dream control and the endless, effortless gratification which comes with it, than with waiting and watching their dreams unfold. By this completely natural process of silently waiting, states of meditation spontaneously arise and many veteran lucid dreamers report increasingly vivid and ecstatic states of consciousness as they become more adept at inducing lucid dreams, and more silent in their witnessing.

According to Ramana the world of things as seen through the mind is just a dream, a common dream in which we all dream together. The only difference is that at night we dream alone. Either way, while the mind is busy with experience, we dream. But when the mind is silent, thoughtless, then, whatever the event, only then is it real.

Here we come to the diverging interests of sage and sorcerer within the holographic multiverse. The mystic is concerned, not with the ever changing realities of the shaman, who is ever altering the location of the point of attention, but to become one with the point of attention. Once at one's own center, one is graced with a glimpse of the center of the holographic flux where nothing happens and nothing will happen, where everything is happening and will always happen. This is the essential suchness of the whole. At the center it is also said that the dreaming gradually stops. The Baul mystics of India call the being at the center *Adhar Manush*, the essential man, and sing:

"Scanning the cosmos you waste
your hours.
He is present in this little vessel,
in this your body He has made his
abode.
You must be single-minded to visit the
court of my Beloved.
If your mind is torn in two
you will swim in a quandary and never
reach the shore.

Only by *intending and being single-minded* are you not split. The dreamer's mind, awake or asleep, will always be split in two, as the dreamer and the dreamed. Be one, and undivided, we are told. Through intention one gains an integration and the crowd within each of us becomes one.

In order to explore that land of no-where within us, it is necessary to travel very lightly. Just as in death you can take nothing with you, so the dream-traveler is stopped at the border of these other dream realms and must continue empty-handed. And that means leaving all traces of the old world behind.

One such trace is our normal way of perceiving reality. This is the first which must be dropped; or rather, that by altering our attitude, it will drop by itself. It is impossible to silence the mind, to force the mind to stop thinking. Rather we have to trick it. We have to use a far more subtle strategy. If someone tells you that you need to relax, all that happens is that you grow more tense trying to relax. Anyone who has ever tried to silence their thoughts will tell you that suddenly there are thoughts everywhere.

A monk who is celibate dreams constantly of women, while a fat man on a diet thinks only of food. It is like the Indian master who claimed that he had a foolproof method for enlightenment which would only take one minute. All you had to do was to *not* think of monkeys for that minute and liberation was assured. Try it!

One marvellous method of leaving the heavy luggage of this world behind, is just to sit watching it all go past. Witness the thoughts passing, keep aware of them but just do not identify with them. This is really the foundation of virtually all meditations, in whatever form they may at first appear. Only be alert and aware of the thoughts, but do not follow any of them or give them any attention whatsoever. For attention is what thoughts feed upon and, having fed, they lead you, as in some eternal relay race, to the next relayer – another thought. This technique of being an alert and yet a silent observer is nothing less than being the witness,

standing on the threshold of the explicate and implicate orders, and watching the unfolding of the manifest world. *It is also the foundation of lucid dreaming.*

Gradually the thoughts begin to fall away for want of attention, as does the mental screening that keeps us all from glimpsing past our habitual perceptions of the world of matter. Once beyond them, perhaps all and everything appears to be luminous vibrations, a vast unending web of light in which all things are interconnected and whole. Unfortunately for the curious among us, only those who have woken up know.

For those of us who still dream, whether we seem awake or asleep, to be lucid allows the possibility to just sit and watch the dreams, like thoughts, go by. This is far easier to accomplish than in our waking hours and is one of the reasons why dream masters pay so much attention to the act of becoming lucid. It is simply that the dreamer is able to meditate far more effectively, undistracted within a dream environment. Just witness the images which arise but give them no identifying attention. Usually only the real veteran of lucidity is able to accomplish this, but even a novice can gain access to deep, meditative states. Eventually, it is said, the dreams will fall away for want of attention and the next moment you will be truly awake for the first time. The Tibetans insist that it will also be the last.

The Cosmic Light of Moon and Sun, Tanjore, eighteenth century. *This side represents the reflected light of the Moon while on the reverse is the radiant light of the Sun. Ramana says that it is like the enlightened one who, being in the heart, sees the light of the mind merged in the light of the heart like the light of the moon in daytime.*

ALERT AWARENESS IN THE NUMINOUS DARKNESS

Mind is neither within nor without,

Nor is it found anywhere else.

It is neither mixed with other things,

nor apart from them.

It is not any-thing whatsoever and therefore

Beings are by nature in Nirvana.

Santideva

I F the Dzogchen Masters of Dream Yoga are right in understanding that we are already enlightened – and in this they are supported by the Taoists – then lucid dreaming is the most natural, and many would agree, far the most enjoyable, way of realizing it.

Lucid dreaming allows you to discover yourself without belonging to any religious club or organization; there is no need to seek a guru or to become a sorcerer's apprentice, no need to suffer or to take it all so seriously. Because it is such a natural process it determines the pace at which you proceed. The deeper layers of your consciousness will find appropriate signposts directing your attention along the road back to yourself.

The only act needed on your waking behalf is to make that initial decision. The single act of intending is the key to both the dreaming and the waking worlds. Once the knack is learned of how to witness your dreams, allowing the events to unfold while remaining blissfully free from identifying with them,

just watching in wonder as it all goes by, then you will have learned how it is to be done in the waking state.

In the meantime lucidity, by its very nature, will already be leading you on the "royal road to awakening." It does not matter if you take the sorcerer's road to power, the therapist's road to integration, the ascetics road to re-birth or the sage's road to reality. It does not even matter if you explore the reality of dreams or the dreams of reality; whichever route you choose, when lucid, will lead you to the same point. For what you will really have done is to question the nature of your own perceptions and your own consciousness. Once lucid you simply have no choice but to question your habitual modes of being. It means that the world about you will never be the same, whether you are asleep and dreaming or awake and dreaming. Whatever happens now, you are already stirring in your sleep. The Dream Maker is about to wake up.

But until then, why not enjoy the dreamings!

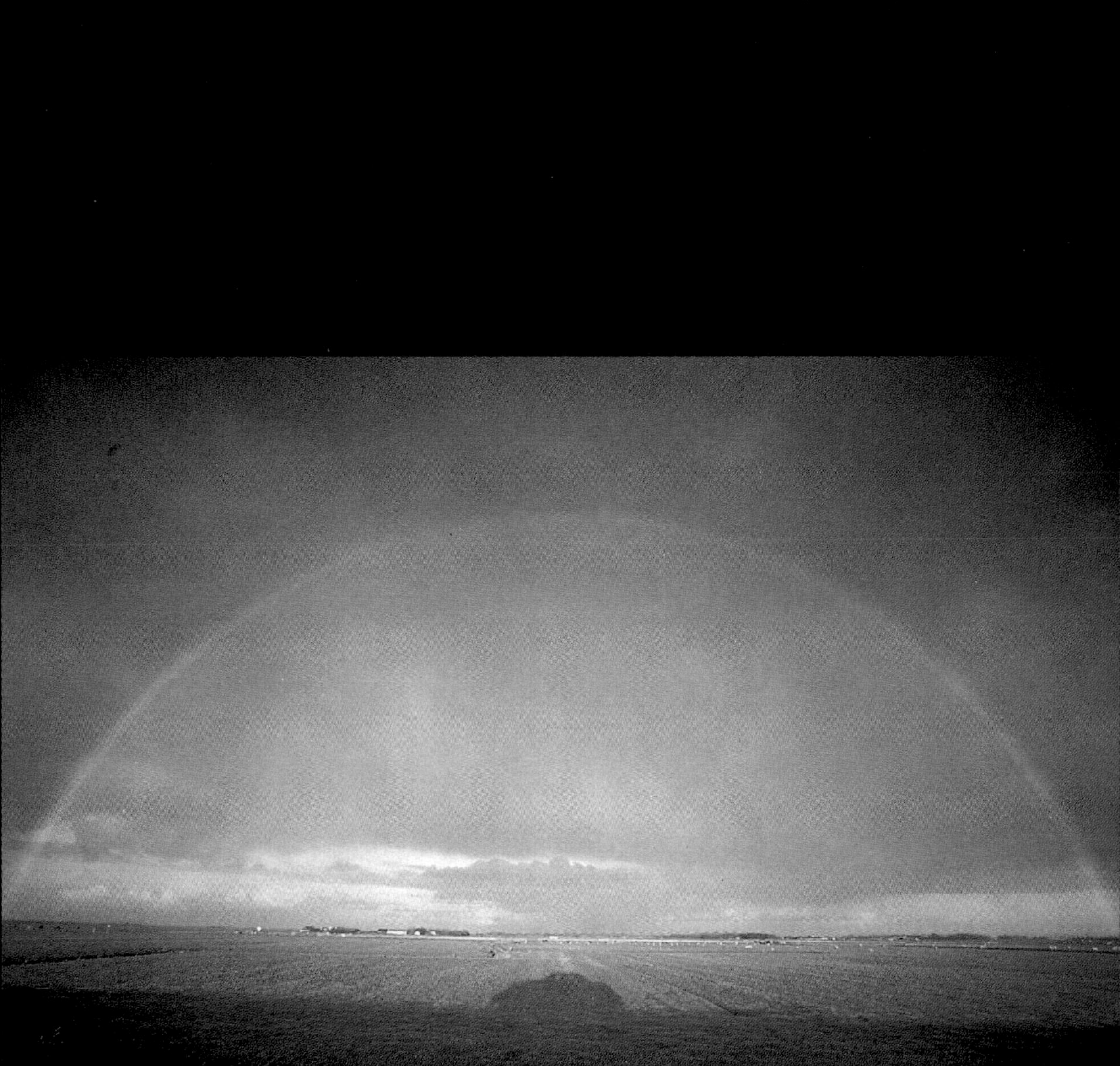

SUMMARY
OF DREAM PRACTICES

BREAKING THE MEMORY BARRIER

THE FIRST and foremost barrier to be overcome in any attempt to induce lucid dreaming is that of amnesia. We forget what happens as we pass between the waking and dreaming realms. All the techniques found in the earlier chapters are devised to break through our habitual, and as some believe, instinctual, mode of forgetfulness. This can be accomplished through the use of mnemonic devices which reinforce certain neural networks in the brain. The dreamer begins to invest energy in building a new bridge across the divide to allow easy access from either side, with no border officials who force you to give up your contraband memories

The major device in building the bridge between the realms is the patient and methodical upkeep of a dream journal. No other single method is so effective or important during the early stages of any expedition into lucid dreaming. The entire ritual surrounding the journal – the pre-sleep activities, the ambience of the bedroom, the techniques of awakening and recalling the dreams – is vital to any success of the venture. All the methods which follow are only designed to reinforce a pattern of alert awareness of that elusive realm.

However, all such devices are empty gestures unless the dreamer has a firm and single-minded resolve to experience a lucid dream. Taking an "oath to essence", willing or *intending* it to happen is the indication of a transforming energy behind conscious effort and attitude. Without that energy, whether fired by a worthy spiritual thirst, psychic curiosity, wonder, a desire to heal oneself, or just because the mountain is there, nothing will happen. *Dream Journal (55), Dream Spot (31), Pre-Sleep activities (56), Oath to Essence (58), Remembrance of the Day (59), Oracle of the Fox (60), Upon Awaking (61), Dream Focus (78).*

INVOKING LUCID DREAMING

WHILE *INTENDING* to have a lucid and consciously alert dream is the driving force behind any attempt at such a summit, and without which nothing will happen, there are a number of simple devices which can help trigger a recognition that you are in a dreaming state. They are all really tricks to trip and shock the unwary and unconscious dreamer into a sudden wakefulness. Probably, of all of them, the deceptively simple trap of the Tibetan master, Atisha, of treating all phenomena as if they are a dream, is the most effective. All such devices are still only methods to trick the mind out of its habitual mode of behavior, and once you have reached the other shore you don't have to continue carrying the boat which took you there. These methods are only a means to induce lucidity and can be discarded in favor of techniques which will spontaneously arise for each dreamer. *Visualization (16), Shamanic Visualization (120), Guided Daydreams (127/132), Pineal Door (98), MILD (140), Hand (141), Self Hypnosis (141), Hypnosis (142), The Methods of Atisha (176).*

REALITY CHECK

As EACH INDIVIDUAL enters lucid states so any further advice is really irrelevant. Each journey is so unique and unknown that little more can be said than *bon voyage*. However, one useful rule of thumb is to get into the habit of checking the reality of each event. Ask yourself whether you are dreaming or not, or if what you are experiencing has any reality at all. Carefully examine the dream happening in minute detail. Turn your full attention to the actual substance of the dream realm and its denizens, including yourself. A reality check made upon the observer in either a dreaming or a waking state can have truly wondrous and unexpected effects. *The Shifting Self (189), Reality Check (220)*

THE OTHER WORLD

Once WITHIN LUCID DREAMS the unique nature of each scenario will gather momentum in different ways for each and every dreamer. These are realms for which there are no tourist guides. You create tracks that birds might make in the sky, so only very general guidelines can be of any help. Most of the techniques given are just indications of possible directions which then will really be up to the creative imagination of the individual dreamer. For this is essentially your own Act of Creation in which you can play God, either imposing your will or letting your creations have free will and watching the results. At first, most lucid dreamers find themselves offered the whole kingdom, with all its myriad delights, wonders and orgies. Each wish can be instantly and completely fulfilled. What seems to happen, however, is that most, if not all, lucid dreamers quickly tire of their unlimited powers and find a balance between witnessing the dream events unfolding without interfering except for an occasional nudge in some favored direction. The exceptions to this are the healing dreams and those in which the dreamer seeks specific answers to outstanding problems. *Dream Room (142/3), Healing Dreams(144), The One Hundred and Twelve (164/9), False Awakenings (174), Dream Body (174)*.

FALLING INTO THE GAP

This is truly a paradoxical method. Instead of aiming to have a lucid dream you intend to witness the gap between wakefulness and sleep. The Tibetan Practice of the Light or the method found in the *Vigyan Bhairava Tantra* of Shiva, both aim for one thing and yet by default appear to bestow lucidity, almost as an after thought. But the attitude towards lucidity is radically different. Many lucid dreamers report that as their tourist-like fascination with traveling between worlds begins to dwindle so a new thirst seems to arise — to really awaken from the dream in both worlds. Then lucidity becomes just one more tool, a device to trick oneself into a final awakening. For those we remain silent. *Practice of the Light (156), Falling Between Worlds (170/1)*.

A C K N O W L E D G M E N T S

I would like to thank all those at Labyrinth Publishing who helped in the production of this book – to Dhiresha and Nishta for sweetly reminding me of things I would prefer to forget; to Philip Dunn who started it all; to my editor, Geoffrey Chesler, who managed to curb most of the excesses and errors to be found in the original manuscript, and to Meaghan Dowling, his trans-Atlantic counterpart at Simon & Schuster, who did some very expert and painless editorial surgery. This book, however, would not have been created without the love and support of my partner, Navyo, both in and out of the design studio, and the guidance and inspiration of my friend and master, Osho, who managed to demonstrate, at first hand, the essential difference between dreams and reality, and the possibility of joyously celebrating both. My gratitude to them all, for it all.

SUGGESTED READING

Allione, Tsultrim, *Women of Wisdom* (New York: Routledge & Kegan Paul, 1987).

Arnold Forster, M., *Studies in Dreams* (London: Allen & Unwin, 1921).

Bohm, David, *Wholeness and the Implicate Order* (London: Routledge & Kegan Paul, 1980).

Briggs, J.P., & Peat, D.,*Looking Glass Universe* (New York: Simon & Schuster,1984).

Castaneda,Carlos, *The Art of Dreaming* (New York: HarperCollins, 1993).

Cowan, James, *Mysteries of the Dream-Time* (Bridport: Prism Press, 1989).

Crick, F. and Mitchison, G., *"The Function of Dream Sleep,"* (Nature, 304, 1983).

Drury, Neville, *Don Juan, Mescalito and Modern Magic* (London:Routledge & Kegan Paul, 1978).

Eliade, Mircea, *Shamanism* (New Jersey, Princeton University Press, 1972).

Evans-Wentz, W.Y., *Tibetan Yoga and Secret Doctrines* (London: Oxford University Press, 1935).

— *Milarepa*, A Biography (Oxford University Press).

Faraday, A.,

— *The Dream Game* (New York: Harper & Row, 1976).

— *Dream Power*, (New York: Coward, McCann & Geoghegan, 1972).

Fox,O., *Astral Projection*, (New York: University Books, 1962).

Free John,Da, The Knee of Listening (Middletown, Calif.:The Dawn Horse Press, 1978).

Graham, A., trans. *The Book of Lieh-Tzu* (London: Mandala, HarperCollins, 1990).

Green, C. , *Lucid Dreams* (Oxford: Institute for Psychophysical Research, 1968).

Hobson, Allan,*The Dreaming Brain* (Penguin 1990).

Jung, Carl Gustav, *Memories, Dreams & Reflections* (London: Routledge & Kegan Paul, 1963).

LaBerge, S.,

— *"Lucid Dreaming: some Personal Observations,"* (Sleep Research, 8, 1979).

— *"Lucid Dreaming: Directing the Action as it Happens,"* (Psychology Today, 15, 1981).

— *Lucid Dreaming* (Los Angeles: Jeremy P. Tarcher,1985)

Lama Lodo, Bardo Teachings(San Fransisco: KTD Publications,1982).

Monroe, Robert, *Journeys Out of the Body* (New York: Anchor Press/Doubleday, 1971).

Moody, R., *Life After Life,* (Atlanta: Mockingbird, 1977).

Nietszche, F., *"Misunderstanding of the Dream,"* from The Portable Nietzsche, (New York: Viking Press, 1954).

Norbu, Namkhai Rinpoche, *Dream Yoga & the Practice of Natural Light* (New York: Snow Lion Publications, 1992).

Osho, (Osho International Foundation)

— *The Book of Secrets* (Vigyan Bhairav Tantra)

— *The Tantra Vision* (Royal Song of Saraha)

— *The Secret of Secrets* (Golden Flower)

— *The Beloved* (Baul Mystics)

— *Yoga: The Alpha and the Omega* (Patanjali)

— *Take it Easy* (Ikkyu)

— *The Book of Wisdom* (Atisha)

— *Hsin Hsin Ming: The Book of Nothing* (Sosan)

Ouspensky, P., *A New Model of the Universe* (London: Routledge & Kegan paul, 1931, 1960).

Pearce, Joseph Chilton, *The Crack in the Cosmic Egg* (New York: Pocket Books, 1974).

Perls, Fritz, In and Out of the garbage Pail (Moab, Utah: Real People Press,1969).

Pribram, Karl, *Languages of the Brain,* (Monterey, Calif.: Wadsworth Publishing, 1977).

Rapport, N, *"Pleasant Dreams!"*, (Psychiatric Quarterly 22, 1948).

Saint-Denys, H., *Dreams and How to Guide Them* (London: Duckworth, 1982).

Sutton, P., ed. *Dreaming, the Art of Aboriginal Australia* (New York: George Braziller & The Asia Society Galleries Publications, 1988).

Talbot, Michael, Mysticism and the new Physics (London: Routledge & Kegan Paul, 1981).

Van Eeden, F., *"A Study of Dreams,"* (London: Proceedings of the Society for Psychical Research 26, 1913).

Wolf,Fred Alan, *"The Physics of Dream Consciousness: Is the Lucid Dream a Parallel Universe?"* (2nd Lucid Dreaming Symposium Proceedings 6, December 1987).

— *Star Wave* (New York: MacMillan, 1984).

INDEX